CRITICAL TRAUMA STU

Critical Trauma Studies

Understanding Violence, Conflict,
and Memory in Everyday Life

Edited by Monica J. Casper and Eric Wertheimer

NEW YORK UNIVERSITY PRESS
New York and London

NEW YORK UNIVERSITY PRESS
New York and London
www.nyupress.org

References to Internet websites (URLs) were accurate at the time of writing. Neither the author nor New York University Press is responsible for URLs that may have expired or changed since the manuscript was prepared.

ISBN: 978-1-4798-9656-1 (hardback)
ISBN: 978-1-4798-2251-5 (paperback)

For Library of Congress Cataloging-in-Publication data, please contact the Library of Congress.

New York University Press books are printed on acid-free paper, and their binding materials are chosen for strength and durability. We strive to use environmentally responsible suppliers and materials to the greatest extent possible in publishing our books.

Manufactured in the United States of America

10 9 8 7 6 5 4 3 2 1

Also available as an ebook

In loving memory of
Dennis J. Struck
and
Elsa Silva

CONTENTS

ACKNOWLEDGMENTS

We first wish to acknowledge the many contributions of the authors whose work is featured in *Critical Trauma Studies*. The book's production has been nonlinear, to say the least, with fits and starts, outright stalls, and numerous points of reinvigoration and reengagement. Truly, without the brilliance contained herein, the editors might have given up the ghost, so to speak, some time ago. We are grateful and humbled that our contributors have exhibited such patience in responding to our many requests for changes and feedback over the past few years, while also continuing to share their excitement about the project. Their enduring support and gracious adjustments have been a gift.

Ilene Kalish and Caelyn Cobb at NYU Press have been consistently forbearing and helpful. We deeply appreciate Ilene's high standards, her warm embrace of interdisciplinary work, and her willingness to reach beyond the edges of what counts as knowledge—while also offering no-nonsense editorial guidance. The anonymous reviewers of the manuscript in its many iterations provided much-needed correctives and enhancements, acting as clear eyes when ours were clouded over with the distractions, seductions, and troubles of other skies.

We would also like to thank the many conference participants of "New Approaches to Trauma: Bridging Theory and Practice," held October 2010 at Arizona State University's West Campus. The insight and energy of the many panelists and attendees made for a conference that surpassed the expectations of its planners and spurred the conception of this collection. This book would not have been possible without the great generosity of mind and spirit it received from our four keynote speakers: Dorothy Allison, Terri Jentz, Jackie Orr, and Maurice Stevens. Each of them went above and beyond the call in helping to make the conference and its textual incarnation something more than a voicing and its echo. This collection became, with their help, a magnification and amplification, a chance to see and hear things we hadn't or couldn't notice in real time. We are grateful for that, and especially for Maurice's keen editorial and theoretical eyes on our introduction.

The work of the conference planning committee was especially important in the gestational phase of this collection. We are grateful for the ideas, commitments, and labor that each of the committee members brought to this project, assisting us in shaping the conference and providing encouragement for this volume: Julie Amparano, Akua Duku Anokye, Joanne Cacciatore, Jeff Kennedy, Martin Beck Matuštík, and William Paul Simmons. We also benefitted from able and collegial assistance from the wonderful New College Division of Humanities, Arts, and Cultural Studies (HArCS) staff: Mary Bauer, Lucy Berchini, Tracy Encizo, Cathy Kerrey, and Dennis Marsollier.

This event was originally sponsored by the New College for Interdisciplinary Arts and Sciences and the Arizona Humanities Council, and the list of supporting contributors grew to encompass a wide swath of academic units within ASU that indicates the reach and interdisciplinarity of critical trauma studies. Substantial backing for the conference was provided by the Center for Critical Inquiry and Cultural Studies; HArCS; the Master's Program in Social Justice and Human Rights; the School of Social Transformation and the Women and Gender Studies Department from the College of Liberal Arts and Sciences on ASU's Tempe campus; the Institute for Humanities Research; and ASU's Project Humanities.

We also want to share some individual thanks.

During production of this book, Monica experienced the loss of her father, Dennis J. Struck, quite unexpectedly following a hospital infection. His death brought painfully close to home, and to heart, the many lessons of critical trauma studies. Monica's mother, Patricia A. Struck, and her three siblings daily manifest a level of resilience that inspires; sometimes, from loss and grief emerges strength, humor, and new connections. As always, especially now, Monica is profoundly grateful for the steady grace, stealth humor, and intellectual partnership of William Paul Simmons. Daughters Mason and Delaney captivate and delight, and they provide numerous enjoyable and mundane distractions from the taxing work of finding the right word or phrase.

For many years, Monica's work has been enhanced by loving and sagacious engagement with Adele E. Clarke and Lisa Jean Moore, and this project is no exception. She is immensely appreciative of her former colleagues at ASU, many who remain dear friends, especially coeditor Eric Wertheimer, who nurtured her kernel of an idea for a trauma studies conference, helping to grow it from a figment of imagination to a fully realized enterprise. Now at the University of Arizona, Monica is grateful to the efficient and good-humored GWS staff—Darcy Román-Felix, Terry Mullin, Leigh Spencer, and Lupita Loftus—who kept her sane, as well as to colleagues in Gender and Women's Studies and the SBS Dean's Office, especially John Paul Jones III, for welcoming her into the fold.

Eric Wertheimer thanks most of all his coeditor, Monica Casper, who has been exceptionally generous with her friendship and intellectual gifts. In the introductory remarks to the conference he was moved to say that Monica put us "on the map" of trauma studies. But she rewrote maps too, charting new practices and theories of intellect and emotion, bringing to the desert a redemptive brand of engagement and energy that has been inspiring. He is grateful too for many at ASU, but most especially Michael Stancliff, Patrick Bixby, and Michelle Tellez. Hank Ridley, Jr., who passed on during the making of the conference and this book, is very much here in the labor and love of this kind of work; Carole and Justine Ridley, too. Eric thanks finally his family—Milagros Cisneros, Daniela Wertheimer, and Ariana Wertheimer—who have been constant and loving in their insistence on growth and struggle; which, if a normative claim can be excused, is what families should do.

We dedicate this book—with an abundance of love and an archive of memories—to the lives of Dennis J. Struck and Elsa Silva.

1

Within Trauma

An Introduction

ERIC WERTHEIMER AND MONICA J. CASPER

As the problematic became absorbed into the taken-for-granted, the vulnerable self merged into biography. Body and self were mutually implicated in that biography of vulnerability.
—Virginia Olesen (1992, 210)

There is no life without trauma. There is no history without trauma ... Trauma as a mode of being violently halts the flow of time, fractures the self, and punctures memory and language.
—Gabriele M. Schwab (2010, 42)

Ground Truths

The Sonoran Desert in autumn, after the heat, is beautiful. Hackberries and wolfberries emerge and barrel cacti blossom. Wildflowers open out in magenta, saffron, Indian red, and burnt orange, feeding butterflies and bees. Snakes map their route to winter sleep, lizards grow sluggish, and winged raptors—wintering hawks, kestrels, falcons, and owls—soar above the cover of fallen petals from summer-blooming perennials. And yet, the pastoral desert is also predatory. Lacerated mesquite trees bleed black sap. Cacti of all shapes and sizes protect themselves with spikes and spurs. Deadly heat, especially in high summer, leeches moisture from flesh, leaf, bone, and tongue. Bullets target humans and animals, leaving corpses and despair in their path. Migratory trails, littered with debris and remains, are haunted by the ghosts of the men, women, and children who walked them, entire families seeking a better life among people who hate and fear.

It is here, in this contradictory desert landscape in which we live and labor, that we began to assemble a working hypothesis about what it means to do intellectual work in the midst of great trouble. We take seriously Bruno Latour's (2004, 239) question, with particular attention to the challenge of his metaphorical pessimism: "Is it so surprising, after all, that with such positions given to the object, the humanities have lost the hearts of their fellow citizens, that they had to retreat year after year, entrenching themselves always further in the narrow barracks left to them by more and more stingy deans? The Zeus of Critique rules absolutely, to be sure, but over a desert."

In the spirit of Latour's inquiry—but refusing the stereotype of the geographically and epistemologically negative space of the desert—we seek to foster a new humanities, one that respects fact and heart even after the disciplines have diverged over arguments about society and imagination, propaganda and information, constructs and cold reality, representation and experience. Our work is thus keen to meld the scientific with the affective, the voices of narrated pain with the determined habits of repair and psychic healing, the archives and realms of theory with the visceral, lived experiences of practice. Our approach is hybrid and interdisciplinary, accustomed as we are to inhabiting geographic and intellectual spaces shaped by plurality, risk, and diverse modes of being.

A Genealogy of Critical Trauma Studies

Critical Trauma Studies: Understanding Violence, Conflict, and Memory in Everyday Life is located both within and after various iterations of the entity known as "trauma studies." In the field's initial configuration, scholars challenged and deliberately moved away from psychiatric and/ or biomedical approaches to trauma, which had dominated the field (e.g., Ball 2000; Fassin and Rechtman 2009). In mid- to late nineteenth-century framings, "trauma" was a disease of the mind, conceptualized as "traumatic neurosis" generated by railroad accidents (Erichsen 1867) and later as war-related "shell shock" and posttraumatic stress disorder, or PTSD (Young 1997). The condition of trauma became a target for biomedical and psychiatric intervention, and in Foucauldian terms, traumatized individuals became subjects of and to various disciplinary practices that congealed around them. To be traumatized meant that one was psychically wounded and vulnerable, unwhole; therapeutic practices were aimed at "restoring" normalcy or stasis.

Epistemological shifts in which historians, cultural theorists, and others unraveled these biomedical and psychiatric meanings of trauma have led to a rich and robust body of work exploring, for example, history and memory (e.g., Caruth 1995; LaCapra 2001), narrative and its limits (e.g., Scarry 1985; Caruth 1996), memorialization (e.g., Sturken 1997, 2007; LaCapra 1998), cultural representations of trauma (e.g., Kaplan 2005), and genealogies of trauma (e.g., Leys 2000; Orr 2006). Taken together, these contributions have brought the study of trauma firmly within the purview of the humanities and social sciences, recognizing and naming "trauma" not only as a condition of broken bodies and shattered minds, but also and primarily as a cultural object. In these framings, "trauma" is a product of history and politics, subject to reinterpretation, contestation, and intervention.

Of course, these epistemological reframings do not diminish the reality of events. Earthquakes strike, buildings fall, and people die; bodies are devastated by bullets and bombs; famine, drought, and genocide decimate entire populations; planes crash (and disappear), trains derail, and cars smash into each other, twisting metal and limbs; loved ones become sick and die, or they are brutally murdered; sexual assault is pandemic; tornados and hurricanes rip houses off their foundations and children from their parents' arms; wars shred lives, communities, and landscapes and send soldiers home in body bags. These events are recursive. Categorizing and responding to them not merely as events, but as *traumatic events*, with its helpful vocabularies, knowledges, and temporalities, is the stuff of critical trauma studies. The field seeks to reveal the processes by which things that happen are denoted as trauma. Critical trauma studies asks: What does it mean to use the discourse of trauma? To represent events as ruptures, breaks, and other deviations from the normal? And what, then, is the normal?

We are speaking here of "trauma studies" as if it is an established area of study. And indeed, there is a significant and influential body of work. But there is relatively little structural coherence to the field, especially compared to other interdisciplinary areas like disability studies, American studies, and gender studies, all of which have become institutionalized to a much greater degree. This is both the virtue and ongoing (albeit productive) problem of critical trauma studies. The boundaries, scope, and content of the field are fluid and contested (Stevens 2011), as they have been from its inception. Yet the field, such as it is, has been forged through shared intellectual considerations of "modern" catastrophes such as war, genocide, forced migration, and 9/11, alongside everyday experiences of violence, loss, and injury. If there *can* be a conceptual heart of critical trauma studies—a domain of inquiry as various and global as its subject—we'd settle on a set of centripetal tensions: between the everyday and the extreme, between individual identity and collective experience, between history and the present, between experience and representation, between facts and memory, and between the "clinical" and the "cultural."

A genealogy of trauma, such as historian Ruth Leys (2000) has provided, must inevitably travel through the historical development and deployment of PTSD, as well as other analytic objects of trauma, such as memory, narrative, representation, and materiality. However, such a genealogy might also travel through social theory, through the epistemes that gave birth to a proliferation of ideas about acute disruptions to the reassuring status quo. Critical trauma studies is, now, a still-evolving product of twentieth-century movements and ideas, including structural functionalism, psychoanalysis and its interlocutors, postmodernism and poststructuralism, the constellation of theories/methods/interventions known as "identity politics," the turn to affect, critical body studies, critical race theory, and the new materialism.

Extending and challenging the focus on psychic breaks and cultural representations and interpretations, the material body is not absent from the imaginings of critical trauma studies. Indeed, the body has always been present if not fully theorized, its material insistence grappled with through investigations of somatic ruptures, such as railroad accidents and traumatic brain injury (Stevens, this volume [chapter 2]; Malabou 2012; Morrison and Casper 2012). The centrality of the brain to considerations (and treatments) of trauma has fostered new scholarly directions that attempt to link neuroscience with cultural analysis. The brain is understood to be "plastic" and thus responsive to interventions, accidental or deliberate. The amygdala has long been a key site for investigations of trauma, connecting as it does to emotion and memory, and "trauma" is now recognized as capable of altering the brain's structure and function. An important task for critical trauma studies is to learn from and make use of these neuroscientific "findings," while also interrogating how neuro-stories are rapidly becoming hegemonic explanations and depictions of human life (Rose and Abi-Rached 2013).

This book follows from the many iterations of critical trauma studies that have come before, but we are especially indebted to what Maurice Stevens (2014) calls *critical trauma theory*. Here, the category of trauma is not taken for granted, but rather unraveled and interrogated to assess the political and cultural work that "trauma" does—both in the world, as well as for those (like us) doing the interrogating. Stevens writes, "Is there something particular or different about the contemporary moment that calls us to reflect upon injury and trauma in new ways? In the forms of mass labor exploitation, proliferating military conflict zones, industrial catastrophe, natural disasters, state austerity plans, and ecological system collapse, the past decade has given evidence of increasing harm being experienced by most of the world's population." In this way, Stevens draws attention to both the epistemological and broader geopolitical contexts in which critical trauma studies is unfolding.

That we are increasingly living in an "age of trauma" (Miller and Tougaw 2002)—that is, that the register of trauma is ever more frequently employed to account for understandings of ourselves, our actions, and the things that are done to us (and that we do to others)—invites consideration and, inevitably, intervention. We suggest that a popular imperative to frame both everyday and spectacular experiences alike as "traumatic" imbues an ethical component into critical trauma studies that must be named, considered, and worked through. There are high stakes not only in studying how and why people are injured, but in assessing, articulating, and even challenging hegemonic modes of diagnosis, rehabilitation, recovery, and redemption. The conceptual spine of this book—embedded within the glue that binds the pages—is that critical trauma studies invokes an ethics of intellectual *and* moral engagement.

Whereas clinical and psychological perspectives respond to trauma as a psychic and/or embodied marker of disruptive experience, a critical approach attends to the ways that the category of "trauma" reveals and unsettles social and cultural classification systems, including how we triage subjects for "help" and intervention (Simmons and Casper 2012; Jackson, this volume [chapter 12]). Indeed, we would argue that twenty-first-century humanities, following on the heels of large-scale disruptions of the twentieth century, are broadly and locally constituted by the study of trauma itself. "Trauma" offers an "imminent" god, as it were, in which the humanities live and breath through the practices and needs of people at the edges—of space, time, and subjectivity—moving forth and back through various borderlands. As a set of intellectual ideas about ruptures in lived experience and transformations of self and being, critical trauma studies engages fundamental questions about our relationships with one another, the "natural" world, and other species (Casper 2014), with events, and with the very terms of our existence. Investigations of trauma are thus both ontological and epistemological, assemblages and intersectionalities, modes of being and ways of knowing.

Thinking and Doing

Critical Trauma Studies is the product of our individual and collective attempts to build on recent work in the field with the explicit goal of linking the domains typically understood as "theory" and "practice." That is, we wanted to put "thinking" alongside "doing" in fresh and provocative ways. Many works have taken up trauma studies and trauma theory, and many have focused on the "doing" of trauma care (the "how-to" and "self-help" genres; see Berns 2011). Seeking to query and bridge this divide, we were motivated by a sense of obligation to find work that would challenge the tired canard that the humanities, supposedly "unmarketable" disciplines, have become irrelevant. In fact, we would instead suggest that we need ever more innovative and atypical convergences of the academic humanities and social sciences with their panoply of practical uses and inspirations.

This volume thus brings together those who think and write critically about trauma with those who work with people who suffer traumatic events, recognizing that *sometimes these groups are the same.* That is, the trauma theorist may also have been traumatized, and may also work as a "fixer" of trauma in some other domain, and may also interweave these varied experiences in and through her own practices. Subjectivities and practices are multiple. The essays in this volume show that it is precisely *within* disruptive moments of wounding and their aftermath that human bodies and subjectivities—and, indeed, families, communities, and nations—become targets for inscription of the always-shifting but deeply divisive categories of normal and pathological (Canguilhem [1966] 1991), and of designations of affliction and appropriate healing.

It is not the case, we believe, that trauma practice is simply an applied version of critical trauma studies. Rather, the ethical and epistemological aims of each domain are different and overlapping. In one, scholars are invested in critically engaging "trauma" as an object of analysis, holding it up to the light, as it were, to examine its interior scaffolding, and often conceptually divorcing it from its deployment as an experience or diagnostic category. Trauma practitioners, on the other hand, are obligated to engage trauma somewhat less critically, and as it actually presents in the clinic, the psychiatric space, the shelter, the prison, the body. As many of us engage in both critical trauma theory *and* trauma work (for example, human rights, counseling, pedagogy, ministry, advocacy), simultaneously and often uncomfortably, we are called to a specific kind of reflexivity. This self-conscious practice offers a way of paying attention to the power dynamics, subjectivities, and meanings invoked in our individual and collective research, writing, and activism about trauma.

As editors, our attempts to see light in the friction between practice and theory are focused by a degree of hopefulness in the face of postmodern skepticism about the integrity of the subject and the ways that subjects are always already assumed to be healthy and whole, or are able to be made so via the classic trauma and recovery narrative. While shaped by and invested in critical trauma theory, this volume is deeply concerned with issues of "practice." We attend analytically to the trauma apparatus while recognizing that we do so *fully within it*. We also recognize it may be possible to discern the theorizing that emerges through practice itself, including the workings of the body (e.g., Siebers 2008; Moore and Casper 2014). If, as Stevens (this volume [chapter 2]) notes, "trauma is as trauma does," then we are firmly entangled within being and doing, living and interpreting, memory and hope, and all points in between.

Mapping the Collection

Critical Trauma Studies is organized around three interwoven themes: politics, poetics, and praxis. Yet these categories are more than a way to "sort out" the book's contents for our readers. Current work on trauma is richly invested in political strategies and operations, in questions of language and representation, and in "grassroots" concerns with how trauma and its interventions are enacted and responded to. The book's chapters take up, embody, and interrogate each of these imbricated themes, with varying degrees of emphasis: some foreground biopolitical traces and processes, while others listen more assiduously to language (including its absence), and still others build narratives from the ground up, heeding lived experiences. In our view, these are the major conceptual and practical spaces at and through which critical trauma studies is unfolding at this particular moment.

Each contributor to this volume is a subject of *traumatization*, in an active sense of the term that is cognizant of trauma's (and the study of trauma's) subject-making features. The volume is deliberately "bookended" with provocative essays by scholar Maurice Stevens and novelist Dorothy Allison, each deeply engaged with trauma, experience, and language but from quite different approaches. Both dare to articulate the investiture of language and narrative and their vital necessity in critical trauma studies—while simultaneously embracing the instability and inadequacy of text. They frame our collection because they make no apologies for gaps and poststructuralist destabilizations. They also, in different voices, tell it like it is. Practice and theory go on together, in spite of and because of all that, in the work of politics and praxis. Conjoined with the other essays in this collection, these offerings show how feeling, knowledge, practices, and power are mutually constitutive and profoundly political.

And so, in "Trauma Is as Trauma Does: The Politics of Affect in Catastrophic Times," Stevens sets the tone for our collective dialogue with intellectual depth, generosity, and creative critique. Working from within a comparative studies tradition, attentive to history, language, affect, and politics, Stevens locates trauma as a biopolitical apparatus rather than "simply" an experience or category per se. He focuses on the affective economies of trauma, how the concept of "trauma" works in both productive *and* limiting ways. For Stevens, the term "trauma" is invoked when subjectivity, assumed to be rational and ordered, has been destabilized. But in relying on trauma as a diagnostic category, we also reproduce the apparatus of trauma. This may constrain the kinds of "posttrauma" reactions (individual and collective) that ensue and also preclude other kinds of openings and avenues for social action. Trauma, in this framing, is interwoven into a key part of a control society. As Stevens reminds us, we need to pay attention not just to what trauma does, but *how* it does as well—especially among those "drawn to the glow of its inchoate affect."

Legal scholar Francine Banner globalizes the trauma apparatus, offering a harrowing account of Chechen women suicide bombers. She suggests that geopolitical trauma produced by the Russo-Chechen conflict was expressed in the embodied subjectivity of the bombers. Interrogating both "trauma studies" and "terrorism studies" as distinctly Western projects, Banner looks to the female bombers to explore gendered, somatic effects of trauma. Rather than positioning the suicide bomber as a deviant figure, she instead reveals the Chechen women as products of an assemblage of occupation, militarization, and gendered inequality. In this assemblage, women's bodies—linked visually and biopolitically to the national body—served as targets for sexual and reproductive violence and as objects of moral and political debate. Banner notes, however, that the women's collective status as victims did not negate their agency; suicide bombing became, in fact, a way for women to assert a kind of political agency in the face of trauma. Here, "the Chechen woman suicide bomber is not a monster, an aberration, or even an anomaly," but rather a spectacular embodiment *simultaneously* of collective trauma, political violence, and social suffering.

Feminist psychologist Breanne Fahs turns our attention to nomenclatures forming the trauma apparatus, specifically the importance of nuance in naming women's experiences of sexual violence. She suggests that in a social context rife with misogynistic violence against girls and women, the binary of "offender"/"victim" obscures rather than illuminates the scope of harm, while also separating people (especially women) from their own experiences of trauma. Fahs locates the language of trauma not in victimized subjectivity that would lead to individual healing (i.e., the psychological framework), but rather in the messy and contentious sphere of politics and power, in which women are systematically disadvantaged. This sphere shapes our cultural fixation on victims (especially women and children) rather than perpetrators, indicating a kind of fascination with and paranoia about sexuality run amok (on view in popular culture in shows like *Law & Order: Special Victims Unit*). Fahs notes that this is not merely a semantic issue: "Regardless of whether women choose to name their traumas as *rape*, or whether we label violent behaviors as *offending*, antiviolence movements should recognize that the very tenets of masculinity and femininity require (masculinized) violence, on the one hand, and the (feminized) assumption of access and consent, on the other." The result of such binaries is a politics in which rape culture finds apologetics at the highest levels of power.

Carmen Goman and Douglas Kelley, representing communication studies, explore an especially vexing issue in critical trauma studies: forgiveness. They note the term's varied meanings in the social sciences, including distinctions made between *inter*personal and *intra*personal forgiveness, one directed outward and the other inward. Both have implications for thinking about trauma, subjectivity, and politics more broadly. Goman and Kelley compellingly suggest that historical traumas often contain within them the logic of forgiveness, reflecting a contextual approach to understanding trauma. Following a helpful overview of forgiveness typologies, Goman and Kelley turn their attention to Simon Wiesenthal's *The Sunflower*, wherein Wiesenthal chronicles a specific incident in which he refused to forgive a dying Nazi. Troubled later by his actions, Wiesenthal invites commentary from writers, theologians, Holocaust survivors, and others, and these responses form the second part of *The Sunflower*. Goman and Kelley analyze the responses, eliciting themes that deepen our understanding of forgiveness and the situations in which it is offered or withheld. They note, "historical trauma calls for a reevaluation of one's collective, the offending collective, and the relationship between the two. Such a massive undertaking may be evaluated only with great care over time, precipitating alternating times of silence and interaction."

One of the most interesting themes to emerge from the essays is trauma's production of silence. As scholars and clinicians have shown, traumatic events disrupt everyday understandings and lived experiences, a disruption most tellingly registered in the realm of speech and writing. Elaine Scarry's *The Body in Pain* (1985), a theoretical subtext for much of this volume, argues that torture tests the limits of language's truth claims in its deterioration of the nexus between body and expression; silence is conceptually and emotionally eloquent when the body is in pain. After trauma, the subject may be voiceless, unable to articulate her experience or who she has become. And into that silence is poured a host of meanings and expectations, including perhaps most painfully the imperative to speak and to act, to recover and to heal. If, as Stevens has noted, trauma makes subjects, then what are the stakes of trauma's compulsion to produce speaking subjects? In various ways, our authors address this question, whether Shahla Talebi's narrative of the child Bahareh, the place of an ethical silence in response to Nazi horrors, or Debra Jackson's account of silently giving witness to rape victims.

What if these silences *are* the interruptions that matter? That is, the spaces in and through which subjectivities are formed may be disruptions constituted by a temporary absence of words; such silences (after Freud, Foucault, et al.) are the biopolitical work of trauma itself. Understanding and narrating trauma as it takes place under the sign of silence offers generative questions, most provocatively in relation to silence in the realm of poetics. As scholars and practitioners, we often must attend to temporalities of re-creation and development in the crushing absence of audible meaning. But what do we miss, analytically and affectively, when we fail to stop at the void, the hush, the space between the inhale and the exhale? When we don't listen to the silences, when we do not remain within the trauma but skip across it like a stone on water, how many other grammars are disabled? And yet, how might we (can we even) speak for the silent (Spivak 1988), those whose voices are muted in vulnerability rather than raised in outrage?

Shahla Talebi's chapter offers a story about the truthful silence that is never fully an absence, how it exists just on the other side of torture's noisily incoherent techniques. Gabriele Schwab's "transgenerational haunting" is embodied in Talebi's narrative voice, a curious chain of mangled but expressive signifiers passing from a mother to a child and, last, to a critical mind with its own story of loss. Bahareh, the child in Talebi's recollection, reshapes language phonologically, taking the typographical signifier and turning it sideways, resulting in a new word, "amama," that is both intensely personal but also bearing a kind of politics, resistant and resonant. Bahareh has indeed "refused to speak the language of her killers." This beautiful narrative attempts to speak outside the frame, through the imagination of a narrator—after the state, after the atrocity, continuous with past and future. Bahareh, for whom Talebi becomes a voice, memory, and future, inhabits an unconsciousness that spans time and space, after her witnessing but never beyond it. Bahareh and Talebi share their loss through the medium of the writerly unconscious, in which the past is brought back and theorized, documenting the possibilities for speech and writing in the face of radical distortion, erasure, and destruction. Bahareh's story, in Talebi's voice, has a narrative end, but never a temporal closure.

Nor are its meanings bounded within our volume. Literary critic and theorist Gabriele Schwab's essay converses with Talebi's narrative, exploring the intersections of trauma, silence, memory, and language. Taking up the story of Bahareh, Schwab articulates the meaning of silence within the confined space of the prison, locating Bahareh's story in a transitional space between individual and collective trauma. The child communicated only through body language and inarticulate sounds, seemingly recognizing that words might be dangerous inside the prison walls. Upon her release, she regained the ability (perhaps the will?) to speak, recognizing that her speech and her life were no longer precarious. Schwab writes, "When it does not come from a peaceful place, silence creates anxiety and fear." Thus, Talebi and others "heard" the child's silence through a world made mute by terror. Listening to the silent child reveals to the imprisoned women connections between them, the speaking. Rather than creating a wall, Bahareh's silence instead engaged "the silenced traumatic core of [the women's] selves." Here, the absence of language actually speaks into existence a vital, if unsettling and pained, community. At the same time, the silent child is interpreted by others—here, two scholars—posing vital questions about who speaks for whom, and when.

Next, we have an intellectually searching, profoundly moving conversation about genocide and the Holocaust between Schwab and philosopher Martin Beck Matuštík.[1] Themes for the interview emerged from Schwab's (2010) book, *Haunting Legacies: Violent Histories and Transgenerational Trauma*. In the interview, we witness Matuštík's psychoanalytically nuanced inquiries eliciting a series of beautifully composed thinkpieces that merge high theory with personal revelation. The dialectic between Matuštík and Schwab reveals two minds alert to the problems of memory in the wake of multiply layered historical atrocities, and the jealous and tender political moralities that trail such histories. Schwab provides the biographies of her ideas and of her transgenerational self—a self-composite of family specters—and, in the process, puts trauma directly into the multidirectional past, ethically charged, poetic, and luminous.

Emergent literary scholar Amanda Wicks addresses a different type of apocalypse, analytically exploring Cormac McCarthy's *The Road*—a landscape seemingly beyond forgiveness. Noting that narrative accounts of traumatic events tend to draw on apocalyptic language and themes, she writes that "it seems increasingly beneficial to turn the tables and read the escalating number of post-apocalypse narratives published since the late twentieth century through the lens of trauma studies." In exploring the language and form of apocalyptic narratives, Wicks is attentive to issues of memory, forgetting, survival, and history. If, as she notes, the apocalypse signifies an "impossible history" that is "not worth recuperating," what does this mean for critical trauma theory? As represented in *The Road* (both the novel and the subsequent 2009 film), memory may be detrimental to the operations of survival, dragging the survivor(s) back into an "impossible history" and overwhelming subjectivity. If self-witnessing and narrative are crucial to recovery and reintegration of the subject, as many trauma practitioners argue, then how does forgetting for the sake of survival figure into this? In the realm of bare-bones survival, as exemplified in the post-apocalyptic narrative, forgetting may trump memory—and indeed, the very work of memorialization shapes both what is forgotten and what is remembered.

Next, sociologist Jackie Orr draws on her astonishing and provocative mixed-media performance piece. Here, in an adaptation of that performance, she offers a version of the artistic piece along with urgent critical thoughts about how live performance might be translated to the page. With attention to imbrications of the visual and the textual, the present and the archival, and the violence inflicted on bodies by technologies, Orr asks what it means to exhibit corpses. Moving back and forth between Gunther von Hagens's Body Worlds, Fallujah, World War I, family history, the Cold War, and popular culture, Orr meditates on the complex, historically shifting relationship among bodies, visibility, weaponry, affect, and the spectacular, and she does so with her trademark playfully serious language. She queries how we *see* the dead (and death) when corpses are so widely distributed across digital networks and sites of display. What does death mean when it happens remotely? And what does it mean to traffic with the dead, to narrate/visualize death, and to (try to) remember the dead?

Writing authority Amy Hodges Hamilton takes us into the classroom, her classroom specifically, and also into her own life as she struggles with her young daughter's leukemia diagnosis. Drawing on a teacher-research study she conducted about the use of personal narratives in academic settings, she offers compelling evidence that such accounts—and the process of writing them—can contribute significantly to a student's educational experience. Focused on the subfield of writing and healing, her moving essay blends her roles as teacher, writer, and mother, and offers a critique of "objective" academic discourse. She writes, "Students come to our classrooms with many literacies or discourses—personal, cultural, global. Why should the academy value one over the other?" As scholar-teachers, many of us encounter personal writing in our classrooms, even when we're not actively teaching memoir and autobiography. Hamilton offers some helpful guidelines for working with students who share "personal" details in their classroom writing. She also vividly illustrates, through the details of her students' writing, that the classroom is a space where "trauma" is narrated, responded to, and occasionally healed. Her work attests to the continuing importance (and difficulty) of critical—and empathically engaged—pedagogy and mothering.

Philosopher Debra Jackson also examines responses to trauma, focusing specifically on sexual violence. She does so from the feminist perspective of witnessing as a crisis counselor—a potential counterpoint to the nomenclature problems described earlier by Fahs. Intimately engaged in questions of practice, Jackson explores embodied effects of trauma, including loss of speech, symptoms recognized in psychiatric literature as PTSD, and anxiety. Often, she notes, recovery of one's subjectivity necessitates the ability to narrate one's story, to name the trauma inflicted so as to contain it. This is a form of self-witnessing. Jackson describes the experience of being a witness to others' trauma, and an ethical participant in the recovery of others' subjectivity. Yet, here again, even in praxis language breaks down. In a poignant scene from the ER, Jackson portrays her own capacity for speech failing in the face of a rape victim's silence. She writes, "The gap between us felt insurmountable." She comes to understand that the witness must suspend her own judgments and bracket her feelings in order to focus wholly on the victim's story, *even if that story is silence.* And rather than a binary with the power to silence and reinscribe, as in Fahs's piece, we have in Jackson's work witnessing as a dialogic and intersubjective process: "An effective witness to trauma connects with survivors without collapsing the boundaries between self and other. In the process, two narratives are written." But it is not a symmetrical process; bearing witness requires empathic and ethical reflexivity.

Sisters Rebecca Hankins, an archivist, and Akua Duku Anokye, a sociolinguist, use oral history methods to document the experiences of their family in the aftermath of Hurricane Katrina. Interviewing twelve of the nineteen displaced members of the Hankins family, the authors chronicle issues of structural disadvantage, including race and class, in the post-Katrina dispersal. Family members evacuated to Texas, and only some returned; each migration impacted lives considerably, wreaking havoc on intimate relationships, educational aspirations, personal and family economies, and quality of life, while also providing some limited opportunities for change. Hankins and Anokye draw important connections between PTSD as it is understood in the psychiatric literature and the phenomenon of posttrauma slavery syndrome, or PTSS. Their essays shows trauma's effects are deeply racialized and historicized, and we often miss both effects at great cost. African Americans experienced Hurricane Katrina in ways that both extended and emphasized their historic structural vulnerability. Hankins and Anokye's work offers a window onto one family's experience of a "natural" disaster, while also showcasing the value of oral history to our interpretations of trauma.

Our final essay is novelist Dorothy Allison's "A Cure for Bitterness," narrated in her inimitable voice. A writer, teacher, mother, and radical feminist, Allison offers up a living theory of trauma, grounded in experiences of violence, pain, damage, and the unspeakable. She poses a vital critique of academic obfuscation, while also navigating the dangerous territory of telling stories about pain and suffering. She tells us that while we may have lived through trauma, this does not entitle us to write about it—a bold claim in the age of memoir. As a teacher, Allison encounters all sorts of horror stories—damaged people who want to put experiences to the page—and there are dangers in doing so, both to the writers and their teachers. She asks: Should all terrors be narrated? What does it mean to tell a good story, one that is believable? Who owns the language of trauma?

Allison tells us boldly that to write trauma, we need to have *already done the work* of engagement with our experiences; the writing itself is not the place to "heal" from our trauma, because that would get in the way of the story. And our stories, she tells us, whether we are writers or academics, are all fiction, no less true for being embedded in language and narrative, and dependent on that which eludes the speaking and listening subject.

***

There are many riches herein, as we've signaled in this introduction, but *Critical Trauma Studies* cannot—and should not—be all things to all people. It necessarily reflects the interests and commitments of those who created this collection—those who are drawn to "catastrophe's glow," to borrow the lovely title of Maurice Stevens's next project. We hope many will seek to join the "chorus" of voices (Griffin 1993) speaking about and within critical trauma studies. The book's contributions reflect what can emerge from the spaces of ethically engaged scholarship and praxis. And while linkages are shared across these pages, readers themselves will perform the connective tissue holding this volume together, animating the politics, poetics, and praxis of which we speak and write. The reader becomes the healer, the visible stitch, in the choreographed but imprecise movement of following "traumatic" pathways through this book.

NOTE

1 The interview originally took place at a symposium inspired, in part, by our 2010 conference, "Memory and Countermemory: Memorialization of an Open Future," Arizona State University, November 6–8, 2011. See http://jewishstudies.clas.asu.edu/memory.

I

Politics

2

Trauma Is as Trauma Does

The Politics of Affect in Catastrophic Times

MAURICE E. STEVENS

I love stories and storytelling, and I love that feeling of being in the presence of a good storyteller. I'm sure you've experienced it. That sense of being spoken to, being spoken of, reflecting or laughing individually and feeling part of something else, something beyond your individuality, your subjectivity. I am fascinated with narratives, too. Sometimes they contain stories, sometimes not, but I have long been interested in how narratives of individual and communal "self-hood" provide us with ideas about who we are, or think we are, and present us with visions of our place in the cosmos, in history, in society, and in doing so relate us to our own sense of interiority. These are narratives of the past, the present, and the future, and they are routed through myriad forms of material, ultimately coming to constitute our sense of identity. These are narratives of science, religion, history, memory, politics, and psyche, and, in their own way, they provide the content that is drawn up, absorbed into, and constitutive of social relations, knowledge objects, and institutions, the operations of which we study and engage.

And if our engagement is deep, both material and immaterial, concerned with individual and intersubjective experience, if it is grounded in the fabric of social relations, even while it depends upon theories of discourse and subjectivity to better grasp the nuances of those interrelations, then I would call it *critical*. If in this deep and critical engagement our subject of study, or our community of engagement, possesses the capacity to inform *us* of the tools necessary to its illumination and understanding, then it may also prove transformational.

So I draw on perspectives from critical race theory, gender studies, studies of visual culture, and critical psychoanalytic studies that grow from both my research and my experience working in clinical settings, to develop what I call *critical trauma theory*. This theory is sensitive to the filaments of social interaction that both inform one's sense of interpsychic experience, and are informed by discursively inflected identity and social subjectivity. At its base is the notion that *trauma* is not simply a concept that describes particularly overwhelming events, nor is it simply a category that "holds" people who have been undone by such events; but it is a cultural object whose function produces particular types of subjects, and predisposes specific affect flows that it then manages and ultimately shunts into political projects of various types. *Trauma does not describe, trauma makes.* That is, trauma is as trauma does, and naming something "trauma" does not always help, and it never only "helps."

A number of theorists have long been concerned with how individuals and communities of people come to understand, represent, and perform themselves as actors, as agents in history. Especially when the subjectivity of racialized ethnic subjects is so often constrained by discourses of difference and denigration that call into question their possession of the very qualities and criteria of being that make one a putative citizen-subject of history. This includes being constructed as without will, for example, or as primitive and without history or literate culture, or as without meaningful psychic interiority. We are all quite familiar with constructions of this type, and we are familiar with how they are repeatedly supported by the exhumed evidence of uncovered mass burial sites or unmarked graveyards, exhibited bones or post-carded atrocities, whispered genealogies. This is not entirely new information, not for people who, sometimes by choice and sometimes not, keep company with the practices that swirl around, within, and through trauma.

One aspect of my work in the academy and in clinical settings has been to confront this kind of denigration and degradation, which has produced two important findings. First, the denigrated and the degraded, if only to beat back the loathing, must create histories that feature themselves and their loved ones as vindicated whole beings who possess the stuff of historical merit—will, self-awareness, culture, humanity, and so on. And second, the absence of this kind of confrontation in traditionally authorized settings (e.g., universities, capitol halls, state archives) has forced the work of representing, and potentially working through, difficult historical events, to fall to cultural production as a locus for memory management.

And so two other questions become relevant. On one hand, we can look to the various modes and sites of cultural production that allow for the representation of history through the mediation of memory—sites like literature, performance work, memorialization practices, visual culture, street art, and the like. On the other hand—and this comes out of my ongoing collaborations in clinical settings in what is very loosely termed "behavioral health"—we can look at how already existing discourses intended to take up issues of history, memory, trauma, and "therapeutic intervention" have remained primarily silent on questions of racialized or intersectional experience or the importance of difference. While various modes of trauma studies are interested in the way individualized effects of traumatic experience might disrupt what Jean Laplanche calls auto-theorization (that piecing together of subjectivity through the weaving of past narratives of self into contemporary stories), and while other modes of trauma studies focus on how traumatic historical events complicate historiography itself, very few theorists take up the question of intersectionality or difference in relation to trauma.

I've been hard-pressed to find discussions of the way memory and forgetting as cultural practices remain the only mode of history making available to abjected groups. So conversations can take place (both in clinical and academic settings) about how traumatic events—individual or communal—disrupt auto-theorization or complicate historiography. But one does not hear many clinicians or academic traumatists discuss the traumatogenic nature of institutionalized modes of psychic denigration that take the form of race-, class-, gender-, and sexuality-based patterns of social differentiation. Instead, one sees the proliferation of discussions about trauma, memory, and historiography that assume a racially unmarked citizen-subject both in the academy and in clinical settings that is understood to respond in various ways to forces overwhelming. And this is where I begin wondering about the work of trauma as a concept that does more than simply describe events or the symptomatology the traumatized subject provides.

***

I have more recently begun to think about committing to engaging this kind of work from a posture that is different from what we have typically done in the past. The kinds of topics that draw us actually require a shifted investment; we can no longer be invested in merely conveying ideas. While we do want to do that, of course, we also need to evoke experiences that can host some of the tensions about which we have such deep interest. What this has meant thus far has been insisting on bodily awareness and breath while speaking of affect in the radically intellectualized contexts academic institutions tend to offer. It has also meant raising caution and suspicion about our desire to "help" and "make better" at social-justice- and community-action-oriented gatherings. In preparing for the conversations we must have, I seek to bring my intuition into some kind of balance with my theoretical concerns and investments, and with my *intention*, with the idea that what I write and how I act in the world might elicit conversation that is meaningful for those who engage my work.

It is for this reason that I have included here "new" writing, writing that is raw and still unfolding. These are reflections that are still growing and seeking, not having clear expectations of outcome and, therefore, inviting of other fresh responses. I cultivate this experimental possibility by conveying, in advance of making any argument or sharing an analysis, some sense of how this piece emerged—to share some old "feeling" with that new writing, perhaps. So more than giving an account of this essay's intellectual trajectory, or nestling it within a narrative of "broader" projects, I want to offer a sense of the affective milieu that is coming to find limited expression in this work. The comments I'm sharing here are actually part of a much smaller project. Smaller in the sense of the micro-relations that constitute our sociality, our memory management, and our affective flows; and smaller in the sense of emerging from the rather mundane impulse of affect to find mediation in the world through features of everyday life. And are we not all involved in work that serves our affect's ardent wish to be translated, or to represent in some way? Are we not all working on projects that are, in their own ways, working us? Moreover, this charge that enlivens my writing, this particular expressive moment, is not and can never be "depleted" in the way we might think of energy being "used up," and any particular manifestation of affect can only be partial, because it finds its way into my classrooms, my parenting, and other forms of social practice. And do not all of us find our affect urgently pressing its way into sensation, dream, memory, emotion, idea, and action?

In some quarters, "trauma studies" seems to be something of a defunct subfield, a "seeming" that has little to do with the flagging usefulness of the field, and more to do with how it has been territorialized by recuperative structures serving ideological masters. In this essay, I both name "trauma" as a "biopolitical apparatus" and seek to articulate a space called critical trauma theory at this historical moment. I offer as a point of departure the need to remain conscious of our own deep affect, feeling, and stakes in conversations about memory, history, trauma, and the biopolitical. That, in fact, to speak and to think about the biopolitical vis-à-vis this cultural concept we call "trauma" necessitates that we pay attention to affect. The way information economies are managed by surveillance, for example, or archival practices, or notions of intellectual property find their analogue in the management of affective economies. Only the latter's technologies come in the form of diagnostic criteria, case histories, and treatment narratives, and notions of "trauma" and its traceability.

When I look back now and put things together, I knew two things for sure growing up. The first was that I carried the heavy and awkward weight of knotted family mythologies on my shoulders. I was the "four winds child," I was the child of many lines of immigrants and indigenous people, and my mothers and fathers told me in broken stories and rare pictures that all of my ancestors were survivors of various types: German Jews, Haitians, Cherokees, Chinese laborers, and Norwegian shipbuilders. Myths. From early on, I carried the myth that I came from a long line of survivors whose primary connection with one another, other than me, was the fact they all had managed to make a way out of no way.

The second thing I knew was that although the world was precarious and psychic coherence fluid, capricious even, it was also consistent in its provision of connection and support, often from places very odd and unpredictable, and in forms nearly unrecognizable, but there nonetheless. And I knew that it always seemed to come back together, to recuperate its coherence. This falling apart and coming together, this expansion and contraction, this breathe and exhale of dissolution and reconstitution of self, would become, or more probably always was, my good-enough love and place of familiar ambiguity. And what a wonder, what one could witness in that movement from individuated selfhood to interpersonal *interbeing* and back again.

It is safe to say that I am called to practices and experiences where one is witness to the ruination of self, an unraveling that sometimes brings the new and sometimes causes its bleeding out; to practices and experiences like watching a body come apart (especially when it is one's own), feeling one's frameworks for knowing strain and fracture and break in the face of the unbelievable noticing, the creeping loss of predictability as one's own compass for reality slips into unreality. Places where dream and waking, consciousness and unconscious, memory and present experience, and dread lose clear or dependable distinction; places where we feel the immanence of direct experience, the unstopping inhale and expansion of overfilling with emptiness to the pop of spiritual annihilation; losing boundedness between individual and collective; and so on. I've sought these boundary experiences in mental health work with psychotic and schizophrenic adolescents, on the streets with homeless veterans, in travels with religious mystics, and through the use of psychoactive substances in controlled and uncontrolled settings. I both have been drawn to these practices and others, and have set up shop there, as it were. My work develops out of the pleasures, sorrows, tensions, excitement, pains, and fears that churn and intermingle in these spaces.

When I think about why this has been so, and try to piece together a justifying narrative (for I must have one when asked, and do not moments of unexplained difference require of us all the production of justifying narratives?); when I justify my persistence, I do so by imagining that it is because these settings of rupture represent moments in which the "fixing"—of which Fanon spoke with such impact in *Black Skins, White Masks*—actually begins to fail, and the dye looses its hold, and coherent narratives lose information, clear pictures become blurry, and above all, dominant logics are dethroned. Indeed, countless philosophers, researchers, theorists, and performers have commented on the ways in which this "fix" has come into appearance for them. And have we not all felt a sense of the multiscalar resonance of our constitution in the social: the cellular, the neurological, the corporeal, the mnemonic, the emotional, the ideational, the familial, the societal, the national, the global, the ecological, and so on? These moments possess tremendous potential energy and are nearly infinite in their possible lines of flight. Their promise looks like Hope, and for much of my life, Hope looked like an answer. That energy for potential, those lines of flight, run in innumerable directions, with innumerable possibilities, all of them Hopeful, yes. But one soul's Hope is another's murder. It is not about Hope for me anymore, just a radical hopelessness and dispassionate fortitude.

This essay offers a series of claims. My first claim is that events we understand through the rubric of "trauma," or the "catastrophe," or the "emergency," or the "crisis," events that constitute the very heart and iterative moment of trauma studies, that these events become meaningful because we imagine them to destabilize senses of being and to trouble subjectivity. Trauma is "trauma," in part, because it disrupts what is otherwise a fairly coherent and seamless object: the subject. Not only do we have particular ideas about the degree of "damage" that counts as trauma (one's sense of being and very subjectivity are destabilized and troubled), but we also have a fairly fixed idea about the "subject" and "sense" and "being" the destabilization of which amounts to "trauma." Indeed, these concepts are at the heart of the conceptual *and* the experienced scaffolding for that subject who is at the center of our own intellectual and political work, which is to say both our "subjects" of analysis and ourselves as researchers and actors.

For the most part, we imagine the subject/self as rationalistic, possessed of agency, and as host to a recognizable interiority. The self that is subject to trauma can be "held responsible," can be expected to respond to intervention with self-restraint or behavior modifications, and, importantly, is assumed capable of providing self-descriptions of their interior experiences and bodily sensations. The subject both *is* coherent and *makes* coherence by providing us with a useful and very particular way to explain and understand action and experience. This subject can be broken, precisely because once it was not.

In general terms, "traumatic" events disrupt and even emaciate language and, at times, the body. "Traumatic" events explode discourse and materiality, and they overflow easy distinctions between and among notions of "individual agency" and institutional practices. Events we believe we come to know as "trauma" and have come to know *through* "trauma" have, it appears, much to do with experiences of interiority and with its absence. The subject of "trauma" is a beleaguered one, and it is also that about which our work speaks and, in some ways, upon which it depends, and certainly, that which it reproduces. We talk about trauma, we rely on trauma, we reproduce trauma. The very and various contexts out of which subjectivity is understood to emerge are disrupted by events we attempt to make sense of through the application of various trauma theories; and the subject thus construed both is the "subject" of trauma study *and* is created through trauma study.

Huddling within this somewhat general claim are, of course, others. Claims that begin to feel, perhaps, more intimate; claims that are closer to home, closer to our own sense of self-knowing. So to begin placing a slightly sharper point on it, let me claim that the events we have come to understand, to see, and to sometimes witness through the lens of "trauma," that these events mangle bodies *and* senses of embodiment, defy mnemonic structures *and* memory's instantiation in/as history. They shake one's capacity to narrate *and* dissolve narrative itself, tangle temporal framings *and* temporality itself. At the same time these events shock social relations, they *also* electrify sociality, and while they obliterate affective regulation, they reduce affect itself to a charged and glowing potential seeking explosive manifestation and symbolization— seeking, that is, mediation. Events we belatedly come to understand as "traumatic" produce enigmatic signifiers, indelible and indecipherable, that "ardently wish to be translated."

It is this coming into "known-ness," this translation or mediation, that fascinates me; it is the cost we pay for the conveyance of this numinous affect into the symbolic that occasionally saddens me; but it is the price of this particular ticket that nearly undoes me. Therefore, moving into the remainder of this essay, I invite you to engage in an activity of wondering that begins with the following consideration.

What Is the Question to Which "Trauma" Has Become the Answer?

By trauma, I mean the sets of practices that provide explanatory narratives, organize interpersonal and material relations, and establish meaningful frameworks for understanding relatedness, temporality, and embodiment vis-à-vis "overwhelming events." Trauma, here, is an ingathering of practices, a cultural object. So what is the question to which this bundle of practices has become the answer? I have come to believe, and currently hold the notion, that the question to which "Trauma" has become the answer is something like: *How can the myth of the independent and isolated ego, the coherent and seamless self, the proper citizen-subject; how can it be asserted, vouched for, and recuperated in the aftermath of the everyday contexts of a "social" that constantly challenges the basic utility of these concepts, which is to say, in the end, their sustainability?* To put this another way, the everyday precariousness and brutality of the social, and the miracles of compassionate interbeing that also populate this unpredictable social, constantly challenge the myth of individuality, independence, and isolated ego, to a degree that essentially requires the emergence of a cultural concept that can do the work of recuperating this myth that is collapsing under contemporary realities.

I also invite you, as you read on, to engage in a kind of witnessing. A witnessing of the type that Kelly Oliver (2001) speaks of in her work, a witnessing based on the notion of relational subjectivity, one that emerges from the social and one that assumes that what we sometimes come to call trauma, and what we remark upon when we note its traces, its symptoms, does not record the event's breaching of an individual's capacity for signification or cathexis, or experience, as most theorists working from a psychoanalytic frame would argue, but rather that it indicates the failure of the social to adequately respond to the event—the inability of the surround to endure the anxiety attendant to the event, to contain or hold it. In this framing, then, the symptom or the trace of the event or agents of injury acts as a kind of memorial to what Peter Shabad (2000) calls "one's lonely suffering," the failure of the surround to hold, more than it does the event itself.

Almost ritualistically, I call upon this particular surround, our surround, this social, to hold a space for my claim that the challenge and possibility that overwhelming events, and our use of the notion of "trauma" to make sense of them, poses to the framing of our concerns, comes precisely in the wake of their force—their power to render ontologies obsolete and inadequate, to melt concrete and reified common sense to slag, to reduce our knowing to a state that calls upon strategies of recuperation and fantasies of healing. Even more so, in few locations outside of those notable for the ruination of subjectivity, does one see at work the operation of ideologies of social propriety and clean and proper citizen-subjectivity so clearly and ruthlessly.

Indeed, it is the trauma, the crisis, and/or the emergent sense of urgency that enlivens state capacities to act. Thus, on one hand the trauma, the catastrophe, the crisis, the urgency of questions like "What shall we do? How can we help? How do we achieve social justice?" all serve to cohere affect. They are the strings to our sweet crystalline rock candy, sites of condensation, circuits or pathways or ecologies, that in meeting the conditions of affect's representability, promise a sense of community, promise a sense of meaningful embodiment, promise the assertion of agency or safety, while also being the site of all the things that undermine these promises and turn them into lies.

At the same time that overwhelming events unmoor the subject that is at the core of our intellectual and political projects, the work of "trauma"—that is, the work not of describing events or subjects, but of actually "making" them—gestures toward new directions of inquiry and new terrains of reflection. As a cultural object that constitutes parameters of proper citizen-subjectivity, "trauma" is exemplary in its ability to do so without regard for national borders, historical boundaries, or claims on authentic membership vis-à-vis the subject as we have known it (be it racialized, ethnicized, classed, gendered, or sexualized). And it does so while also and sometimes simultaneously complexly linking the community gathered under the banner of an affect by the past-perfect or future-perfect sense of no-longer-whole-coherent-seamless-innocent-proper-etc., linking this community of "traumatized" to already extant templates functioning at various scales: Nation—when it's useful, Race—when it's useful, Class—when it's useful, Community—when it's useful, and so on.

So, as you are holding space for these claims, allow me to discuss a few of the particular contexts in which I imagine that reflecting on the ways that "Trauma is what trauma does" might actually offer possibilities for an increasingly capacious enactment of our work, without recourse to some idea of the future, and without recourse to a fixed status; and that we might find the "new" here among the wreckage of the "old," among the found objects that once again found, may be rearranged. I offer this reflection in three gestures, three breaths, almost ritualistically.

First Breath: Body and Embodiment

Usable theories of the body and embodiment have proven essential, and even elemental, to the emergence of trauma studies and in conventional understandings of trauma and interventions considered appropriate and adequate to the damage associated with trauma. For in every instance out of which a theory of trauma has arisen—a theory, that is, describing or accounting for the disruption of experience and its representation, the rupturing of the subject's capacity to regulate its own sense of embodiment—there has also been a substrate that functions to record the suffering or rupture that has given trauma meaning; a medium in or through which traces of the event, real or imagined, find their expression. "Trauma" allows us to register these traces, appearing as they do in the form of scars, or symptoms, or lapses, or repetitions; and it does so upon "bodies" of various types: corporeal entities, psychic projections, narratives of selfhood, informational archives, and so on. Indeed, beginning with "marks" like the bloodied body, the ruptured mind, the incomplete narrative, or the riddled archive, the idea of trauma provides explanatory narratives that, by offering one telling of how the subject achieved its ruination, support fantasies of an originary time before the fall; a time of whole, coherent, innocent selfhood, and uncorrupted, clean, and proper subjectivity. And now, as much as at any other time, the proliferation of affect and informational economies, the society of control and surveillance thus occasioned, and the precariousness of existence inherent to this stage of globalization, almost necessitate a very powerful recuperative fantasy. What better time for the ascendancy of a way of knowing injury that presents individual, whole, coherent bodies as its objects of analysis; discrete and spectacular injuries that can be identified and healed, while at the same time providing technologies for managing large pools of affect and the populations understood to be defined by them.

This lens of trauma, through its tender and unfaltering facing of the sacrificial horrors of disintegration, holds out the promise of our own ritualized healing, our own recuperative imagining, our own admission to the global community of the healed, the cured, and the normative. This notion of trauma, and its organizing myth, can make these promises, however, only after the assumption of significant injury has been accepted, and a sign of damage proffered. Whether it is the body as the autopoietic self-sustaining system that Freud imagined whose "protective shield" is breached; or the organismic body whose capacity to experience or signify, some suggest, is simply overwhelmed by the immensity of the "traumatic" event; within the terrain determined by and articulated through the emergence of "trauma" as a kind of singularity, imperfect bodies and examples of hobbled embodiment, do this work. These injured bodies provide the constitutive outside to our dreams, trajectories, and fantasies of wholeness and control.

As it is popularly and often clinically configured, "trauma" describes events unique in their ability to disrupt or confound both what we believe we know about bodies (our own and those of others), and our ways of knowing about embodiment. In most renderings, trauma's power is daemonic, it is scourge to ontology and epistemology, "unmaking worlds" (Scarry 1985) and disorienting time and space. Trauma viewed from these heights is the site of the Dionysian rupture that signals the Apollonian return of order, the overturning of earth that promises new crops.

With the proper application of technique and the perseverance of survivors, their resilience, integration, orientation, and ordered sociality will return. This vision of trauma—our popular and clinical imagining of the concept—is a heroic narrative. At the same time that overwhelming events split the past off from the present by unmaking rituals of the familiar that promise timelessness, the concept of "trauma" and its theorizations suggest a futurity, and in doing so, put history back on track. Bringing always the undoing, and always the promise, the daemon "trauma" names is neither evil nor beneficent, but simply a force of superficial upheaval. Our conventional understandings of trauma promise to bring the overwhelming, the numinous, the maddening, and the ruining under control and into management by providing a narrative of/for understanding.

That bodies are both the site and stake of the explanatory narratives that trauma proffers should perhaps come as no surprise, given that discursive practices that depend upon and reproduce concepts of trauma have historically been critically restricted by classifications based on race, class, gender, age, and sexuality. While *harm* may be a universally applicable notion, exempt in the abstract from the fetters of politics or prejudice, *having been harmed* is quite another matter, for it is an assessment whose conditions of possibility are entirely determined by cultural context. *Having been harmed* is as much a situated knowledge (Haraway 1988) and experience as knowing one's injury as "trauma."

Second Breath: Affect and Feelings

By now, threats of biological, nuclear, environmental, and explosive attack have become ubiquitous as tropes in American cultural discourse. Stoked by iconic narratives of the sacrificial individual whose suffering will "save" or otherwise bring about the restoration of the primordial and pure community, individual sentiments of vulnerability and outrage have been universalized, cast out into the public sphere and repetitively territorialized. Once imagined, these sentiments—residing as they do somewhere between embodied sensation and sentimental framings—are deftly mobilized in the service of complexes of group identification and action. Affect and information economies and their management provide vectors for the mediation and manifestation of affect (through sites of intensity like activity, symbolization, symptom, or their shadows—declivities, oblivions, absences) and always in the service of capital and the control of reproduction of relations of production.

Moreover, while atomic iconography, millennial imaginings, and visions of contamination have been commonplace within the American cultural imaginary, and have often been festooned with eschatological biblical imagery, contemporary threats are represented as entirely new emergencies; emergencies, in fact, that cohere affect, and that require immediate action and produce immediate effects. Indeed, these actions and effects result in the production of communities of practice that, on one hand, interface with technologies of self-protection like gas masks, duct tape, thyroid tablets, security systems, hand guns; and on the other hand, exhibit signs of emotional distress, with sleep disturbance, nightmares, irritability, an inability to concentrate, and restlessness having all been reported and spectacularized through their very normalization.

Popular therapeutic readings have framed these responses to emergent dangers in the terms of posttraumatic stress disorder, or PTSD, and more recently traumatic brain injury (TBI) and within the theoretical rubric of "trauma" and its effects. "Trauma" functions as a kind of state servant and ideological apparatus, because it helps to perform the work of shunting affect into "appropriate" and state supporting practices. Yet just which version of the state trauma is invoked to support is ferociously contested.

Of course, every closure represents an opening somewhere, and every effort to territorialize, define, discipline, and police will also produce possibilities. The stoking of affect does not always nor only produce the responses that one might expect or desire. Affective intensities seek symbolization through lines of flight that may, or may not, be predetermined, and novel formations do emerge.

Whether it is the anxiety elicited by visions of terrorism and surges in religious, political, and martial fundamentalism throughout the world in spaces considered "the very heart" or the "bordering edge"; or mounting worries in the face of warnings about global financial collapse, or viral pandemics, or border breaches, communities of practice and affect come to be drawn together without having to actually imagine their membership in any specific ways. There is no need for a sense of national belonging or identification with the nation-state for these formations to take on meaning and produce material effects, even while these effects often come to be coupled with or articulated in nationalist terms and in relation to local community and regional relations; or are cast back into already existing narratives of national identity, citizenship, religious, and/or class affiliations.

Third Breath: Memory, History, and Temporality

Like trauma and memory itself, the *study* of memory and the formation of the memory sciences have a milieu, and they have taken their shape and cue from social contexts that, over the course of modern industrialization's inexorable cultural speedup, have come to privilege the production of history over the production of memory. Spaces of history like the archive, the memorial, or the "official story" are often *figured* in binary opposition to spaces considered the purview of memory: the performance, the repertoire, or the ephemera of public culture and spaces.

Moreover, through the rhetorics of provenance, authenticity, and the originality of the record, institutions that manage memory increasingly wear the robes of truth's arbiters. In repositories of facts and in conglomerations of evidence, memory management *takes place* while historicity is conferred by the archive and through its objects. Authority to produce "real" narratives that can be read as true shifts as remembering bodies are replaced by bodies of information that constitute history.

So while they are often *posed* in opposition, both memory and history contribute to a regime of remembrance whose logics and functions are familiar and, in some ways, comforting. The logics of this mnemonic regime, the arcs of its movement, are those of the photograph or the gene or the eyewitness testimony; its functions converge to convey truth, to represent the real, and to reproduce the Same. Thus, one need not accept the opposition between history and memory to appreciate the effects produced by the solidification of their polar relation. History posed against memory works. It works like science against culture or data against interpretation, its cultural leverage deriving not simply from the binary opposition, but from the meanings ascribed to those oppositions and the material relations those meanings justify, the ideologies they reproduce, and the incommensurability they convey.

So when it comes to "trauma," the way it privileges a particular concept of the body and embodiment, and its posture vis-à-vis "feelings," the science of memory has shifted from conceiving of its object, *memory*, as an evolving entity open to processes of contestation, reframing, appropriation, diffraction, or simple dissolution, and has moved, again, with seeming inexorability, toward a focus on *history* as the fraught and always problematic recording of what has "gone on," as the recitation of actions and events contained within the past-perfect grammar of description, and the body's sometimes inaccurate keeping of the record. There and then was an event, it occurred in a place and at a time that are, by definition, distanced from here, from now; and the historian (or the psychologist, or other technician of memory recuperation) heroically does the work of salvage, approaching the event through documents, archives, psychological artifacts, patient narratives, corroborating testimony, and images believed to shed evidentiary light on the always-already past event, to link it through an ideal provenance of its traces to the present. The labor of recuperation, then, and the measure of one's "healing" agency or ability lies in getting as "close" to the event as possible and determining what should be memorialized in objects of historical and psychological inscription.

Unlike "the history," as the story goes, memory exists continually, inscribed in the ongoing production of a narrativized self or community of practice or affiliation. The muscle remembers, the space is haunted, the landscape is scarred; always, with memory, a trace remains. A trace remains, defiantly, sometimes hinting, sometimes pressing, sometimes roaring, but always insisting in/on its ubiquitous return. Reading and writing this "natural" history, engaging in this kind of "reconstructive" archaeology requires sifting through *remnants* instead of *traces*, and speaks the past differently. Events captured in history are located in the mythos of temporal progressions, in the relation between moments and events; the distance imagined between here/now and there/then is the necessary condition to this kind of history taking. The recuperative work associated with "traumatized populations" does similar work.

Indeed, history as a trope with rhetorical force is memory's nemesis, pushing it ever flatter, out of the flesh of bodies, gestures, objects, and spaces, and into the amber of dominant signs and symbols, or the architecture of archives cataloguing ash and bones, or the taxonomy of etiology or morbidity—but not in the bodies whose experience it purports to record, as it is carefully peeled away, disentangled, distanced by the practice of "history taking."

And yet history (and the practice of "taking histories") is haunted by stories that have gone unincluded in the realm of the historiography "trauma narratives" require. History grows gaunt and distracted in its confrontation with events that test its ability to represent, and in its encounter with affect that won't stay still and is difficult to inscribe with any accuracy, if at all. Hunched over, squinting, and losing its flexibility, these taken histories worry at the frayed ends of incomplete narratives, hidden transcripts, dream images, and unruly sensations. Still, we see that when and where history struggles, when and where it collapses in the face of the body's absolute truth of *having* pain or being harmed, and the clinging and inexorable suspicion that accompanies *documenting* it, we see, in fact, trauma's mnemonic regime providing support. Here, trauma interventions can begin the work of putting narratives together enough for them to be legible to the archives of history taking, and History making.

Just as the invisible genome vouches for the validity of phenotype, or the effaced technologies of the photo argue the "fact" of its real representation, the past and completed unrepresentable trauma supports claims about the coherent subject of history. It says, "You see, there once was a whole, seamless, and modern subject/body. Our effort to repair it, by making legible its injury, is proof enough of its having been there at one time, whole, pure, and mature. Trauma has rendered this particular example of proper subjectivity and able-bodiedness damaged, where once, in a moment of innocent possibility, it was not."

An Inhalation: Control Societies and Trauma as Bio-political Apparatus

Catastrophe, and the "trauma" we imagine it to convey, that is, the sense we make of the injury and suffering inherent to catastrophe's upheavals, is quite central to forms of imperialism and global neoliberalism that seem to be coming so fully into their own over the past decade. That is, what sentimentalism was to the imperial and colonial projects of the last century, where laboring subjects were brought into modernist economies as to-be-subjectified, to-be-disciplined citizen-subjects— what sentimentality provided this great shift, "trauma" now provides the control society. Where instead of, or rather, in addition to, disciplined citizen-subjects, we might speak of observing the emergence of controlled populations of affective flow and practice, the emergence of bio-affective-political economies.

"Trauma" as a particularly understood catastrophe calls for relief and strategies of recuperation. It acts as the point of the sword that opens lines of entry, vectors for economic and political flows operating under the best intentions and deep longings to "help," to achieve justice, and to document. Operating in such a way that allows us to imagine ourselves enacting our "best selves," the best of humans, true humanitarians. This activity of opening economic and political flows is salved with our own pleasurable affect and sentiment. Thus, while laboring to manage affect, to improve emotional states, or to alleviate suffering, it is precisely our own affect that is turned to the work of globalizing capital and political flows.

Indeed, information technologies, diagnostic practices, biotechnological expertise, and analytic frames born of American academia follow these flows. And with them flow the instruments of their management:

archives, inventories, histories, analyses, tables, outcome measurements, best practices, and so on. The great globalizing science of what I call "eu-affectics," then, requires the ready emergence of political economies that accompany securitizing and the bringing under control, the calming down, the pacification of the subject of the state. These come best and most warmly through the provision of "safety," "hope," "somatically grounded resiliency treatments," and "neurologically based trauma treatments," to and for the traumatized.

These are, in part, questions of scale. The fact that we can talk about individual bodies, social embodiment, communal memory, history, and global flows of affect suggests as much. This work, the work of critically examining trauma, requires that we keep one eye on what trauma does, while keeping another on *how* it does it, for whom, and with what consequences. And so I urge my fellow traumatists to keep in mind and heart the points of constraint and lines of unfolding that emerge in our work and passionate engagements with injury and upheaval under the rubric of trauma.

3

"She Was Just a Chechen"

The Female Suicide Bomber as a Site of Collective Suffering in Wartime Chechen Republic

FRANCINE BANNER

They physically have lost their desire to live. *Physically.*
Not psychologically. Not in thought. Do you understand
me? There are some people who want to become suicide
bombers because something happened in their heads, but
there are more people who physically don't want to—who
can't—live. . . . And this, this is what I think happened to
those girls.
—"Irina," human rights worker, to the author (Moscow,
October 2008)

From 2000 to 2004, Chechen women composed more than 40 percent of those who committed suicide attacks against the Russian state.
While male fighters engaged in suicide missions, driving explosive-
laden trucks into military compounds, it was women alone who donned
the visceral suicide belt. This chapter explores the ways in which these
suicide bombings by women manifested within their own bodies the
geopolitical trauma written on the Chechen national body during the
Russo-Chechen Wars.

Anthropologists, sociologists, and trauma studies researchers have
made vital inroads into documenting and explaining the somatic effects
of profound trauma (Wilson 2004; Kleinman 1997; Weiss 1997; Kleinman and Kleinman 1994; Lock 1993; Leder 1990; Martin 1987; Scarry
1985). Scholars also have begun to unearth complex interconnections
between individual and collective bodies during times of stress (Mallot
2006; Todeschini 2001; Argenti-Pillen 2003). To date, however, few have

interrogated the ways in which traumatic experiences differently impact men and women in societies in conflict.

Trauma studies and terrorism studies are Western inventions.[1] Post-colonial and feminist scholars question whether European perspectives on these issues, focusing primarily on the effects of conflict on male combatants, can be transferred to study across cultures and genders (Kienzler 2008; Sideris 2003; Argenti-Pillen 2000).[2] Mallot (2006) suggests that a way to adapt this problematic research paradigm—to "decolonize" trauma studies—is to step away from psychological investigations and toward considering the ways in which trauma physically is incorporated into the human body (see also Kleinman and Kleinman 1994 and Lock 1993).

The most common definition of the term "normal" is "accepted" or "customary," but another is "corporeal." Despite the intimate connections between the body and suicide bombing, in most studies, the role that a person's experiences as a member of her community plays in her self-immolation—the interplay between her status as a body in the world and the processes by which she comes to engage in terrorism—is deemed insignificant. A feminist approach, which treats the body not as peripheral but as the center of shifting locations of power, can help us to understand the ways the self is entrenched in and formed by societies experiencing prolonged oppression (Sideris 2003, 714; Merleau-Ponty 1969). The case of Chechen women suicide bombers provides a unique opportunity to explore gendered, somatic effects of trauma. Looking closely at Chechnya also provides an entry point toward exploring women's engagement in suicide bombing as the spectacular embodiment of social suffering.

Rather than categorizing the woman suicide bomber as deviant, an outcast, or an aberration, this essay frames the Chechen female militant as a figure exposing the tensions of a society in crisis. It argues, furthermore, that women in particular were uniquely suited to represent the suffering of this traumatized population. I do not dismiss the actions of women suicide bombers as unusual or abnormal, but instead argue that the actions of women militants were a distinctly normal product of the "state of exception"[3] wrought by postmodern occupation.

The first part of the essay provides an overview of the injuries that Chechen society experienced from 2000 to 2004, focusing specifically on the ways in which torture, forced disappearances, and rape impacted the Chechen collective experience during this fragile time. In the second part of the essay, I discuss Chechen women's roles in Chechen society and in Russo-Chechen conflict, particularly focusing on the ways in which women's bodies, treated simultaneously as both central in and alien to Chechen society, have functioned as a field of moral debate during times of crisis. Last, I offer that suicide bombings by Chechen women should be viewed not as a product of individual psychosis but as a form of collective, political violence. I interrogate the processes by which protracted and brutal wars on the Chechen national body may have led to the nation, paradoxically, enacting further injury upon itself.

The Wall of Silence: War and the Collective in Chechnya

In the *banya*, you would see chunks of body parts missing from all the fighters
—"Lincoln," filmmaker, to the author (Salt Lake City, November 2008)

Not all harms constitute trauma. Herman (1997) offers that trauma arises from the extraordinary. "Unlike commonplace misfortunes . . . traumatic events generally involve threats to life or bodily integrity, or a close personal encounter with violence and death" (33). Others argue that trauma is a result not simply of exposure to dramatic events of violence but also of structural violence that is inherent in everyday lived experiences under extreme oppression (Fassin and Rechtman 2009; Miller and Rasmussen 2010; Stevens 2010; Betancourt and Williams 2008). Whether one takes a narrow view, attributing traumatic suffering to extraordinary encounters with violence, or accepts the position that trauma can result from the structural violence that inheres in the ordinary, the Chechen Republic unquestionably qualifies as a site of extreme stress. Between 1994 and 2004, the Chechen people lived under a state of terror in which the Russian state, local authorities, and religious zealots competed to restrict the most basic human rights and freedoms. The republic was embroiled in two brutal, long-standing wars with the Russian state during which an estimated hundred thousand people—a tenth of the population—were killed. On an everyday level, there was an unemployment rate upward of 60 percent, a lack of health care, and a dearth of opportunities for education. Libraries housing linguistic resources and relics deliberately were destroyed (Williams 2000, 126).

Nongovernmental organizations have documented thousands of forced detentions, summary executions, and disappearances occurring between 1994 and 2004 (Nivat 2003; Politkovskaya 2001, 2003; Human Rights Watch 2000a, 2000b, 2000c).[4] Since the conclusion of the wars, more than sixty mass, unmarked graves have been discovered in the republic, one containing nearly eight hundred bodies ("Russia: Chechen Mass Grave Found" 2008). The graves evidence not only widespread practices of torture, but, equally significantly, the state's persistent refusal to preserve evidence and to identify the victims and perpetrators of crimes of war (Knight and Narozhna 2005).

In the original Greek, the word "trauma" means a physical wound or injury. Over time, however, the word has become associated with suffering of the soul and spirit (Mallot 2006, 166). The story of the Russo-Chechen Wars is a story of incursions on bodily integrity leading, gradually, to the disintegration of emotional and social frameworks. A hallmark of the Second Russo-Chechen War was *zachistki*, "mopping up" operations, effected by the Russian military as a part of antiterrorist strategies (Politkovskaya 2002). During such operations, a village would be surrounded by tanks, armored vehicles, and trucks, one of which, the "purification car," was designated for torture (Kurczab-Redlich 2002). While the stated purpose was to check civilians' papers, zachistki often devolved into a "free-for-all" (Conley 2004, 335–36).[5] Politkovskaya (2002) described a typical blockade: "Russian soldiers have to be paid 1000 roubles [approximately $40], and then a man won't be taken to the filtration point [usually a military facility such as Khankala or Chernokozovo] . . . . The fee for soldiers to give up the rape of local women was around 300 to 500 roubles [around $20]." Soldiers serving in Chechnya suffered from severe shortages of supplies, hazardous conditions, and rampant drug addiction. The result for Chechens was a constant lack of security—in their property and in their persons. When the *Los Angeles Times* interviewed conscripts returning from Chechnya, they described their actions as *bezpredel*, without limits (Reynolds 2000).

So many people suffered during the Russo-Chechen Wars. However, social, historical, and biological factors meant that Chechen women faced harms different from those faced by Chechen men. As I show, distinct injuries necessarily foster unique approaches to resistance.

Trauma in Chechnya: Gendered Effects

For four days, I slept, I worked. The grenade was a part of my
body, a part of my body—and if they touched me, I swear to
God, I'd have pulled the ring.
—Gabrielle Giroday, interview with war survivor (2008)

In societies under occupation, often figures emerge that express the tensions at work in a particular culture. What Pitcher (1998) deems "liminal" persons direct "the trauma of occupation away from individual incapacity and internalized 'pathology' and toward a collective and proactive affirmation of . . . identity" (121). Chaudhry and Bertram (2009) similarly discuss how in "limit societies"—societies experiencing extreme trauma—a few persons may carve out unique possibilities for resistance. For example, during the intifadas, some Palestinian young men were able to transform ritual imprisonment and beatings by Israeli soldiers from a demonstration of brutality by the occupier into a transformative experience that "galvanized participants into unsettling power arrangements" (Peteet 1994, 31). By becoming martyrs, Pitcher (1998) and Peteet (1994) argue, these young men were able to carve out spaces for resistance within the strictures of oppression. Acts intended to entrench the power of the occupier were "transformed into a ritual expression of political agency, masculinity and construction of self" (Peteet 1994, 31). Chaudhry and Bertram observe, similarly, that within "'limit situations,' suffering is revealed, negotiated and transformed as a collective dynamic" (Chaudhry and Bertram 2009).

Although the scant research that exists on the relationship between suicide bombing and social embeddedness focuses on men, as Chaudhry and Bertram (2009) identify, it is women, based on their realization of "interlocking oppressions" of class, gender, and state violence, who may be uniquely suited to "identify[ing] fissures within structures of power and, if only momentarily, subverting those structures" (299).

This is because, during times of catastrophe, women's bodies become central in the struggle for control over public space (Cooke 2000, 175; Eisenstein 2000; Dowler 1998; Yuval-Davis 1996, 1997). In most—if not all—societies, women are, paradoxically, insiders and outsiders, "the symbols and the 'others' of collectivity" (Yuval-Davis 1996, 1997; Anthias and Yuval-Davis 1989). Across cultures and ethnicities, women historically have been denied rights and privileges afforded to men. However, as Enloe (2000) points out, in times of conflict, "womenandchildren" constitute the heart of society. It is in the name of defending and protecting these "most vulnerable" members that communities most frequently (claim to) go to war. And it is "enemy" women who are targeted in campaigns of mass rape and ethnic cleansing, because to soil or shame women is tantamount to debasing the values of a society as a whole (Raccioppi and O'Sullivan 2000; Yuval-Davis 1997; Card 1996).[6]

In the Chechen language, there is a proverb that, to survive, women need "both looks and an axe." Women must be serene in outward appearance; however, they must also be willing to safeguard their bodies even at great personal cost. Embedded within Chechen culture is the idea of *Nokhchallah*, which cannot be translated directly but "implies moral and ethical behavior, chivalry, generosity and the will to safeguard the honor of women" (Unrepresented Nations and Peoples Organization 2009). The centrality of women's chastity to the Chechen national project is evident in a common parable:

> Here is a story about a man who asked to spend a night in a house that stood on the outskirts of a Chechen village, without knowing that [his hostess] was alone. The hostess . . . gave him something to eat and made a bed for him. In the morning, the man realized that the woman was alone. . . . As he was hurriedly washing up, he brushed the woman's hand with his small finger by accident. The man cut the finger off with his knife before leaving that place. Only a man brought up in the spirit of "nokhchallah" will go to such pains to protect a woman's honor. (Chechen 2007)

Today, Chechens continue to hold women, the members of society tasked with preserving cultural heritage and national identity, in high esteem. Refugees consistently identify respect for women as among the highest values in their culture, and they view the primary role of the

Chechen woman as a wife and mother (Szczepaniková 2004, 43; Bersanova 2004, 2). Chechen President Ramzan Kadyrov offers guidelines for women's behavior: "I want our women to be *samie nedostupnie*—[the most] inaccessible" (Seierstad 2008, 219). On International Women's Day in 2007, President Kadyrov called all female students to the auditorium at Chechen State University. He made a speech indicating that women were Chechnya's "most treasured possession" and therefore must be "honored and protected" (Seierstad 2008, 179). He announced that he had brought gifts for all women—headscarves—and that he would be offended if they did not wear them (Seierstad 2008, 180). Today, the government requires that female students attend class in head coverings (Israilov 2008). Women who dare to walk the streets without a headscarf risk being targeted by government thugs wielding paintball guns (Weir 2011). Although couched in the language of respect and protection, the deliberate placement of women as embodying the nation's moral and cultural norms is precisely what renders them targets in times of crisis.

Written on the Body: Women, Modesty, and Chechen History

Besides the wars, the Deportation is perhaps the defining event in Chechen history. In 1944, as Russians celebrated victory in the Second World War, nearly the entire Chechen population was forcibly deported to the steppe at the behest of Joseph Stalin (Pohl 2000; Nekrich 1978).[7] One of the most vital occurrences in any refugee population is the development of what Tambiah (1996, 27) calls an anthropology of displacement, wherein disbursed peoples reconstruct their experiences of suffering in mythohistorical terms. The mythology of the Chechen Deportation is in many ways a fabular construction of women. For example, a key narrative of the 1940s is that of fecundity. In most populations, at times of excessive hardship the birth rate falls. In the Chechen case, however, the birth rate remained high from 1940 to 1960. Although an estimated seventy thousand Chechens died in the first year of exile alone, the population that returned to the homeland was as vibrant in number as that which left (Williams 2000, 112). Although sociologists have identified the youth and health of deportees as the primary reasons for high birth rates, in the retelling, the births of children during Deportation have become an expression of communal solidarity, a way for the population to recover from losses and to outlast their Russian counterparts (Jaimoukha 2005; Lieven 1998, 189; Lapidus 1984). One Chechen scholar describes "procreation" as "self-defense in the face of possible liquidation" (Jaimoukha 2005, 130). In the postwar context, women's fecundity again has taken on mythic proportions. A Chechen obstetrician observes, unrealistically, "From personal experience, I can say that [during the wars] the birth rate went up 20 to 30 percent. It's to make up for the loss of population" (Baiev and Daniloff 2006; Daniloff 2007). Sonia, a human rights worker notes, "There is an urban legend that during this past fifteen years of collapse, Chechen women had more children than before. The explanation is that there was nothing else for them to do. *Women reverted to the natural state*" ("Sonia," personal communication with the author, 2007). As Ranehod-Nillson and Tetreault (2000) observe, "Because women are biological producers of national collectivities, the conditions under which, when, how many, and whose children women will bear are questions of national importance (to men) and matters of civic duty or oppression (to women)" (6; see also Woliver 2002; Yuval-Davis 1996, 1997).

For Chechens, the Deportation also provides an object lesson about women's preservation of chastity at great personal cost. When Russian soldiers arrived in 1944, they herded villagers into train cars for exportation. Thousands died during the weeklong journey, many of them young women. The deaths of these women have taken on a heroic status based on a bizarre exercise of resistance. The cars, the narrative unfolds, were not segregated between men and women, so that young girls were transported alongside men. Legend provides that the young women were so demure that they refused to urinate in the presence of male passengers (Pohl 2002). The women went so long without relieving themselves, the myth continues, that they perished when their bladders burst (Pohl 2002).[8]

Another story known among Chechens is that of the mass suicide at Dady-Yurt. Chechnya and Russia have a protracted history of violent engagement dating before the 1600s. In 1819, one of the most heavy-handed Russian officers, General Yermolov, gave troops orders to raze the Chechen village of Dady-Yurt. When Russian soldiers attempted to rescue the forty-six female survivors by taking them across a nearby river by ferry, the women reportedly threw themselves into the river rather than risk being defiled by Russian soldiers (Basayev 2009; Ka-vkazcenter 2011). In 2010, President Kadyrov declared a new holiday, Chechen Women's Day, to honor these women who drowned rather than succumb to the advances of their rescuers (Kishovsky 2010). The advent of Chechen Women's Day was accompanied by a series of mod-esty campaigns, during which the Kadyrovsky, thugs employed by the local government, forcibly took women's cell phones, restricted their In-ternet use, and penalized women for failure to dress in conformity with government-disseminated ideals of modesty (Weir 2011; HRW 2011).[9] Resurgent mythologies about and restrictive rules regarding women's chastity highlight that the ideal Chechen woman is one who stands at the heart of the preservation of traditional morals and who, further-more, is expected to sacrifice her life for the greater good of the com-munity when those morals are threatened.

As conflicts escalate, the risk of sexual and gender-based violence typically increases (United Nations Entity for Gender Equality and the Empowerment of Women 2011). This is true in regard to both "pub-lic" crimes, such as mass rape by troops, and "private" crimes of do-mestic violence.[10] As women, the keepers of the collective, increasingly are threatened, the focus of the national body becomes dependent on reclaiming and rebuilding intact and unharmed female bodies. Ironi-cally, as women become increasingly visible icons of cultural norms, the needs, desires, and accomplishments of individual women are pressed into the background, in Chechnya as elsewhere.[11] The ways in which these processes functioned during the Russo-Chechen Wars are dis-cussed next.

The Gendered Body at War: 2000 to 2004

During the Russo-Chechen conflicts, the role of Chechen women most visible in the West was that of perpetrators. This conspicuous role, how-ever, obfuscated Chechen women's far more frequent status as victims. After coming to power in 2000, Prime Minister Vladimir Putin ini-tiated a campaign of carpet bombing, with the promise to "waste the terrorists in the outhouse" (Russell 2008, 107; Williams 2000, 109). In a 102-day siege, twenty thousand people were trapped underground in the Chechen capital city of Grozny (Williams 2000, 109). From 2000 to 2001, four hundred thousand Chechens fled the republic as refugees (Memorial 2000). Because men were prohibited from crossing checkpoints and were also recruited by local groups as fighters, more than 80 percent of the refugee population were women (United Nations 2006).[12]

In 2004, Doctors Without Borders surveyed more than three hundred refugee families in camps in Chechnya and Ingushetia. Two-thirds of interviewees reported that they "rarely felt safe" (Médecins Sans Frontières 2004). The same survey found that more than 70 percent of Chechen refugees had "heard about" someone who was raped (Médecins Sans Frontières 2004, 15). Medical Care for Victims of Torture, one of the few organizations to document sexual violence in Chechnya, reports that, of the thirty-five clients who sought assistance, seventeen (sixteen women and one man) had experienced sexual torture (Medical Foundation 2004, 2).[13] Stories abound retelling how families hid young girls in cellars or attics in order to evade Russian soldiers (HRW 2000a, 2000b, 2000c).

The highly publicized rape of eighteen-year-old Hedda Kungayeva is emblematic of the sexual violence committed against Chechen women by Russian forces. On March 28, 2000, Colonel Yuri Budanov, stationed in the Chechen Republic, was celebrating the second birthday of his daughter, back at home in Russia. The colonel told subordinates to fetch him a Chechen girl with whom he could celebrate (Wines 2001; BBC News 2001). Hedda was at home with her three siblings when Russian soldiers knocked at the door. After unsuccessfully trying to take her thirteen-year-old sister, soldiers bound Hedda in a blanket, saying, "We'd better take the pretty woman" (HRW 2000a). Later that evening, Budanov raped and sodomized Hedda, then strangled her to death. Subordinates buried her body in a nearby forest. Although Budanov confessed to the rape, his first trial resulted in a verdict of not guilty by reason of temporary insanity. Those who assisted him in dumping the body were pardoned. Russian citizens were outraged that he had been prosecuted at all (Wines 2001; BBC News 2001).[14] One Russian man echoed his fellow citizens' dismay, observing, after all, "She was just a Chechen" (Zarakhovich 2001).

In its stark and deliberate violence, the story of Colonel Budanov's attack on Hedda Kungayeva is, sadly, typical. What makes her story rare is that her family actually came forward to discuss the assault. The profound emphasis on women's roles as keepers of the national culture has made disclosing and documenting the widespread sexual violence that occurred during the Russo-Chechen Wars a gargantuan task. Kungayeva's father observed, "As a Chechen ... I am ashamed that I have to talk about my daughter's rape. In our culture, we don't. ... *Hedda's death isn't the worst thing.* Her rape humiliates my family, my clan, and the whole Chechen people" (BBC News 2001, my emphasis). While there is disagreement as to the prevalence of honor killings in Chechnya, stories regularly surface regarding male family members harming sisters or daughters in the name of protecting familial honor. President Ramzan Kadyrov recently remarked matter-of-factly to Russian newspaper *Komsomolskaya Pravda*, "According to our tradition, if a woman fools around, her family members kill her. ... That's how it happens, a brother kills his sister or a husband kills his wife. ... As a president, I cannot allow for them to kill. So, let women not wear shorts" (HRW 2011, 10).[15] A report from the International Rescue Committee released in 2006 found that 95 percent of female focus group participants had heard about or witnessed an incident of violence against women (IRC 2006, 48). Stark statistics such as these reflect both the centrality of honor in the Chechen culture and the extent to which it is considered women's responsibility to guard that honor—to the point of death if necessary.[16]

State restrictions on dress, honor killings, and repeated instances of domestic violence evidence that, when a woman is victimized or behaves in a way deemed inappropriate under contemporary societal standards, her individual body becomes a metaphor for the social body. Her individual suffering brings shame to the collective. As Berko and Erez (2007, 496) observe, in highly patriarchal societies, for women, honor is passive and can only be "lost or tarnished, whereas 'honor' for men is active, and can be retrieved, increased and expanded." The import of this is that, in some cases, men may be able to "redeem" their own or their family's honor within the community only by punishing, ostracizing, or exacting physical harm on dishonored female relatives. In times of collective trauma, the revival of the national body becomes contingent on the restoration of a moral female body. Paradoxically, restoration may hinge on women's sacrifice—or, rather, the sacrifice of women.

In times of peace, it is men who engage in the political sphere, whereas women in highly patriarchal societies are consigned to the private realm of home and family. Stories such as Hedda Kungayeva's, however, illustrate the extent to which, during conflict, women are relocated at the heart of negotiation of the parameters of identity. As Eisenstein (2000) observes, "Shame [the mother], shame her family, and her nation, and they are defeated" (47). Deceased fighter Ruslan Yamadayev (2002), critical of Movsar Barayev's and Shamil Basayev's decision to have women suicide bombers participate at Dubrokva, observed, "Using a woman in war is a matter of great shame for a Chechen. If a man allows a woman to interfere in an everyday family fight, we say that he is . . . worse than a woman." Shcheblanova and Yarskaya-Smirnova (2009, 250) argue that this statement evidences the extent to which being a woman is nonidentical to being Chechen. However, in times of conflict, it is in fact women who come to symbolize the very heart of the nation. At peace, the woman may be consigned to the domestic sphere, tasked with inculcating morals and traditions in future generations (Yuval-Davis 1997; Walby 1992). She is, merely, a woman. However, at war, the body of the woman becomes representative of the body of the collective (Yuval-Davis 1997). In times of conflict, she is "just a Chechen."

Loyal to the End: Women as Suicide Bombers

It started in different areas—Basayev, the woman killing the general who killed her husband. It never came back after Beslan. It is not grassroots. It is not a mass of women wanting to do this because of revenge. The notion of revenge is very complex. . . . I am skeptical of revenge. . . . If there is a crime, there needs to be revenge, but . . . revenge is the business of men. Because all law is the business of men.
—"Sonia," human rights worker, to the author (New York, 2007)

It is important to highlight that women's collective status as victims during the Chechen wars did not preclude their acting, simultaneously, as agents. Chechen women took on varied roles during conflict as family breadwinners, activists, nurses for rebel operations, and militants

(Szczepaniková 2004; Liberakina 1996). However, what may seem to be "novel" engagements of women during war often rely on traditional linkages between women and the private, domestic sphere (Dowler 1998; Ridd and Calloway 1986). This, too, was the case in the Chechen Republic. For example, during the wars, many Chechen women became sole providers for their families. However, this was not because women took on unusual tasks but because the available paid tasks within refugee camps—cleaning, cooking—were traditionally "women's work" (Szczepaniková 2004, 43). Similarly, women's engagements with militant operations were not primarily as fighters but as nurses and caregivers (Speckhard and Akhmedova 2006).

Chechen women also were activists. In recent years, the vocal participation of Russian, Chechen, and Dagestani women in defending and advocating for victims of conflict has been recognized by numerous international organizations, including the International Rescue Committee, the nonprofit organization Reach All Women in War (RAW), and the Norwegian Nobel Committee. As Eliza Moussaeva, director of the Ingushetia Office of the Russian human rights organization Memorial, notes, "the real protectors of rights in Chechnya are women" (quoted in Conley 2004, 332).[17] Conley (2004) suggests in the post-Soviet period, there was almost no civil society in Chechnya. "What protests there [were], against government policies, against the war, in the hopes of finding information about detainees, generally [were] spearheaded by women [because] they [were] . . . less likely to be suspected of being guerillas" (Conley 2004, 334–35; Politkovskaya 2002). It was Chechen women who were tasked with claiming the bodies of dead Chechen militants from the Russian military because they were the "most mobile" members of society during the wars (Conley 2004, 333). Bersanova (2004, 3) observes, "By claiming a blood relation to the victim, [women] save[d] men completely unknown to them." Rather than stepping out of domestic roles, women's activism *relied on* associations with maternity and pacifism to achieve political objectives (Oushakine 2006, 303; Liberakina 1996).

Das (1997, 81) reminds us that acts of mourning traditionally have been "gendered activities." She writes, "In the course of everyday life, men dominate the public domain in terms of control over speech, but in the case of death they become mute." In traditional Chechen society, women were key participants in death rituals, sitting with the body for a week, uttering lamentations, and striking themselves on their faces (Jaimoukha 2005, 132). Historically, mourning rituals called for widows to cut off an ear at their husbands' deaths, then a topknot of hair (Jaimoukha 2005, 132). Aset is a fairly common Chechen name today, derived from Isis, Egyptian goddess of the dead and funeral rites (Meier 2005, 70). In Chechen society, it is women who are deemed most capable of and thus responsible for exhibiting emotion and publicly mourning deaths (Manchanda 2001, 120–21; Das 1997, 81). In these rituals, as in the activism premised upon them, men are silent. It is women who give voice to collective trauma. This may also be said of women's participation as suicide bombers.

Altruistic Suicide? Suicide Bombing as Collective Political Violence

Many narratives about societies that have experienced the deep, collective trauma of long-standing conflict hinge on the idea that the act of suicide bombing is one way in which heavily scarred communities can express their pain to the world. Rhetoric from supporters of Palestinian bombers, for example, describes militants' actions as violent "narratives" that may help to explain the circumstances of living under occupation.[18] These narratives highlight that suicide bombing is not a manifestation of individual psychosis or psychopathology (Speckhard and Akhmedova 2006; Pape 2005; Atran 2003, 2004; Kreuger and Malecková 2002; Hoffman 1998; Reich 1998; but see Schweitzer 2006). Rather, suicide bombers typically emerge from those who are most embedded in their society or culture (Pape 2005; Ricolfi 2005; Victoroff 2005; Atran 2004; Haddad 2004). In this vein, suicide terrorism has been described as an act of "altruistic suicide," sacrificing one's life for the perceived good of the community (Pape 2005, 22), a "prosocial behavior" in which the bomber risks his or her life for the social welfare (Victoroff 2005, 12), and a manifestation of borderline personality disorder, in which "governmental abuses and violations . . . extend beyond the political parameters to encompass the emotional borders" of actors who are particularly invested in their societies (Lachkar 2006). As Weiss (1997, 813) observes, "the dialectic between the individual and society [is] altered by the advent of conflict." This is especially evident in the case of suicide bombers.

Despite widespread recognition of suicide terrorism by men as an expression of collective political violence,[19] when it comes to women, the majority of research attributes involvement in suicide bombings to personal frailties. In a universe in which "normal" women are altruistic, peacemaking caregivers, female suicide bombers are considered a glaring exception. Aside from a very few works focusing on women militants,[20] women suicide bombers most often are discussed as a footnote to the actions of men. By and large, women's participation in terrorism across cultures and ethnicities is attributed to outcast status, premised on factors such as advanced age, nontraditional education or career choices, divorce, drug abuse, sexual abuse, infertility, or extreme grief (see, e.g., Von Knop 2007; Skaine 2006; Schweitzer 2006; Bloom 2005, 143; Fighel 2003, 3; Myers 2004; Beyler 2003, 2006; Victor 2003). The most prevalent theories regarding Chechen women bombers are that they have been "zombiefied" by Islamic extremists via the use of psychotropic drugs, coerced into seeking vengeance after losing male relatives, or shamed into participation via tactics such as sexual assault (see, e.g., Skaine 2006; Krasnov 2008; Groskop 2004; Shermatova and Tait 2003a).[21] Whereas for men living under occupation, committing political violence is within the parameters of expected behavior, when women act violently, we mark them as deviant, assuming that they must have been overcome by personal, psychological frailties (Sjoberg and Gentry 2007; Jewkes 2004; Pearson 1997).

It is unquestionable that shame, loss, and frustration play a powerful role in women's decisions to become suicide bombers. However, the way in which these emotions are interwoven with the bodily experiences of women suicide bombers cannot be fully explored using the current language of terrorism studies, which by and large focus on identifying motives for or "root causes" of political violence. The vast majority of academic research regarding terrorism treats the body as a constant physical object rather than something culturally and historically constituted. Suicide bombers are labeled as anticorporeal, motivated by the *rational* desire to defend home, family, or territory, or über-corporeal, irrational zealots who have "lost their minds" and surrendered wholly to bodily desires or frailties. In each conception, the body is "bracketed" as a "black box" and disregarded (Lock 1993, 133). Needed are new approaches toward articulating the ways in which the relationship between the individual and the collective is fostered. It is here where explorations of trauma are useful.

During the wars, via torture, mass rapes, and zachistki, Russian soldiers and local militants systematically attempted to silence the Chechen population. The oppressions wrought by the Soviet state were compounded by an authoritarian local government, persistent ignorance of the global community, and local stigma surrounding discussions of torture and sexual violence. As Pohl (2004, 8) observes, "There has been a wall of silence around the Chechens not just for the last ten years of genocidal war, but for sixty years." Rather than reliving traumatic events, many Chechens simply want to get on with their lives after years of suffering. More than half of nearly three hundred respondents interviewed by Doctors Without Borders noted that, when confronted with painful situations, their strategy was to "look the other way" (Médecins Sans Frontières 2004). By denying or downplaying the extent of sexual violence that occurred during recent wars, men and women have been able to "save face" and continue to preserve the familiar, gendered roles that they assumed in peacetime. However, as I discuss below, there is substantial evidence regarding the collective and personal harms wrought by keeping silent. As human rights advocate Gistam Sakaeva observes, "[After the wars] I was hearing stories from 40–50 women . . . all these women it was like, you know, they were suffering so much . . . that they couldn't have some place to go to share their feelings . . . to get some assistance. . . . They were so vulnerable" (Open Society Institute 2008).

Although some scholars are critical of the remedial effects of truth commissions and testimonials (see, e.g., Mallot 2006), others have documented the ways in which collective resilience to conflict is developed when survivors are provided with vehicles for achieving social justice and accountability (Sideris 2003). Das and Kleinman (2001), for example, articulate how the creation of "alternative public spheres" in which trauma survivors can voice demands for justice assists survivors in "remaking the world" after acts of violence (see also Sideris 2003). Medical researchers similarly have found that women in conflict situations who "just tried to forget" about their experiences reported significantly worse mental health outcomes than those who used active strategies of coping, such as talking to relatives and friends (Usta, Farver, and Zein 2008). For example, Usta, Farver, and Zein, who conducted research among female conflict survivors in postconflict Lebanon, found that constructing a coherent narrative of painful events ameliorated posttraumatic stress and depressive symptoms and improved the overall functioning of survivors of violence. On the other hand, when attempts to discuss traumatic occurrences were resisted, interviewees exhibited poorer psychological functioning (Usta, Farver, and Zein 2008, 795).

Today it has become common in the West to speak about trauma in terms of PTSD, an individual psychological issue that stems from participation in, subjection to, or witnessing of conflict. However, Doctors Without Borders cautions that the silence found within societies in conflict is not solely a product of individual psychological disorders (Médecins Sans Frontières 2004). The suffering in societies that have experienced long-standing conflict is "much more than the deep subjectivity of the afflicted person, the psychology of the individual" but transcends the individual as "cultural representation, as transpersonal experience, and as the embodiment of collective memory" (Kleinman 1997, 316–17; Grosz 1994, 50, 51). Argenti-Pillen (2003, 11), who studied the Tamil population in Sri Lanka, notes that, in situations of extreme conflict, "terror and horror ... become sedimented into the body" (see also Das 1997, 2001; Scarry 1985).

During peacetime, the *individual* body is the site of everyday domination and aggression (Olujic 1998, 46; Csordias 1994). However, at war, this individual body is transformed "into the social body as seen in genocidal rapes, ethnic cleansing, and purifying of the bloodlines" (Olujic 1998, 46; Weiss 1997; Scheper-Hughes and Lock 1987). Weiss's (1997) research on communities at war echoes these sentiments. Weiss asked Israeli university students to draw their bodies in periods of war and peace. Uniformly, and regardless of gender, the body drawn in war was different from the everyday body. The "peace" body was drawn alone, while the body at war was surrounded by others (Weiss 1997, 820). The relationship between the individual and society was altered by the advent of conflict (Weiss 1997, 813). The work of these scholars evidences that trauma is not an "intra-psychic but a psycho-social phenomenon" (Chaudhry and Bertram 2009, 301; Silove 1999). As Kleinman (1997) articulates, under brutal oppression, the collective "cartography" of trauma may become mapped onto the bodies of individuals, "direct[ing] the trauma of occupation away from individual incapacity and internalized 'pathology' and toward a collective and proactive affirmation of ... identity" (see also Pitcher 1998; Chaudhry and Bertram 2009).

Chechnya does not have a "culture of martyrdom" as there is in Palestine, where suicide bombing at times has inspired reasonably widespread grassroots support (Speckhard and Akhmedova 2006, 2). However, at least until the kidnapping of schoolchildren at Beslan in 2004, the perception that suicide bombers were engaging in individual actions in order to convey the angst of the collective appears to have existed among Chechens. After the 2002 hostage taking by Chechen militants at Moscow's Dubrovka Theater, a Russian television station interviewed Chechens in refugee camps in Ingushetia and found that the vast majority considered chief hostage taker Movsar Barayev "a national hero" and a "defender of the nation" (BBC News 2002). All of five women who agreed to be interviewed on camera stated that they themselves would have agreed to take part in Dubrovka as suicide bombers. As one explained, "I would do anything now. I'm already fed up with living, you understand? Living as if we're not people" (BBC News 2002). A friend of one woman militant who participated at Dubrovka spoke to psychologist Anne Speckhard (2005, 125, my emphasis) about her acquaintance: "I understand and I feel very sorry for her. *Certainly, I need her*. She was very brave. It seems to me, if there were no war, she would have entirely another life and I also."

Recent clinical research suggests that women's bodily incorporation of trauma may be not only discursive, but also literal. Studies regarding populations in conflict and those postconflict have begun to explore the differentiated effects of trauma on men and women. Findings show that women are more likely than men to bodily manifest trauma symptoms. Ashford and Huet-Vaughn (1997) hypothesize that women are at greater risk for developing mental health problems during conflict due to the combination of their responsibility as primary caregivers for children, their lower social status, and their increased risk of being rape victims. Renner and Salem (2009), for example, conducted interviews with refugees from Chechnya, Afghanistan, and West Africa in order to assess how clinical symptoms of posttraumatic stress disorder were revealed in men versus women. While the measures of depression, anxiety, and posttraumatic stress did not yield significant gender differences, researchers found that women were significantly more likely to report somatic symptoms. For example, women reported lack of interest in sex, feeling a lump in their throats, and experiencing a "heaviness in the whole body" more often than men (2009). The authors concluded that women, particularly women in collectivist societies, were more susceptible to developing PTSD as a consequence of traumatic events than their male counterparts (Renner and Salem 2009; see also Waas, van der Kwaak, and Bloem 2003). Ai and Peterson (2004, 135), who interviewed Kosovar refugees, also found that although both men and women both reported some level of PTSD, "women experienced higher levels of physical reaction to matters that recalled their traumas, greater alertness, more troubles in sleep, [and] more feelings of numbness." Although Betancourt et al. (2010), who studied the effects of trauma on child soldiers in Sierra Leone, did not find many significant gendered differences in PTSD, they did discover higher levels of PTSD among those who suffered social stigmas or discrimination. Individuals who experienced greater social stigmas, particularly as a result of rape, were more likely to exhibit mental health symptoms (Betancourt et al. 2010).

Hage (2003) cautions that one must be careful in attributing suicide bombing to the Durkheimian concept of altruistic suicide, since men, regardless of altruistic objectives, tend to be competitive and individualistic. For Chechen men, historically, it is considered better to die than to back away from a challenge. The image of the fierce Chechen warrior is embedded in the works of Tolstoy, Dumas, and Lermontov dating back to the 1800s. Chechens themselves embrace this warrior ideal in the persona of the *abreki*, noble bandits who have periodically descended from the mountains to single-handedly battle Russian or tsarist forces.[22] Perhaps unsurprisingly, while Chechen men have engaged in suicide missions, such as driving trucks into military compounds, very few men have donned the infamous "suicide belt."[23]

While men in Chechnya are driven by a culture that enforces bravery, revenge, and blood feuds in protection of clan and family, at least outwardly women are passive and protected. Although scholarly literature claims that women suicide bombers are, at worst, deviant vengeance seekers or at best, outcasts from traditional, patriarchal cultures, Speckhard and Akhmedova (2006), who conducted interviews with thirty-four friends and family members of Chechen women militants, found little evidence to that effect. Only two of thirty-four women suicide bombers they researched did not fulfill "traditional" roles. Nearly half of the women had been married, and several had children (Speckhard and Akhmedova 2006, 39).

Pitcher (1998, 17) speaks of occupation as a time in which a traumatized population tries to "recapture" its identity. During the Second Russo-Chechen War, the parameters of Chechen identity were delineated in large part through the actions of women. Women's activism and retrieval of soldiers' bodies were reminiscent of traditional roles in which women's bodies were deliberately engaged in expressing the grief of the Chechen collective (Ramphele 1997, 105). Although in some cases conflict may have opened up new spaces for women, most commonly Chechen women's actions depended on their role as keepers of the home fires rather than transgressing such roles (Jordan and Denov 2007; Dowler 1998). As wives and mothers, as nurses, as resisters, as activists, and as mourners, women transformed traditionally established societal roles in order to form "a mimesis . . . between body and language that serve[d] to render loss communicable" (Das 1997, 81). Women were tasked with "displac[ing] the emotional pain [of the collective] onto their physical selves and transform[ing] their bodies into ongoing testimonies of loss" (Mallot 2006, 168). In times of conflict, engagement in suicide bombing may extend this maternal, self-sacrificing role further into the public sphere (Manchanda 2001, 107).

Conclusion

"Late-modern colonial occupation differs in many ways from early-modern occupation . . . in its combining of the disciplinary, the biopolitical, and the necropolitical" (Mbembe 2003, 14; Agamben 2005). Via "smart" bombs, zachistki, everyday structural violence, and imposition of "traditional" morals via domestic violence and honor killings, during the Second Russo-Chechen War, each collective of which Chechen women were a part—global, state, and local—asserted an absolute right to decide whether, when, and how they lived or died. At a historical time in which the state of exception became the rule, Chechen women were triply disempowered. As the holders of national morality, women faced a greater threat to bodily sovereignty than their male counterparts. On an individual level, vulnerability to rape left them open to abuse by male relatives in the name of preserving their collective honor.

Rather than being about "making a change in the political status quo," Argo (2006) argues that suicide bombing may be about attaining "a type of empowerment." Speckhard and Akhmedova (2006, 34–35) hypothesize that, for Chechen women, suicide bombing enables participants to provide "an active response versus a passive role in relationship to their traumas" and "[gives] meaning to their suffering and offer[s] a promise of social justice." For liminal figures who emerge within societies that have experienced massive, collective trauma, suicide bombing may be an individual, physical manifestation of the awareness that life under occupation is unlivable, the "expressive articulation" of "a self less vulnerable to the occupier" (Pitcher 1998, 21). As Mbembe (2003, 11) observes, "To exercise sovereignty is to exercise control over mortality."

Although many people suffer greatly, there is a "politics" involved in characterizing experiences as "traumatic" (Fassin and Rechtman 2009; Stevens 2010, this volume [chapter 2]). Historically, the experiences of a few (white, male) sufferers have been legitimated by the clinical community, while the experiences of other (nonwhite, female) sufferers have been overlooked. Approaching the actions of Chechen women suicide bombers as the embodied expression of collective trauma provides a fresh way in which we can come to understand others who at first may appear radically different from ourselves. It enables us to recognize that, despite the extremity of her act, the Chechen woman suicide bomber is not a monster, an aberration, or even an anomaly. Hers is a subjectivity constituted in a historically, geographically, and culturally specific time and place (Merleau-Ponty 1969; Spivak 1988). Foregrounding the body in discussions of suicide bombing and, specifically, considering how the body carries and transmits the memory of suffering may provide vital insights into how experiences under severe oppression, both extraordinary and mundane, may lead some individuals to believe that death is preferable to life.

The exalting of the self-sacrifices made by Chechen women during the period of Deportation through the present illustrates the profound connection that exists in the Chechen national narrative between women's self-immolation and acts of resistance.[24] For Chechen men, even under horrific conditions of occupation, public suicide may have been an act of shame and cowardice. For Chechen women, however, in cases of collective dishonor, suicide is not only accepted, it may even be expected—part and parcel of what historically it has meant to be a "good Chechen." In 2002, twenty-year-old Aiza Gazueva approached a Russian general who had brutally tortured her husband, asked "Do you remember me?," and then blew herself up with a handful of grenades. When asked about her daughter's actions, Aiza's mother responded, "Her husband had been dragged away by Russian troops in front of her eyes. She had neither father nor brother anymore—no reason to live. *She was a loyal woman*, to the end" (Nivat 2005, 415).

NOTES

1 Fassin and Rechtman (2009) describe the birth of trauma psychiatry in nineteenth century London. See also Maurice Stevens (2010), discussing the field of trauma studies as subject to political agendas and investments.

2 See Kienzler (2008) for a comprehensive overview of the debate regarding the application of PTSD scales to measure the impact of trauma on non-Western societies.

3 The term "state of exception" was popularized by theorist Giorgio Agamben (2005), who observed that numerous societies today are living under "a situation in which the emergency becomes the rule, and the very distinction between peace and war (and between foreign and civil war) becomes impossible" (14).

4 The Society for Russian-Chechen Relations, in collaboration with Human Rights Watch, reported that, in the span of *just one month* during 2002, 59 civilians were murdered, 64 were abducted, 168 were seriously wounded, and 298 were tortured (Kurczab-Redlich 2002).

5 For example, in July 2002, Russian soldiers occupied the village of Meskyer Yurt, where they bound twenty-one men, women, and children, blew them up, and threw the remains into a ditch in order that the bodies would evade identification (Kurczab-Redlich 2002).

6 Das (1997), Card (1996), and others have discussed how wartime rape is less about desire than communicating "man to man" in a shaming gesture that men are not able to protect their women.

7 In the period after Deportation in the 1950s and 1960s, Chechens were granted the right of return but were treated as "second-class citizens" in their own homeland, where jobs and homes had been occupied by Russian settlers (Pohl 2004; Nekrich 1978).

8 Historian Michaela Pohl conveys to the author that she has investigated this alleged phenomenon and has concluded, based on scientific data, that this is a physical impossibility.

9 "We want to remind you that, in accordance with the rules and customs of Islam, every Chechen woman is OBLIGED TO WEAR A HEADSCARF. Are you not disgusted when you hear the indecent 'compliments' and proposals that are addressed to you because you have dressed so provocatively and have not covered your head? THINK

ABOUT IT!!! Today we have sprayed you with paint, but this is only a WARNING!!! DON'T COMPEL US TO RESORT TO MORE PERSUASIVE MEASURES!!!" (poster disseminated by Chechen government in 2010; HRW 2011, 21).

10 Catharine MacKinnon (1994, 14) importantly cautions against characterizing rape as an *either/or* situation, an attack of soldiers on civilians or an individualized act of men against women. She observes that because "[w]omen are not typically raped by governments but by what are called individual men," most rapes are legally characterized as "private" crimes and, thus, placed outside the human rights discourse.

11 Miriam Cooke (2000) discusses the idea of "visible invisibility," arguing that, in Western discussions of Muslim cultures, the collective, gendered body of Arab women often is a central focus, while the personal, lived experiences of women are obfuscated. This highlights that even what may appear to be preferential treatment of one identity group may in fact harm that group by ignoring the value and diversity of individual experiences.

12 According to Amnesty International (2000, 6), at the start of the second war, concerned that Russian soldiers were being too "tenderhearted" toward Chechen civilians, General Viktor Kazantsev ordered internal borders closed to men and that all Chechen men between the ages of ten and sixty be rounded up and taken to filtration camps.

13 Human Rights Watch and the Medical Foundation for the Care of Victims of Torture have documented numerous instances of sexual violence against Chechen men, suggesting that such violence was prevalent during the Russo-Chechen Wars. Although beyond the scope of this chapter, the topic of rape against males deserves further study.

14 During and after his trial, Colonel Budanov became a folk hero to the nationalist movement in Russia. In a poll taken during his trial, more than half of the respondents thought that he should be set free (Arutunyan 2011). However, in March 2003, facing pressure from the international human rights community, the Russian Supreme Court retried Budanov and sentenced him to ten years in prison, with credit for three years served (BBC News 2003). He was released in January 2009 and murdered in 2011, in what Russian authorities believe was a contract killing. More than a thousand people attended Budanov's funeral, where the officiant referred to him as "a saint" (Arutunyan 2011).

15 The number of honor killings taking place in the republic is impossible to ascertain, as the deep shame associated with women's perceived immodest behavior means that families do not discuss these crimes. Furthermore, Chechen law enforcement admits that they do not pay a great deal of attention to those cases that do surface, as they are "seen as just punishment for insulting the honor of the family" (Caucasian Knot 2011).

16 For example, an interviewee during a focus group held by the International Rescue Committee observed, "A sullied daughter is worse than a dead one to her father. It's a terrible disgrace. She'll never get married and no one will say a kind word to her, even though it is not her fault she was dishonored" (IRC 2006). A Chechen respondent to a United Nations survey noted, similarly, "If [raped women] come home, they would

be better off shooting themselves. If anyone laid a hand on them, they'd be written off for good here in Chechnya" (United Nations 2006, 16).

17 Interestingly, the most prominent activists who have been killed in connection with their work in Chechnya, Natalia Estimerova and Anna Politkovskaya, have been women.

18 Consider the actions of Palestinian bomber Wafa Idris, as reported by an Egyptian weekly, "[She] did not sit in the coffee shops of rage to which our intellectuals are addicted. . . . She did not go out to demonstrations. . . . She did not sign petitions aimed at the international community. All she did was don a belt of explosives and talk to Israel, America, and the world in the only language they understand" (MEMRI 2002).

19 See, e.g., Pape (2005); Gunawardena (2006, 82); Speckhard and Akhmedova (2006); West (2004-5); Tilly (2002); Reich (1998); Crenshaw (1998); Hoffman (1998); Victoroff (2005).

20 See, e.g., Sjoberg and Gentry (2007); Bloom (2005); Victor (2003); Skaine (2006).

21 Acts of violence by female Chechen militants were so frequent and dramatic, the women earned a nickname in the Western media—the "Black Widows" of Chechnya. Although the term "Black Widow" is not native to the Chechen language, Western scholars nearly uniformly have adopted the pejorative label to characterize Chechen women who engage in political violence (see, e.g., Guletkin 2007; Lahnait 2008; Garrison 2006; Skaine 2006; Krasnov 2008; Pape 2005; Bloom 2005). The nickname highlights that violence committed by women is described in terms distinct from those used to depict violence undertaken by men and used to signify militant women's status as apart from "traditional" culture (Sjoberg and Gentry 2007, 29; Balasingham 2003, 8).

22 In the late 1700s the Russian Empire entered the region that would become Chechnya and stormed the home of Sheikh Mansur, who folklore notes was told by God to lead a *ghazavat* (holy war) on the Russians (Jaimoukha 2005, 40). Six hundred Russians were killed in the resulting ambush, setting off a struggle that continued until 1917. Throughout this period, *abreki*, or "noble bandits," repeatedly attacked Russian settlers in the region, earning a Robin Hood–like image in the Chechen and Russian imaginations (Rotar 2002, 109; Nekrich 1978, 187). A person acknowledged in Chechen society to have been the last *abrek*—Khasukhi Magomadov—escaped Russian forces in the 1940s and launched guerrilla attacks from the hills until 1979 (Jaimoukha 2005, 147).

23 As Reuter (2004) discusses, the suicide belt is a weapon originally developed by the Liberation Tigers of Tamil Eelam specifically for use by women Black Tiger suicide forces. Until 2009, there was only one reported incident in which Chechen men allegedly donned suicide belts. Since 2009, there have been a few instances of men engaging in suicide bombings using the device; however, the vast majority of events categorized as "suicide terrorism" involve "suicide missions," such as car bombings, but do not implicate the body in the same way as the wearing of the suicide belt.

24 The categorization of suicide as an act of war is not unusual. It has been adopted by the US government in the context of detainees at Guantanamo Bay, where military officials labeled inmates' simultaneous hangings "an act of asymmetric warfare" rather than a mental health issue (Savage 2011).

4

Naming Sexual Trauma

On the Political Necessity of Nuance in Rape and Sex Offender Discourses

BREANNE FAHS

Access and definition are fundamental ingredients in
the alchemy of power, so we are doubly, and radically,
insubordinate.
—Marilyn Frye (1983)

The question of naming—that is, the deployment of language to describe
and create meaning around our experiences—remains as fraught with
power, culture, and conflict as any in critical trauma studies. Choosing to put words to violent and frankly unspeakable experiences is a
task often undertaken under duress, and this is particularly so within
the complicated terrain of *sexualized* violence (Brison 2003). When
considering the power of a name to shape experience, I recall a recent
experience I had watching *The Girl with the Dragon Tattoo* (2010), the
much-acclaimed film based on Stieg Larsson's (2008) bestseller. It is
about a woman, Lisbeth, who undergoes repeated sexual traumas only
to emerge as a sidekick in a crime-solving pact with an investigative
journalist, Mikael Blomkvist. Upon my first viewing, scenes of seemingly unending violence against women led me to react in horror. How
had a film so gruesome garnered such widespread positive acclaim?
Could this suggest that sexual violence is so deeply engrained in the
American psyche that people uncritically digest Lisbeth's suffering or,
more troublingly, find it amusing?

When reading reviews of the film (Ebert 2010), I discovered that
Larsson had originally titled the work *Men Who Hate Women*, implying
that the book intended to illuminate conditions of misogyny. My panic

about the fetishization of violence within the film suddenly dissipated. The author *meant* these works as an exposé of misogyny with a clear focus on perpetrators of violence, yet Hollywood had stripped the project of its political edge to make it more palatable to wider audiences (just as they turned her into a *girl* rather than a *woman*). As one *New York Times* reviewer noted, this version "covers up something the filmmakers seem loath to reveal and simultaneously eager to exploit" (Dargis 2010). Why does the *naming* of "hating women" carry such drastically different symbolic and political weight? Can such naming transform the context of what we view or, more significantly, what we *experience*?

This essay considers the naming of sexual violence not simply as a categorical strategy, but as a *political tool*.[1] While naming has certain legal or social implications—by naming rape, victims can prosecute their rapists and then identify and seek treatment as a rape survivor—it also has certain *political* implications related to broader narratives of power, identity, morality, and consent. By tracing cultural panics about "sexting" and sex offending combined with women's own often-ambivalent accounts of naming sexual violence, I pose a rather radical claim: because sexual violence is so pervasive—where men internalize the perpetration of such violence as *normal* and women internalize sexual violence done *to* them as *normal*—categories of *rape* and *sex offending* obscure the pervasive qualities of perpetration and victimhood in the culture at large. The "rape victim" and the "sex offender" become categories of "Otherness"—often seen as *outside the norm* and *outside of ourselves*—that blur and erase the many different ways sexual violence disrupts, traumatizes, and circulates within women's lives. As such, categories of "rape victim" and "sex offender" encourage a widespread failure to recognize, act upon, or become disturbed by the overwhelming numbers of women who experience some sort of sexual violence ("named" or not), and the overwhelming numbers of men who use violence in their "normal" and "everyday" sexual practices with women. Furthermore, experiences outside these dichotomies—for example, sexual violence between women, men as rape victims, those who *both* perpetrate and are victimized by sexual violence—fall further and further out of focus.

Several questions arise when considering the complexities of naming rape, especially pertinent to this volume: What does it mean to remember and recollect trauma, particularly if traumas are situated in and on the body? How are naming and witnessing trauma informed by power and social identities (race, class, gender, sexual identity, and so on)? How are narratives and labels forms of "debased power" *and also* sites of resistance? How do sexual biographies form, change, and rupture? Finally, how do the politics of naming transform not only individual narratives of trauma, but also larger institutions that evaluate, label, minimize, treat, and potentially discard traumatic experiences?

Moral Panics of Sexuality

One of the more disturbing features of our current sexual climate is the near-incessant propensity to dichotomize people's sexual experiences in binary terms. Gayle Rubin's (1993, 3–4) work, drawing on poststructuralist challenges to hierarchical binaries, identified several divides prevalent in ideologies of sexuality: procreative versus nonprocreative; free versus for money; coupled versus alone or in groups; in a relationship versus casual; at home versus in the park; heterosexual versus homosexual; married versus single; and monogamous versus promiscuous. She warns, "It is precisely at times such as these, when we live with the possibility of unthinkable destruction, that people are likely to become dangerously crazy about sexuality. . . . Disputes over sexual behavior often become the vehicles for displacing social anxieties, and discharging their attendant emotional intensity." One such displacement involves the imagining of sex within this dichotomous framework, rendering nearly all sexual acts and choices as good *or* bad.

Notions of sexual pathology and sexual normality are deployed in nearly every major social institution, including school, church, marriage, religion, and the government. Competing values about sexuality permeate each of these institutions and create new climates of panic. One cannot have sex when one is too young, too old, too fat, too disabled, unmarried, unpartnered, non-monogamous, too queer, too traumatized, or non-reproductive. Further still, harsh penalties await those stepping outside of these boundaries. Recent moral panics about teenagers "sexting" their friends (that is, sending naked photos of themselves via their cell phones to friends and boy/girlfriends) have led to headlines like "Her Teen Committed Suicide over 'Sexting': Cynthia Logan's Daughter Was Taunted about Photo She Sent to Boyfriend"; "Sexting

Girls Facing Porn Charges Sue D.A.: Underage Girls Launch Lawsuit Against Prosecution over Allegedly Lewd Pictures Found on Classmates' Cell Phones"; "'Sexting' Teens Can Go Too Far Sending Provocative Images over Cell Phones: It's All the Rage, but It Can Go All Wrong"; "'Sexting' Surprise: Teens Face Child Porn Charges"; and "Teen 'Sexting' Craze Leading to Child Porn Arrests in US."[2] Such headlines generate, and respond to, ideologies that place teens who violate notions of their presumed nonsexuality in the category of "sex offender." That few teens have actually been charged with sexting-related crimes or misdemeanors is irrelevant; the culture of panic condemns teen nudity as *dangerous* and in need of control, portraying the frankly sexual teenager as pathological.[3]

Similar mechanisms have entered public discourse around adult sex offenders, as many states require a sex offender registry to identify and delineate the sexually dangerous and deviant. Some counties have websites to identify the residence and type of crime committed by each sex offender. Other areas have "concerned citizens" groups who call neighbors to inform them if a sex offender has moved into the neighborhood. All of this frenzy fosters a flawed underlying premise: The only sexually dangerous men are those categorized as "sex offenders." Only men perpetrate sexual violence. And, most insidiously, one is *either* a sex offender (who may not have been caught yet!) *or* is sexually normal. Moreover, empirical evidence suggests that programs based on these premises are generally ineffective at preventing sex crimes, protecting children, or increasing public safety (Casper and Moore 2009; Levenson and D'Amora 2007).

Feminist scholars have rightly noted, however, that there is greater pop cultural interest in victims than in perpetrators, particularly *women and children* victims of sexualized crimes. With the sex offender registries as a notable exception, most interest focuses on women as repeated (and, in a Lacanian sense, fetishized) victims of sexual violence. Popular television shows like *CSI* and *Law & Order: Criminal Intent* regularly depict young, dead rape victims combined with nationalistic, pro-America discourse (Harrington 2007). News coverage of rape primarily uses passive voice to describe crimes committed by men against women (Bohner 2001); for example, headlines like "Deputies: Woman at Bus Stop Kidnapped, Raped" and "Police: Woman Raped" leave out the fact (later mentioned in both articles) that a man—notably unnamed—raped a woman.[4] Efforts to determine women's missteps in "encouraging" sexual violence overshadow interest in perpetrators' motives or actions. Furthermore, adult women are always assumed to have provided consent unless they can prove otherwise, as cultural assumptions about sexual access to women permeate legal literatures about sexual violence (Rubin 1993). The frequent appearance of "rape victims" in television, legal, and social discourses also signals that women fall into a dichotomy wherein they are portrayed as rape victims to the exclusion of all other identities. The "rape victim" has become a media trope that obscures the pervasiveness of sexual violence more broadly.

Social Science Research on Naming Rape

Contributions from the social science literature paint a more nuanced picture of women's rape experiences, as conflicts about rape statistics, labeling and naming rape, and the effectiveness of *treating* the sexually victimized clearly reject notions of the "rape binary." Though always provided with the caveat that women underreport rape, statistics reporting frequencies of rape advise that rape and sexual assault against women in the United States carry a high prevalence, hovering around 21 to 25 percent (Campbell and Wasco 2005; Koss, Heise, and Russo 1994), with the United States having the highest rate of any industrialized nation (e.g., four times higher than Germany, twelve times higher than England, twenty times higher than Japan) (Rozee 2005). While American women generally struggle within a culture of violence that normalizes rape, some groups of women report especially high rates of sexual assault—a fact often related to lower social status and vulnerability associated with those identities. These women include those with sexual abuse histories (Parillo, Freeman, and Young 2003; Sarkar and Sarkar 2005), those under age eighteen (Tjaden and Thoennes 2000b), those who identify as Native American or Alaskan Native women (Tjaden and Thoennes 2000a), or women in college who used drugs, lived in a sorority, drank heavily in high school, or attended a college with normative heavy drinking (Mohler-Kuo et al. 2004). Indeed, *nearly half* of women in college described a history of some type of sexual victimization (Koss, Gidycz, and Wisniewski 1987), and most rape perpetrators were men women knew intimately rather than strangers (Marx, Van Wie, and Gross 1996). While women represented 91 percent of rape victims, men committed 99 percent of rapes (UCSC 2008). At least four in ten rapes occurred in women's homes, and the vast majority of nonconsensual sex acts remained unreported (Tjaden and Thoennes 2000b).

Still, these statistics often fail to account for women's "mislabeling" and underreporting of sexual violence, which has led to new research that specifically inquires about *why* women underreport rape. Research on the degree to which women name and label coercive events *as rape* varies dramatically, revealing the slippages women have about naming sexual trauma. Social science research has found that nearly half of college women who reported a rape experience did not label it as rape (Bondurant 2001; Kahn et al. 2003; Koss 1985). Furthermore, the use of the term "rape" seems contingent on the qualities of both the perpetrator and the victim. Women who labeled their experience as rape more often experienced forceful assault by an acquaintance, awakening to someone performing a sexual act on them without consent, or experiencing the assault as a child. Women less often called their experience rape if they submitted to a whining or begging boyfriend, gave in to an emotionally needy man, were assaulted by a boyfriend, were severely impaired by alcohol or drugs and unable to resist, were forced to engage in oral or manual sex rather than penetrative intercourse (Kahn 2004), or reported that they initially wanted the sexual intercourse more (Peterson and Muehlenhard 2004). Women did not label acts as rape when their scripts about the rape experience did not match the events in which rapes occurred (Littleton, Rhatigan, and Axsom 2007) or if they had experienced sexual violence during their youth (McCloskey and Bailey 2000). This suggests that situations that dictate men's sexual access to women—particularly dating and longer-term relationships—led more often to *underreporting* of rape if and when it occurred.

Labeling rape also maps on to broader ideologies of gender and power, revealing how *naming* remains inextricably intertwined with gender roles, constraints, and expectations. For example, many women expressed difficulty labeling certain behaviors as rape and more often labeled the event as rape if more violence and less alcohol use took place. Women who felt less stigma about their sexual assault experiences also felt less likely to label the act as rape than did those who experienced more stigma (Littleton and Breitkopf 2006), implying that some women may find it empowering to resist the label "rape." When women were asked to judge other women's experiences, women avoided the label "rape" more often if the victim had an extensive sexual history or if they engaged in a lot of foreplay (Flowe, Ebbesen, and Putcha-Bhagavatula 2007), suggesting that women, too, shun labeling rape based on perceptions of "slutty" behavior or "wanting it more" at first.

Naming and labeling rape can impact women's well-being, though studies find conflicting results about whether labeling is positive or negative for women. In general, the label did not correlate with a higher or lower likelihood of recovering from the rape experience (McMullin and White 2006), but labeling rape correlated with higher incidences of health complaints (Conoscenti and McNally 2006). Women's feelings of shame, guilt, embarrassment, concerns about confidentiality, and fear of not being believed (Sable et al. 2006) also affected women's likelihood of labeling rape. Women who named their rape experiences tended to be met with varied reactions ranging from highly supportive and nurturing to complete disbelief (Guerette and Caron 2007). Women had more positive mental health outcomes if they reported rape within one month of its occurrence compared with those who waited longer (Ruggiero et al. 2004). When women did report rape, the relationship between the victim and perpetrator, whether the victim had consumed alcohol (Tellis and Spohn 2008), and the victim's demeanor and dress (Jordan 2004) affected legal outcomes of rape trials, perhaps indicating that "blaming the victim" ideologies are enhanced by the perception that women drank too much or otherwise "asked for it." This may help in part to explain women's hesitation to name and report rape.

This variability in labeling rape may also stem from the long-standing history of failing to criminalize marital rape in the United States and failing to adequately and successfully prosecute other types of rape. The cultural script for married couples' sexuality allows husbands to have sexual access to their wives by arguing that women should not (and sometimes legally could not) refuse their husbands' efforts to initiate sex. Marital rape became illegal in all fifty states only in July 1993. Studies show that 10 to 14 percent of all married women experienced rape by their husbands, while 40 to 50 percent of married women were battered by their husbands (Martin, Taft, and Resick 2007). Marriages in which marital rape occurred had significantly higher rates of nonsexual violence and marital dissatisfaction as well as lower ratings of marital quality. Most marital rape victims felt unable or afraid to resist sexual aggression by their husbands, and often reported depression, posttraumatic stress disorder (PTSD), gynecological problems, and negative physical health symptoms (Martin, Taft, and Resick 2007). These social scripts of marriage and consent have only recently received broad attention, as notions of presumed consent have been challenged.

Despite women's inconsistent labeling of rape, research consistently shows that women who describe coercive sexual encounters experience a range of mental health consequences, including PTSD, depression (Wolitzky-Taylor et al. 2008), anxiety, mood disorders, sexual disorders (Faravelli et al. 2004), and borderline personality disorder (Clarke, Rizvi, and Resick 2008). Negative social reactions from others and avoidance coping mechanisms correlated most strongly with PTSD symptoms (Ullman et al. 2007). Victims most often suppressed the event or resorted to self-blame and self-loathing following sexual assault (Littleton and Breitkopf 2006). Many rape survivors also reported more risky sexual health behaviors after sexual assault, including increased frequency of sex without the use of condoms and increased use of drugs and alcohol during sex (Campbell, Sefl, and Ahrens 2004). Compared to women without sexual assault histories, sexual assault survivors also had more marijuana use, diet pill use, eating disordered behaviors, and suicidal ideation and were far more likely to experience sexual victimization again (Gidycz et al. 2008). Thus, the consequences not only of naming, but also of living and perhaps minimizing violence provoke questions about how women make meaning of sexual violence. How is naming or not naming rape a gendered case of naming trauma? Also, how does one label, categorize, and speak about something as complex and difficult as rape?

Speaking about and Naming Women's Experiences of Rape

Elaine Scarry's (1985, 14) work on torture articulates a particularly compelling view of why narrating pain can subvert the mechanisms of power that enforce silence surrounding trauma. She writes, "The difficulty of articulating physical pain permits political and perceptual complications of the most serious kind. The failure to express pain . . . will always work to allow its appropriation and conflation with debased forms of power; conversely, the successful expression of pain will always work to expose and make impossible that appropriation and conflation." Similarly, articulations of sexual trauma—particularly narratives that both directly label rape and also skirt such labeling—allow a reimagining of the relationship between labels and narrative. In the case of women's sexual trauma experiences, their accounts require a deeper consideration of not only *whether* labeling benefits them, but also the *political, power-laden purposes* of such labeling.

The narratives described in this section draw from a qualitative sample of forty women interviewed between 2005 and 2007 in Ann Arbor, Michigan, and Phoenix, Arizona. These women participated in face-to-face, semistructured, two-hour interviews during which I asked them about their sexual beliefs, practices, and histories. The sample included women ages eighteen to fifty-nine (with an even distribution across age brackets), and diversity of race (65 percent white, 35 percent women of color) and sexual identities (58 percent heterosexual, 24 percent bisexual, 18 percent lesbian). During these interviews, I asked them to describe what they consider to be their worst sexual experience. This question did not include any reference to loaded terms like "rape" or "assault"; hence, any use of these terms was introduced by participants themselves. Women divulged a remarkable array of sexually traumatic experiences ranging from unambiguous sexual trauma labeled as rape to more ambiguous or "unlabeled" sexual traumas that involved obvious coercion. Over two-thirds of women sampled described sexual coercion in these narratives, though under 50 percent labeled these experiences as rape.[5]

To illustrate the differences between the unambiguous and the more ambiguous sexual trauma narratives, women with unambiguous sexual trauma most often described childhood sexual abuse, violent rapes, and stranger rapes, while women with ambiguous sexual trauma typically described events that included a romantic partner, events that started with some degree of consent, or an internalized belief that they should "go along with" the sexual coercion. As an example of unambiguous trauma, consider Maria's description of a rape that occurred in a campus parking lot:

> I was raped last year. It was very bad, very degrading. I got knocked out in a parking lot on school grounds so I went to official people and they didn't really seem to do anything. They didn't care. It was kind of horrible. I left town for a couple of weeks to go to a safe house. It was an awakening experience for me. I always knew that rape and domestic violence were issues, and violence against women was real, but when it happens to you, it changes you.

Maria's story implies that she now recognized the similarities between her experience and experiences of other women, giving her solidarity with other women who experienced rape. Similarly, Geena's description of sexual molestation at the hands of her uncle clearly establishes the sexual trauma as labeled coercion:

> I was abused sexually by my uncle, who would sit in such a way with his robe open. He would expose himself and fondle himself in front of me. . . . I remember feeling that it was gross, definitely gross, and I wanted to ignore it and not be affected but I was upset. There was a part of me that didn't want to have a strong reaction one way or another so that I was impervious to what was happening to me. Then, when I was sixteen, in a family cottage in the middle of the night, he actually raped me. . . . I remember feeling trapped, and I was angry because I knew that this was wrong and he was doing this to me. I did not ask for this. I was sixteen and my body was responding, but I'm feeling nauseous and sweaty and I want to throw up, so you know, there's a definite conflict.

Even as Geena recognized the emotional and physical conflicts she felt during the rape, she also gave herself agency to squarely label it as *unwanted violence*.

On the other hand, the majority of women who experienced sexual trauma described it more ambiguously, often resisting the explicit label of "rape." This often occurred because they perceived themselves as complicit in the encounter, as if they did something to inspire sexual violence—itself a highly gendered phenomenon. To name rape seemed to absolve themselves, something most women would not and could not do when reflecting on experiences of sexual violence. Margaret's language conveyed the self-blame inherent in many women's minimizations of their rape experiences: "I got really drunk and went to a country club and got taken advantage of. I remember feeling pretty grimy and not wanting anyone to know about it. I wanted a good scrub down when I got back home and realized what had happened. I didn't want to get into that situation again. I shouldn't have drunk like that and expected everything to turn out okay." Margaret's description implies that women may resist labeling rape because they perceive that they deserved it—a narrative of "rape myths" perpetuated in popular and cultural discourses of sexual violence (for example, women's clothing choices are still permitted as evidence in many rape trials).

Perhaps even more complex are situations where women described events that *clearly* seemed like rapes, though they refused the labels altogether, preferring instead to portray the event as something they (at least partially) wanted or chose. For example, Brynn recalled her worst sexual experience:

> The worst sex I would have to say would be forced sex, not actually rape, but not so nice. I was in a relationship once where I kind of got put into a situation I did not want to be in. I was handcuffed and put over the side of a Jeep. We were driving out to the middle of nowhere, in the middle of the day, just out and about, and we wound up at the river bottom. Fooling around, we went from one thing to another to me being halfway over the back end of the Jeep, handcuffed. He decided that he thought it would be fun to cram a "penis top" [commonly known as a "cock ring"] inside of me to see how it would feel and it got stuck behind my pelvic bone. When he went to yank it out, it pulled out the whole inner wall, and it was just painful like no other. I went to the hospital and was in bed for a day and a half. Thinking about it now, I feel small, belittled by the fact that I knew that I didn't want him to do that and I allowed somebody to do that to me.

This may give women a sense of agency that the label "rape victim" denies them; if they *chose* this encounter, then someone else did not victimize them. When I asked her why she did not define the experience as rape, she blamed herself for the event, citing her lack of protest:

> I didn't really protest, but we were kind of playing around and it stopped being fun real quick. I was scared and wanted out of there but it wasn't rape. My body tensed up and it was just not fun anymore. He was rough

with me all the time too, or at least a lot of the time. It was one of those things I kept saying we should work on, but it never really happened that way. From that experience now, I can't get pregnant because of everything it ripped from inside and all the scarring.

Brynn's description that managing *his* violence was something *she* should work on suggests that she may characterize herself as both complicit with, and responsible for, his behavior. Resisting the label "rape" may also help her to fight back against feeling victimized in light of having experienced intense violence during this encounter.

Women also resisted labeling rape to protect a male partner from blame for the rape, revealing the heightened complexities of women labeling rape when the perpetrator is a sexual partner rather than a stranger. Sally recalled an experience with her boyfriend: "It was hurting me and he just kept going and he just kept going and he just held me down. I was like, 'Stop! Stop! It really hurts,' but he kept going. I was still with him for two months after that, justifying the kind of person he was." When I asked her whether she considered this rape, she minimized the coercive dimensions of the event:

I don't consider it rape. I felt scared and I felt like he wanted to dominate me. I bet he wouldn't even remember to be honest. I wouldn't say it was rape because I don't feel that he intended to do that. I don't feel that he did it on purpose. I think that he was just being arrogant. . . . I was really scared and sad because I guess I wasn't a strong enough person to get up and leave. I trusted him a lot and I couldn't even talk to him about it afterwards, but I felt belittled.

Women's self-blame about these events not only prohibits them from fully naming the experience as *violence*, but also articulates a sense that men deserve unmediated access to women and their bodies. That women feel pressured to *allow* coercion to occur suggests that women internalized dual pressures to "give in" to sex and to construct a flexible boundary between consent and nonconsent. Such descriptions may stem from trauma bonds or from contemporary gender roles, where women's refusals of sex—including sex with other women in front of men—occur less and less often.[6]

Women also resisted labeling rape when sexual violence occurred during sexual encounters other than intercourse, particularly oral sex and anal sex. Several women described forced oral sex as fraught with ambiguity about consent and power, as if rape based not on intercourse *should* feel less violating. For example, Kate recalled wanting to feel "sexually normal" while being coerced into oral sex:

> I'm angry at myself that I let it go on as long as I did. I didn't tell my friends what was happening. There were just a lot of coercive incidents, typically around oral sex. He would force me to perform oral sex on him and since then, I just can't do it to anyone. It was a feeling of wanting to please him because I had a strong desire to please, like a feeling that I should be having these experiences because I'm an adult now and this is part of being an adult, part of being an independent woman. You've gotta do all these sexual things.

Conflicts between conforming to perceived norms and asserting her needs and desires informed Kate's decision to avoid the label "rape," as she associated adult womanhood with putting up with coerced oral sex with her partner.

Finally, women who resisted the label "rape" sometimes did so because they later had a positive relationship with someone who raped them. Two women in the study married men who raped them, including Ruth, who described substantial conflicts about her characterization of her husband:

> It was our wedding night and I said no, but he didn't listen. It was just so unlike him, because he's a very sweet, gentle man and always puts me first. I told him, "I don't want this tonight." I wish that our wedding night hadn't happened that way. I was dead tired and stressed out and my husband had been waiting for sex, you know? We went ahead and had intercourse that night but I did not want to. I've suffered from depression most of my life and I remember one time I snapped at him that I felt raped on my wedding night and he was like "Whoa, where did that come from?" That's been kind of hanging out there and we've talked about it over the years. I feel deeply sad when thinking about it. If we had just waited one night, I think it would have just been better. Both of us were virgins and neither of us had a lot of sexual experiences and such.

For Ruth, her "outburst" of labeling rape met with disbelief, resentment, and anger. The dissonance between having a decades-long marriage and recognizing sexual victimization early in their marriage required her to minimize the significance of the rape.

Collectively, these narratives challenge more traditional ideologies that separate the categories of "rape victims" from "not rape victims" in a clean binary by instead suggesting that coercion (and, to a lesser degree, sexual violence) occurs as a pervasive, pandemic, and almost universal experience in women's sexual lives. The articulation of traumatic experiences along with women's rationale for minimizing or avoiding labels of rape reveals the frightening normalization of sexual violence—a condition that we might ethically and politically consider *pathological*—as much as it speaks to women's individual choices about labels. Most centrally, the way women described sexual violence along a vast continuum—here ranging from clear incidents of sexual molestation and stranger rape to more ambiguous occurrences of spousal rape, drunken sexual encounters, and shame about forced/coerced oral sex—disrupts the notion that rape is a dichotomous and "identifiable" experience. Rather, women define and develop their core identities as girls and women within a context that normalizes sexual violence, so binary labeling only obscures this politically significant process.

Trauma as "Culture Bound Syndrome"

Just as labels of rape implicitly divide women into dichotomous categories of victim/not victim—thus obscuring the pervasive qualities of sexual violence for *all* girls and women—labeling sex offending similarly skews cultural definitions of "normal sexuality." By defining rapists as a *separate category* of men outside of "normal" masculinity, this binary conceals the overwhelming links between hegemonic masculinity and sexual violence that occur in multiple spheres of men's lives. "Normal" masculinity dictates men's control of, and access to, women's bodies and blames women for sexual violence (teaching women to hold tightly to their keys when walking through deserted parking lots or entering buildings late at night—see Valentine 1989). "Normal" masculinity dictates consent as an assumed and enforced norm of heterosexuality, leading to violence and discrimination toward women who refuse to have men as sexual partners. "Normal" masculinity unites sex and violence in language (e.g., "fucking," "banging"; see Caputi 2003), imagery, and experience while fetishizing women's powerlessness. Thus, the category "sex offender" merely obscures these facts, preferring instead to relegate "perverted," "sick," or "illegal" sex into a category of Otherness that falsely assures people that everyone else is "healthy."

Ideologies of sex offending arise in part because "the sex offender" has developed as a person-based identity rather than a particular set of (offensive) sexual crimes. As Hocquenghem (1980) noted in his dialogue with Foucault and Danet, "But today's overall tendency is indisputably not only to fabricate a type of crime that is quite simply the erotic or sensual relationship between a child and an adult, but also, since this may be isolated in the form of a crime, to create a certain category of the population defined by the fact that it tends to indulge in those pleasures." Consequently, sex offender registries assert that certain *people* are dangerous, immoral, and frightening rather than applying these labels to *behaviors*. Similarly, these discourses imply that certain people (primarily white women and white children) are also *vulnerable*, which thus gives definition to the sex offender's identity. This leads to false constructions of safety and danger. If women avoid dangerous people, the logic goes, they will avoid sexual trauma. Of course, this is patently false: women typically know their rapists and, in many cases, live with them; still more, women are much safer outside of their homes than inside their homes (Valentine 1989).

Perhaps sexual trauma should more accurately be considered a "culture bound syndrome" or, as Susan Bordo (1993) calls it, "the crystallization of culture," as these experiences cannot be divorced from a culture that largely constructs sexualized violence in binary terms. By nuancing the category of "sex offender" to include *actions* of violence rather than divides between "safe" and "unsafe" people—and by nuancing the category of "rape victim" to recognize the astonishingly common occurrences of sexual trauma in people's lives—we not only will more accurately describe people's experiences of sexual trauma, but also can begin to tackle the way sexualized violence pervades the most mainstream stories about men and women. Further still, removing these binaries can bring forth new conversations about ties between deviance and power and the largely uncontested assumptions about gender and sexuality that underlie the semiotics (and somatics) of rape and sex offending.

Regardless of whether women choose to name their traumas as *rape*, or whether we label violent behaviors as *offending*, antiviolence movements should recognize that the very tenets of masculinity and femininity require (masculinized) violence, on the one hand, and the (feminized) assumption of access and consent, on the other. There is a political urgency to these matters. Headlines daily reference the campus rape crisis in the United States, for example. What kinds of possibilities emerge from the deconstruction of rape and sex offending as taken-for-granted binaries? How can those working within and outside the field of trauma studies rupture damaging assumptions about sex, violence, and consent? These questions are not simply an issue of semantics. Rather, they unsettle the most basic assumptions about sexual biography and narratives of trauma, locating sexualized violence not merely as within Other People's stories, but also as soundly within our own.

NOTES

1 Note that throughout this piece I refer to the *political implications* of naming rape by referencing the strategic, often subtle forms of power mapped onto the body. As this differs from a more traditional or legal use of the word, I have used the word "legal" as sharply distinguished from the more Foucauldian word "political."

2 These headlines were found in the following articles from major US and British news sources: Mike Brunker, "'Sexting' Surprise: Teens Face Child Porn Charges," MSNBC, accessed May 1, 2011, http://www.msnbc.msn.com/id/28679588/ns/technology_and_science-tech_and_gadgets/t/sexting-surprise-teens-face-child-porn-charges/; CBS News, "Sexting Girls Facing Porn Charge Sue D.A.," accessed May 1, 2011, http://www.cbsnews.com/stories/2009/03/27/earlyshow/main4896577.shtml; Mike Celizic, "Her Teen Committed Suicide over 'Sexting,'" MSNBC, accessed May 4, 2011, http://today.msnbc.msn.com/id/29546030; Ed Pilkington, "Sexting Craze Leads to Child Pornography Charges," *Guardian*, accessed May 3, 2011, http://www.guardian.co.uk/world/2009/jan/14/child-pornography-sexting; Gigi Stone, "'Sexting' Teens Can Go Too Far," ABC World News, accessed December 12, 2010, http://abcnews.go.com/Technology/WorldNews/sexting-teens/story?id=6456834.

3 Note that controversies about teen "sexting" also eerily mimic discussions of public health discourses surrounding the HPV vaccine, which construct teen girls as frankly sexual, potentially promiscuous, and in need of control (see Casper and Carpenter 2008 for a discussion of US rhetoric, while Carpenter and Casper 2009 explored its global implications).

4 Both headlines appeared in the *Orlando Sentinel*: "Deputies: Woman at Bus Stop Kidnapped, Raped" (http://articles.orlandosentinel.com/2011–01–10/news/os-orange-rape-suspect-20110110_1_orange-deputies-wooded-lot-bus); "Police: Woman Raped" (http://articles.orlandosentinel.com/2000–12–05/news/0012050052_1_groveland-lake-county-man-who-raped).

5 For a more complete exploration of this data, see chap. 5 in Fahs (2011).

6 Women's descriptions of accommodating male partners' wishes for group sex, or women "hooking up" with other women at parties in front of men, also reveal such dimensions, as refusing sexual encounters becomes increasingly more threatening when sexual access to women (often in multiples) is assumed.

5

Conceptualizing Forgiveness in the Face of Historical Trauma

CARMEN GOMAN AND DOUGLAS KELLEY

Men are unable to forgive what they cannot punish and . . .
they are unable to punish what has turned out to be
unforgiveable.
—Hannah Arendt (1959)

A common response to transgression is confusion about how one goes about the process of forgiveness and, perhaps more centrally, whether one should forgive at all (Tracy 1999; Mullet, Girard, and Bakhshi 2004). Consider Simon Wiesenthal's *The Sunflower: On the Possibilities and Limits of Forgiveness*, in which he asks religious and political leaders if they, in his place, would have forgiven a Nazi SS officer who, on his deathbed, asked Wiesenthal for forgiveness for crimes he committed against the Jews. Responses from those who reply to Wiesenthal's question (fifty-three responses constitute the second half of his book) reveal that the understanding and application of forgiveness is a complex task. How one understands and applies forgiveness is fundamental to how one operates as a social being. As Robin Casarjian (1992, 12) proposes, "The beliefs that you hold about forgiveness open or close possibilities for you, determine your willingness to forgive, and, as a result, profoundly influence the emotional tone of your life."

Forgiveness is, it almost goes without saying, a historically problematic concept, and it has been variously defined by laypersons and researchers alike.[1] Scattered conceptualizations have resulted, in part, from the multitude of academic disciplines studying forgiveness, including communication studies, psychology, sociology, philosophy, and religion. In addition, Vincent Waldron and Douglas Kelley (2008, 11) note that forgiveness may vary depending on cultural setting and level of analysis, such as international conflict versus interpersonal conflict. This lack of a singular forgiveness conceptualization that crosses disciplinary boundaries no doubt contributes to the general conceptual confusion regarding forgiveness (e.g., does forgiveness require apology or reconciliation?).

Although lay definitions typically lack the sophistication of researcher-derived definitions, the ways that laypersons define forgiveness influence how forgiveness is typically enacted (Waldron and Kelley 2008). For example, common understandings of forgiveness integrate reconciliation and time as integral parts of the process and view forgiveness as both *felt* (an emotional process) and *thought* about as a choice (an intellectual process) (Kelley 1998). The goal of the present study is to understand forgiveness as a response to trauma, giving particular attention to lay conceptualizations of forgiveness for trauma.

In this essay, we use forgiveness conceptualizations from social science to understand possible responses to trauma. With this framework, we examine forgiveness themes in key chapters of Wiesenthal's *The Sunflower* in order to broaden our understanding of forgiveness. A social scientific perspective on forgiveness distinguishes between interpersonal and intrapersonal forgiveness. Everett Worthington (2005, 841) argues that intrapersonal forgiveness is a focus on the self, and interpersonal forgiveness is a focus on the other or on the relationship, usually with the intention of reconciliation. Intrapersonal forgiveness is a process that one goes through individually, usually involving the general themes of "acceptance, dealing with the event, or getting over it" and "reduction in negative feelings, letting go of grudges." This process does not involve the transgressor, only the victim. By contrast, interpersonal forgiveness includes a focus on the offender and on preserving the relationship. This view regards the forgiveness process as a dialogue rather than a monologue; that is, it is something that happens between two (or more) individuals, and not just within the victim herself. Interpersonal forgiveness influences the attitude of the victim toward the transgressor such that reconciliatory behavior may be enacted.

To understand forgiveness within the context of trauma, and specifically historical trauma, one must view forgiveness as both an intrapersonal and interpersonal process. Gordon, Baucom, and Snyder (2005, 1394) define a traumatic event as one that "violates basic assumptions about how the world and people operate." Their research suggests that forgiveness may be an appropriate response to traumatic events because it helps individuals manage the emotional impact and search for meanings of the trauma, while at the interpersonal level also helping determine the future of the relationship. Likewise, Waldron and Kelley (2008, 5) offer the following relationally embedded definition that emphasizes both intra- and interpersonal aspects of the forgiveness process: "Forgiveness is a relational process whereby harmful conduct is acknowledged by one or both partners; the harmed partner extends undeserved mercy to the perceived transgressor; one or both partners experience a transformation from negative to positive psychological states, and the meaning of the relationship is renegotiated, with the possibility of reconciliation."

Various elements of this definition are essential to individuals who have experienced trauma. For example, this definition clearly distinguishes between forgiveness and *reconciliation*. Lay conceptualizations that see forgiveness and reconciliation as synonymous may inhibit individuals' willingness to forgive. Clear conceptual distinctions at this level allow damaged individuals to forgive without the potential "trauma" of prematurely reconciling the relationship. In a study focusing on differentiating forgiveness from reconciliation, Suzanne Freedman (1998, 202) states, "Forgiving, as the overcoming of resentment, does not necessarily restore relationships, although that may be the first step. A primary characteristic of the forgiveness ... is that forgiving is something the injured person can do on his or her own without the offender's involvement or knowledge." An important consideration when contemplating reconciliation as a possible outcome of forgiveness is that in order for a healthy reconciliation to occur, a change in the offender's behavior/ attitude must occur. This underscores the assumption that forgiveness is under the complete control of the victim, whereas reconciliation requires cooperation of both the victim and offender; therefore, reconciliation between a victim and his or her transgressor is not always possible, even for a victim who desires it (Stoop and Masteller 1991).

Other concepts commonly confused with forgiveness include pardoning, forgetting, acceptance, condoning, excusing, justifying, and denying (Stoop and Masteller 1991; McCullough, Pargament, and Thoresen 2000; Derrida [1997] 2001). Although some religions may refer to forgiveness as a form of *pardoning*, the concepts differ in terms of who offers forgiveness and who offers pardoning. Typically, a pardon is a juridical term that is offered by a judge or someone of a higher power, whereas forgiveness is offered from the transgressed to the transgressor (Enright and Fitzgibbons 2000). *Forgetting* is also distinguished from forgiveness and is problematic in numerous ways. First, if one "forgets" before forgiving, the process can become one of avoidance of the transgression as opposed to an intentional process to deal with the transgression. Second, Waldron and Kelley (2008, 15) argue that typically when victims desire to, they are unable to forget a transgression because "forgetting is not a simple act of will." An exception to this may occur in response to extreme trauma (e.g., abusive relationships) where victims may forget as a survival mechanism. Yet this survival mechanism is not an intentional act, nor directed toward forgiveness. Third, for many, forgetting means to *live as though the transgression never happened*. In these cases, "forgetting implies that moral violations have been overlooked," that the injury is trivial, and that any lessons learned from the experience can also go forgotten (Waldron and Kelley 2008). As such, the common understanding about forgiveness among laypersons, "forgive and forget," may lead to feelings of invalidation and impede the choice to forgive.

Acceptance, condoning, excusing, justifying, and denying are also challenging ways to understand forgiveness, in that all three deemphasize the significance of the transgression. Robert Enright and Richard Fitzgibbons (2000) define *condoning* as an "acceptance" of a moral infringement. Those who confuse forgiveness with condoning may choose not to forgive their offender because they feel that forgiving implies their approval of the transgression; thus it can be expected that someone who understands forgiveness as condoning will be very reluctant to extend forgiveness. Similarly, *excusing* relieves the offender of responsibility for his act because it offers a reason that reframes the act in a nonthreatening way and causes one to "no longer perceive [the act] as a moral infraction" (Waldron and Kelley 2008, 15). If a victim accepts an offender's excuse, then the forgiver shifts blame from the offender to the reason itself. Finally, forgiveness is also not *denying* because denying simply claims that "no transgression took place" (Waldron and Kelley 2008, 15). Those that relate forgiveness to denying may also have a very hard time forgiving because they fear that what happened to them will no longer be acknowledged and their feelings of hurt will be invalidated. In contrast, forgiveness is a process that, rather than denying, intentionally remembers what happened so that the problem can be dealt with, lessons can be learned, and relational negotiations can be made based on recognition of the transgressions.

Forgiveness acknowledges transgressions because it is a *response* to transgressions. Most narratives of forgiveness involve a particular harmful act between a transgressor and a victim. A *transgression* is a "deliberate and harmful act" and often requires extensive relational work in order for the relationship between the victim and offender to be restored (Waldron and Kelley 2008). However, transgressions fall on a continuum of severity and "the perceived severity of a transgression is a primary predictor of how [people] approach forgiveness" (Waldron and Kelley 2008, 29). People often minimize the need to forgive relatively mild transgressions, but in contrast severe transgressions may precipitate forgiveness with conditions in order to maintain the relationship but protect one's self from further injury.

Thus, conceptualizing forgiveness as a response to traumatic events is challenging. Yet historically traumatic events create unique conditions for the exercise of forgiveness. By historical trauma, we mean events that take place in the midst of national transgressions, have affected a great number of people, and persist in their historical and national memory; examples include the Nazi genocide of the Jews during World War II, the genocide of the Armenians by the Ottoman Empire following World War I, and the murder of hundreds of thousands of Tutsis during the Rwandan Genocide. As Desmond Tutu (1999) states, effective reparation between national groups and individuals representative of these groups requires some type of forgiveness response. Our study seeks to understand the nature of interpersonal forgiveness within the context of a historically traumatic event.

Trauma is commonly understood as some terrible event(s) a person undergoes that can cause continual residual psychological suffering. Neil Thompson and Mary Walsh (2010, 382) define trauma as "experiences [that] produce feelings of anomie, powerlessness, frustration, vulnerability and confusion which, in turn, are likely to produce a destabilisation of meaning and therefore create the need for the re-establishment of meaning." Critical trauma scholars point out that traumatic experiences have both psychological and sociological dimensions—that is, both the experience and the treatment of trauma need to be approached through a social perspective because human experience (e.g., trauma) cannot be abstracted from social context (Thompson and Walsh 2010). That is, what individuals count or name as trauma emerges from their social context. Derek Summerfield (2004, 241) writes that "suffering arises from, and is resolved in, a social context: shaped by meanings and understandings applied to events, evolving as the conflict evolves. It is subjective appraisal that determines what a stressful event means: one man's trauma is another's heroic sacrifice."

Whether experienced individually or collectively, trauma can cause a sense of "disorientation," a loss of a sense of self or group identity. Thompson and Walsh (2010, 379) argue that trauma is an "existential injury" in that "it can damage, distort or even destroy our sense of self and how we fit into the wider world. It undermines the basis of our existence, severely altering how we see the world and how we make sense of it—in effect, de-establishing or even shattering our frameworks of meaning, our spiritual and existential foundations." Understanding this on a collective level means that whole groups of people can experience trauma and in effect feel their group identity threatened within the larger social context. For example, beyond the individual suffering that victims of the Holocaust experienced, the Jewish community as a whole underwent existential suffering in that collectively they were symbolically tortured and completely disenfranchised. Although experiencing trauma as a group can establish a helpful, supportive community as members attempt to cope together, it can cause dissension among members if coping is handled in different ways. Respondents in Wiesenthal's text have divergent ideas as to how Jews and specifically Wiesenthal, *as* a Jew, should cope with their trauma—to forgive or not forgive.

And so Wiesenthal's *The Sunflower* provides opportunities for studying layperson conceptualizations of forgiveness in light of our discussion so far. *The Sunflower* chronicles Wiesenthal's harrowing experiences as a Holocaust prisoner and survivor. One senses Wiesenthal's despair and hurt from his expressive writing: "What in this Nazi world was reasonable and logical? You lost yourself in fantasy merely in order to escape from the appalling truth. And in such circumstances reason would have been a barrier. We escaped into dreams and we didn't want to awake from those dreams" (1998, 37). The story begins with Wiesenthal already in a Nazi death camp, living desperately, hopelessly, with fellow Jews and friends, without faith for God's intervention (or even existence, for some of the prisoners) or the war's end. From his descriptions of the minutest daily annoyances to those of unbearable tortures and even finally to ultimate death, Wiesenthal's ironic, even cynical, tone offers the Holocaust narrative in a way that speaks loudly about his disposition toward forgiveness, even before he broaches the issue.

In the first half of the book, Wiesenthal finishes with a story of his unique encounter with a Nazi SS man, Karl Seidl. While in the Lemberg Concentration Camp worker's group in 1943, Wiesenthal is singled out as a Jew and summoned to a Nazi army hospital and the bedside of Karl, who is dying. Karl forces his story upon the reluctant Wiesenthal, a story about his part in the slaughter of nearly two hundred Jews who were burned alive, all forced together in a small three-story house. Those who dared to jump through broken windows were shot by Karl and his comrades. Karl then desperately expresses his desire for Wiesenthal to forgive him, on behalf of the Jews, so that he may die in peace. Wiesenthal does not grant Karl his wish; he says nothing and simply walks out of the room. He soon becomes troubled about his silence, however, and he wonders whether or not he did the right thing in not responding, and in not forgiving. He shares this story with his comrades upon his return to the camp, and he receives an array of responses, most of which are a passionate endorsement that Wiesenthal did the right thing and that Karl did not deserve forgiveness. Despite the support from his comrades for the decision he made, Wiesenthal remains very troubled about this experience, and he eventually solicits others to write and respond to this question: "You, who have just read this sad and tragic episode in my life, can mentally change places with me and ask yourself the crucial question, 'What would I have done?'" (1998, 98).

Among those whom Wiesenthal asked to respond were writers, theologians, human rights activists, Holocaust survivors, jurists, and survivors of other attempted genocides (in Bosnia, Cambodia, and Tibet). The second part of *The Sunflower* consists of these fifty-three responses; of the fifty-three respondents, only twelve espouse forgiveness, sixteen are opposed to it, and twenty-five express ambivalence. The very fact that almost half of the respondents are undecided on whether or not forgiveness was the "right" response is evidence of the complexity of forgiveness as a response to historical trauma, situated within its social and cultural contexts. Many of these responses are confounded with forgiveness-related themes, such as forgetting, pardoning, condoning, excusing, and reconciliation. We move now to an analysis of various excerpts from these responses and the understanding(s) of forgiveness they espouse. The perspective of this essay is interpretive in nature, with the intention to understand how laypersons conceptualize forgiveness following historical trauma.

We analyzed the respondents' own words as they appeared in *The Sunflower* and thus were able to arrive at a summative understanding of layperson conceptualizations of forgiveness in relation to national trauma. Embedded in the essays we analyzed are implicit definitions of forgiveness. These definitions both confirm some of the social science definitions but also expand upon those perspectives. Of the fifty-three responses to Wiesenthal, we analyzed every fifth response (a total of ten responses) and used theoretical saturation as our measure for comprehensiveness (Strauss and Corbin 1998). Both of us had previously read all fifty-three responses multiple times. However, neither of us had previously systematically analyzed the responses. Using a systematic process of analysis, we individually read two responses and identified emerging themes regarding implicit and explicit conceptualizations of forgiveness (Smith 1995). We then came together to compare themes and ensure that there was relative consistency between our independent assessments of the responses. Finally, we read and analyzed the remaining eight essay responses separately and came together again to compare our findings.

Overall, there was a high degree of consistency between our assessments. We agreed on how to combine our results to create one common set of themes. We developed themes using William Owen's (1984) method of interpretation that derives themes based on the criteria of recurrence, repetition, and forcefulness. Finally, we collapsed our findings into themes and their appropriate subthemes. We felt that after analyzing ten responses, saturation was reached, and thus we created a finalized list of themes and subthemes that provided a comprehensive understanding of how the respondents conceptualized forgiveness in the historical trauma context.

Our interpretive analysis uncovered five themes, each of which grouped subthemes that illustrated how laypersons conceptualized forgiveness.[2] These themes were (1) nature of forgiveness, (2) processes of forgiveness, (3) functions of forgiveness, (4) conditions of forgiveness, and (5) the dark side of forgiveness. Grouped within these themes were a total of twenty-two subthemes. The numerous and varied understandings of forgiveness illustrate the elusiveness of the concept and thus the difficulty in developing a universal definition of forgiveness. One might suppose, due to the specific context (historical trauma), there would be significant continuity of forgiveness perceptions across *The Sunflower* responses, but this was not the case. Very few respondents were neutral on the issue of forgiveness. While some participants found forgiveness an inappropriate response, at best, others deemed forgiveness a positive response, if not necessary. For example, some respondents described forgiveness as a sacred concept, while others considered it a desecration. Some believed it to be always the best response, even in the most hurtful situations, yet others argued that forgiveness was a useless concept that benefited only the offender, who did not deserve it.

Under the first theme, *nature of forgiveness*, responses reflected varied beliefs about the overall character of forgiveness. These included the appropriateness and/or morality of forgiveness, whether forgiveness is a public or private process, collective or individual, and whether forgiveness is a religious or secular issue. The eight subthemes reflected individuals' perception of forgiveness as psychological/theological/social, forgiveness as a moral response, forgiveness as the best response, forgiveness as public or private, forgiveness as dyadic or collective, forgiveness as sacred, forgiveness as grace, and forgiveness as true humanity.

Respondents wrote from different perspectives, which reflected views of forgiveness as being either a psychological, religious, or social process. Catholic priest Theodore M. Hesburgh believed that the willingness to forgive stems from one's religiosity; thus he linked the decision and process of forgiveness to religious belief. Eugene J. Fisher commented that differences in reaction to Wiesenthal's question most likely stem from existential stance, regardless of the theology that one has. Some commented that forgiveness can be granted only from within a psychological state that allows one to do so, ascribing forgiveness as a psychological (intrapersonal) process. These responses reflect Casarjian's (1992, 12) insight that one's particular beliefs about forgiveness determine one's willingness to forgive.

Forgiveness was viewed as a type of moral response to the transgressions of the Nazis. For example, Fisher noted, "Christians simply do not have the experiential base to make a moral judgment on Jewish behavior with regard to the Shoah" (Wiesenthal 1998, 131). Thus, forgiveness in the face of historical trauma was viewed within moral constraints as to when it is or isn't appropriate to grant or ask for forgiveness. Some respondents noted that it would be immoral for Wiesenthal to have forgiven on behalf of the murdered Jews, while others argued that forgiving would be immoral because it condoned the criminal acts of the Nazis. Still others believed that it was even immoral for the SS officer to have asked for forgiveness.

Although many respondents reflected an unwillingness to forgive, for some forgiveness was seen as the best response, even in cases of severe trauma. Martin E. Marty wrote, "In every circumstance that I can picture, more value would grow out of forgiveness than out of its withholding" (Wiesenthal 1998, 211). This view is based on the belief that forgiving would be freeing (an overlapping concept we discuss later) for both the victim and the perpetrator. Marty contrasts the feelings associated with forgiveness to those associated with unforgiveness (groveling, self-hate, loss of self-pride); he points out that victims have two choices, to forgive or not forgive, and considering the negative feelings and prolonged suffering of unforgiveness, he argues that in every situation to forgive is the best choice.

Forgiveness was also framed within a public/private dialectic. Hesburgh, who believed that forgiveness is always the best response, viewed forgiveness as something that should be asked for and granted privately. Terrence Prittie noted that forgiveness is something a person should ask of God, not of their victim or anyone else. In contrast, several respondents argued that one should repent and ask for forgiveness publicly. For example, Fisher wrote that repentance and forgiveness are "done . . . publicly, as the Pope has done it, since the offense is not only against the Jews but God and humanity as well" (Wiesenthal 1998, 134). In relation, there was also a sense of forgiveness as a dyadic (private within the relationship) versus a collective (public by definition) process. Since Karl asked Wiesenthal to forgive him on behalf of other Jews, the issue was raised as to whether it was right for Wiesenthal to forgive as a "proxy" for the Jewish victims. Prittie wrote that "a persecuted Jew could only forgive wrongs done to him personally; he could not possibly forgive genocide" (234). Tzvetan Todorov argued that "the only one who can forgive is the one who has experienced the injury. Every extension by analogy, from the individual to the group, seems to me illegitimate: one cannot forgive by proxy any more than one can be a victim by association or uphold the existence of a collective guilt" (265). For such respondents, forgiveness for Karl seems impossible, as it is only the dead victims who would have the right to grant Karl forgiveness.

Rodger Kamentez objected to the way in which Karl solicited Wiesenthal for forgiveness; he wrote, "You were not addressed as a person. You were addressed, from his perspective, as Jew. Not as *a* Jew, a Jewish person, as an individual, with a life, a history, a heartbreak of your own, but merely as *Jew*. For his purposes, any Jew would do" (181). This response reflects the potential dehumanizing effect of Karl's request for forgiveness. Kamentez presumes that when a person is asked for forgiveness, he or she undergoes a very individual and unique process. It isn't something that one can do, experience, or be asked on behalf of another or in a collective form. Respondents, such as Kamentez, thought it offensive for "any Jew" to be asked to grant forgiveness on behalf of all Jews. However, some responses reflected the belief that all Nazis, as a whole, should be forgiven by all Jews, as a whole. For example, Fisher argued that the Catholic Church as a whole must change its teachings and behaviors before it can be forgiven by the Jews. Thus, in this case, forgiveness is seen as a process engaged by a collective group and granted to another collective group.

Related to a discussion of the conditionality of forgiveness, some also framed forgiveness as sacred. Mary Gordon wrote, "The sinner must publicly acknowledge guilt, and only then ask for absolution. Anything less than that is, I believe, a perversion of the sacrament" (153). Alan L. Berger argued that "to have forgiven would have been a desecration both of the memory of the Jewish victims and of the sanctity of forgiveness" (118). Thus, forgiveness was seen as something sacred, not to be granted casually. If granted when undeserved, the sanctity of forgiveness would be destroyed. Furthermore, the sanctity of forgiveness could make it virtually unattainable between people, as Hesburgh wrote: "I think of God as the great forgiver of sinful humanity . . . can we aspire to be as forgiving of each other as God is of us?" (169).

Likewise, forgiveness was also framed as grace that is costly but that sometimes can be given cheaply. Marty remarked, "Nothing should happen that would let haters or murderers off the hook by assuring them that grace is readily available . . . we do not want cheap grace, a casual people, or a forgotten victim" (211–12). Some expressed the fear that forgiving Karl on his deathbed would be an unearned and "cheap grace" that invalidates the enormity of the Nazis' crimes against the Jews. Berger further argued that if Karl were to be forgiven, he would have earned cheap grace, as he would be absolved yet without moral accountability for his actions. At the same time, Marty also warned against the dangers of not offering the grace of forgiveness: "Gracelessness helps produce totalitarianism as much as cheap grace might. If there is to be grace, it must be mediated through people. We have to see potentials in the lives of even the worst people, have to see that it is we who can dam the flow of grace" (212). Thus, forgiveness is seen as a grace that can absolve one's transgressions, yet it is costly and should not be cheaply and easily given.

The final subtheme related to the nature of forgiveness was reflected in a response by Albert Speer, a high-ranking Nazi officer, who regarded forgiveness as an expression of true humanity. Speer differentiates between legal guilt, which the court can punish then erase, and moral guilt, which nothing can erase, except perhaps forgiveness. Speer wrote to Wiesenthal,

No one is bound to forgive . . . but you showed empathy, undertaking the difficult trip to Stuttgart in 1946. You showed compassion by not telling the mother of her son's crimes. This human kindness also resounds in your letter to me, and I am thankful for it. You showed clemency, humanity, and goodness when we sat facing one another on this May 20th, too. You did not touch my wounds. You carefully tried to help. You didn't reproach me or confront me with your anger. I looked into your eyes, eyes that reflected all the murdered people, eyes that have witnessed the misery, degradation, fatalism, and agony of your fellow human beings. And yet, those eyes are not filled with hatred; they remain warm and tolerant and full of sympathy for the misery of others. (245–46)

Wiesenthal's comportment toward Speer is what, for Speer, embodies forgiveness and its effects. He relates forgiveness to such positive character traits as clemency, goodness, and kindness, and seems to almost elevate forgiveness to an action beyond human capability, yet claims that one's humanity is acknowledged (for both the forgiver as well as the forgiven) when forgiveness takes place. For Speer, forgiveness is a true reflection of humanity.

The second theme that emerged through our analysis was the conceptualization of *forgiveness as process*. Parts of the forgiveness process included the nature of the transgression(s) that called for forgiveness, the emotional damage caused, and the presence/absence of repentance. These issues were salient as respondents discussed forgiveness as a response to a personal injury and as a response to the past. Some respondents wrote that forgiveness is a response specifically to repentance, yet others suggested that simple forms of repentance are manipulative attempts to assuage personal guilt. Berger referred to repentance as "formulaic: a learned ritual which soothes the troubled soul yet does nothing for those who were murdered" (119). For Berger, mere repentance is not enough—forgiveness should be a response only to evident behavior change and obvious remorse. Forgiveness was also defined as a response after emotions tied to the injury subsided. Prittie wrote, "The Jew was facing death every day that he remained alive. He knew that the very most that he could achieve for himself would be to face death bravely and to maintain his faith in his own identity up to the end" (234). Prittie suggests Wiesenthal was under too much emotional duress and pain to be asked to forgive at the time because forgiveness is more easily granted when one has greater emotional distance from the injury. In this light, the deep hurt and pain experienced during trauma make forgiveness prohibitive until the intense emotional response subsides.

Forgiveness as process also emphasizes the element of time. As previously discussed, some believed that a victim must have emotional distance (gained over a period of time) in order to grant forgiveness. Others noted that forgiveness takes time because the victim must see true repentance and behavior change in the perpetrator. For example, Fisher wrote, "I believe that if I were Jewish, I would wait a generation or so to see if the official documents and statements of the Church do, in fact, bring about the transformation toward which they confessedly aim"

(132). Thus, forgiveness is conceptualized as a process that isn't instantaneous but can take months and even years to work through, a response embedded in a long process of social and cultural transformation.

Finally, respondents understood forgiveness as a step toward something (e.g., reconciliation, healing). Kamentez argued that Wiesenthal was correct in not forgiving Karl because he was dehumanized when asked, as a "Jew . . . not as a person," to forgive Karl (181). For Kamentez, forgiveness was framed as a step toward rehumanization of the victim and the relationship between the victim and transgression. Others saw forgiveness as a step toward the restoration and reconciliation of relationships (victim-transgressor, transgressor-God, etc.). For example, Fisher argued that first, the Christian collective must repent and show behavior/doctrine change, and then perhaps Jews could forgive and as a consequence begin to repair the damaged relationship that continues today between the two groups (132). In addition, Deborah Lipstadt noted that forgiveness "is designed to make our relationship with both God and those around us whole again" (193). She also argued that forgiveness is a step that opens up other possible steps for transgressors—an important step that sinners must achieve before they can atone for their sins and become whole again. Evidently, laypersons understand that, in the face of trauma, forgiveness accomplishes something beyond itself and is especially consequential when transgressions are particularly grave. The common laypersons' conflation of forgiveness and reconciliation is made clearer by certain of Wiesenthal's invited essays.

The third prominent theme that emerged from *The Sunflower* is the conceptualization of *forgiveness as serving a particular function*, whether to heal, liberate, eliminate guilt, or facilitate something else. The functions were not only beneficial; there were also frameworks for understanding negative/deleterious functions of forgiveness. Some respondents referred to forgiveness as a "cleansing" of one's soul (119). Related is the idea that forgiveness "cleans one's slate" and thus eliminates guilt. Lipstadt remarked, "Even if the prisoner had offered the soldier verbal forgiveness, that would not have resulted in an automatic cleansing of slate. Such atonement would only have come when the guilty man had borne the consequences of his act and had demonstrated by his subsequent behavior that he had returned to that 'place' he had occupied prior to committing his heinous crime" (196). Thus, forgiveness is a step toward the cleansing of one's slate and consequently the atonement for one's guilt.

Forgiveness was also viewed as fulfilling a healing function for the victim, the perpetrator, and their relationship. Lipstadt proposed that repentance and forgiveness are "designed to make our relationship with God and those around us whole again" (193). Marty emphasizes freedom and liberation for both victim and perpetrator, "If I forgive in the face of true repentance and new resolve, I am free. . . . Forgiving and being forgiven are experiences that allow me to be free for a new day" (212–13). Marty particularly points out the freeing function of forgiveness for the victim, but also notes that the forgiven person becomes liberated toward new possibilities and a new future through forgiveness.

Similarly, Berger noted that forgiveness functions to heal the conscience of the offender. Berger's response to Wiesenthal was that he was right for not forgiving Karl, but Wiesenthal would have "sealed his own guilt" had he spoken to and forgiven Karl (120). Berger conceptualized forgiveness as a dyadic process in which only the victim is allowed to forgive the offender, thus making it impossible for Karl to be forgiven. In addition, Berger argued that forgiveness requires repentance, and repentance "is a process rather than a single act," which Karl, being on his deathbed, could not have the opportunity to enact (119). Thus, according to Berger, forgiveness *should* function to cleanse one's conscience, yet undeserved (cheap) grace can actually undercut this possibility.

Forgiveness was also understood as a means to something else, whether to future possibilities, to heaven, to the elimination of fear (of hell), or to the undoing of the past. Negative perceptions were often woven through these various functions of forgiveness. For example, Lipstadt viewed forgiveness as an "easy way out" that is sought upon one's deathbed; she argued, "Would he [Karl] have felt so contrite if he had not been at death's door? It is also important to note that the soldier's apparently genuine struggle with his past did not obviate his responsibility to bear the punishment for what he had done" (196). Prittie also spoke of forgiveness as a means to relieve the fear of hell: "Men under fire who have never prayed before, pray and promise 'to be good' in the future—if God will oblige by rescuing them from impending death. The certainty rather than the mere possibility of death can only reinforce the plea for mercy" (233). Some also regarded forgiveness, upon its granting, as a means to heaven, and thus condemned Karl's request to attain forgiveness without first atoning for his crimes. In a similar vein, forgiveness was regarded as an undoing of the past, or as Gordon put it, as a "magic eraser" that in a sense denies the reality of what happened (152).

A final subtheme was conceptualization of forgiveness as a dialectic between forgetting and remembering the past. Most common was the perception that forgiveness could function to erase or forget the past, and thus invalidate the atrocity. For example, Berger argued, "to have forgiven [Karl] would have been a desecration of the memory of the Jewish victims and of the sanctity of forgiveness" (118). Another respondent noted that forgiveness becomes a way of denying and forgetting the past unless there is recognition of guilt by the victim. Thus, forgiveness was placed within a dialectic of forgetting and remembering—it was possible for forgiveness to take place while the crimes and victims were still remembered; yet, there was a predominant sense that forgiveness most easily falls into the trap of forgetting the past.

The fourth theme that appeared in our analysis was that *forgiveness was conditional*. Wiesenthal's respondents noted various conditions on the forgiveness process, such as forgiveness being granted only by certain people, after certain actions (on the part of the victim) take place, and when the victim is in a particular state (mental, physical, psychological). For some respondents, forgiveness was defined as something that could be granted only by God. Prittie believed that Karl should have asked God, not man, for forgiveness; Berger argued that humans can forgive only sins committed against themselves, but that only God can forgive crimes against humanity. Others argued that forgiveness is a right that belongs only to the victim and cannot be granted by anyone else. For example, Gordon wrote, "No one can grant forgiveness as a private person in the name of another, for that would be theft of the wounded person's right to forgive or not to forgive" (153). In this sense, forgiveness is understood conditionally and can be granted only by someone who has the right to do so.

Many saw remorse as a necessary precondition of forgiveness. Some questioned the validity of Karl's remorse and suspected that had he not been dying, he would have continued his crimes against the Jews. Respondents wrote that Karl needed to have shown drastic behavior change in order to have been granted forgiveness. On a more collective level, Fisher argued that the entire Catholic Church needed to be observed over a generation and could be forgiven only if there was evident transformation in its teachings regarding the Jews. Some spoke specifically of the need for atonement as a condition of forgiveness. Gordon specified further that "atonement must match the crime" in order for forgiveness to have any meaning (153). Lipstadt suggested that one must first bear the consequences of one's actions before achieving atonement and consequently forgiveness. Thus, punishment for crimes was seen as a condition for forgiveness, as well as remorse for the crimes and subsequent behavior change.

Some responses reflected the notion that one must be in a particular psychological, emotional, and physical state before one can be "free" to offer forgiveness. Because Wiesenthal was being asked for forgiveness while he was still a prisoner and victim of the Nazi regime, he was considered to be a "captive . . . [who] did not have the full freedom to speak" (p. 181). Kamentez argued that Wiesenthal was not granted his "humanity," and only when his humanity was acknowledged could he have the freedom to grant forgiveness. Prittie also touched on this point, writing that "as a badgered, brutalized concentration camp inmate," Wiesenthal could not have been graceful and forgiving because he was not in a healthy enough place to be able to do so.

The final theme that we discovered, *the dark side of forgiveness*, overlaps with many of the aforementioned themes, as forgiveness was often defined in negative terms. Most respondents did not believe Wiesenthal should have forgiven Karl, and this seemed mainly due to their conceptualizations of how forgiveness can function negatively. At times, forgiveness was referred to as desecration and victimization, or as a narcissistic act and as cheap grace. Although the subthemes in this category overlap with previous categories, they deserve attention because of the common negative perspective on forgiveness.

The Holocaust was viewed by many as a memory that the Jews must preserve, to show respect for the suffering they as a people had undergone. From this perspective some viewed forgiveness, in this almost unbelievable situation, as a desecration of both that memory and the sanctity of forgiveness (118). It was also argued that forgiving the Nazis would have been a perversion of the sacrament of forgiveness (153). Thus, forgiveness was seen as sacred but also as having the potential of desecrating the Jewish memory of the Holocaust. Some respondents argued that Karl had no right to ask Wiesenthal for forgiveness and that doing so further victimized Wiesenthal and the Jews. Fisher wrote, "We have no right to put Jewish survivors in the impossible moral position of offering forgiveness, implicitly, in the name of the six million. . . . Placing a Jew in this anguished position further victimizes him or her. This, in my reading, was the final sin of the dying Nazi" (133). It was also noted that forgiveness victimizes when it is granted without offenders repenting and atoning for their crimes. Gordon noted that forgiveness becomes a form of forgetting, and thus a victimization of the victim, if the offender does not admit guilt.

Some respondents believed that forgiveness is more beneficial for the Nazis and less beneficial (if at all) for Wiesenthal and other Jews. Gordon wrote that "[forgiveness is] a narcissistic rather than a moral act because it places the perpetrator's need to be purged of guilt ahead of the victim's need for restitution or simple recognition of having been harmed" (152). Berger's argument illustrated the benefits that the SS officer would have reaped by receiving forgiveness and noted that Wiesenthal would have gained nothing for himself: "[Karl's] desire is to 'cleanse' his own soul at the expense of the Jew" (119). Forgiveness from this perspective is a way for the perpetrator to feel good about himself or herself, and it is self-serving for the perpetrator, lacking any value for the victim.

Some argued that forgiveness was a way for Karl to seek an easy way out and a ticket to heaven, which served only him and did nothing for Wiesenthal or the Jewish victims. Such a perspective conceptualized forgiveness as self-serving, making the offender feel better but in no way benefiting the victim(s).

It was also mentioned in a previous subtheme that some respondents conceptualized forgiveness as cheap grace. Grace was viewed as something costly to be earned, and forgiveness was argued as a "cheap" way of earning that grace. Various respondents noted that forgiveness is to be earned through a long and sincere process of repentance and atonement, and that if forgiveness is offered before such a process took place, it is a cheap form of grace. This "dark" forgiveness is of no benefit for the forgiver and does not uphold the standard of costly grace.

***

We have highlighted important considerations when examining for-giveness of traumatic events. The many ways in which forgiveness was conceptualized in regard to Wiesenthal's dilemma emphasize the com-plexity of understanding forgiveness within the context of historical trauma. Based on our reading of *The Sunflower*, further investigation of forgiveness and trauma should consider possible motivational ele-ments such as religiosity, victim-offender relationship, the effect of social constructions of transgressions on willingness to forgive, and length of time after the traumatic event(s). Forgiveness literature would also benefit from a theoretical synthesis of the vast amount of concep-tualizations into a more comprehensive understanding of forgiveness in the context of historical/national trauma. Such an endeavor would benefit from more extensive studies of dialogue and conversation on this topic. Concepts that surfaced several times yet remain underdeveloped in forgiveness literature, such as functions and conditions of forgiveness, could be expanded upon in subsequent individual studies.

We also want to highlight how historical trauma events include el-ements that are both interpersonal and intergroup/nation. Few re-spondents saw Wiesenthal's dilemma as one that merely involved an exchange between two young men. Rather, Karl's approach and request for forgiveness unleashed a variety of responses targeted at understand-ing the nature of humanity and, subsequently, individual and group identities. Equally important was the struggle to determine the place of "God" in human interaction.

We close with recognition of a concept that emerged several times throughout the responses and seemed to support the obscure relation between forgiveness and trauma—silence. Kamentez writes, "I feel si-lence, under the circumstances, was the best response . . . you were under duress—the best choice was to remain silent" (Wiesenthal 1998, 181). Kamentez argues that words may properly come only from "per-sons." In his dehumanized state, Wiesenthal was not able to condemn or forgive—his silence alone confronts Karl with both justice and mercy. Forgiveness at an interpersonal level takes place only between two per-sons; perhaps, Kamentez seems to say, in the absence of personhood, silence is the best response.

Silence also protects forgiveness from becoming its own form of con-trol and manipulation. Marty writes that, as a Christian speaking on a nominally "Jewish issue," "[he] can only respond with silence" (210). To judge unforgiveness without full recognition of cultural, social, and relational contexts runs the risk of revictimizing the victim. Trauma itself calls for a deep reformulation of one's self, the offending other, and one's relationship (Kelley 2012). Likewise, historical trauma calls for a reevaluation of one's collective, the offending collective, and the relationship between the two. Such a massive undertaking may be evaluated only with great care over time, precipitating alternating times of silence and interaction. Thankfully, Wiesenthal's own silence before Karl was eventually broken with the writing of *The Sunflower*.

NOTES

1 Mullet, Girard, and Bakhshi (2004).

2 The term "layperson" references that none of the essays were written by forgiveness researchers or theorists.

II

Poetics

6

Bahareh

Singing without Words in an Iranian Prison Camp

SHAHLA TALEBI

Listen to the song of the reed,
How it wails with the pain of separation:
"Ever since I was taken from my reed bed
My woeful song has caused men and women to weep.
I seek out those whose hearts are torn by separation
For only they understand the pain of this longing . . ."
—Rumi

The Encounter

It was a hot summer in 1983 when I first saw Bahareh, in an overpopulated ward in Evin, one of the most notorious political prisons in Iran. The ward was crowded with hundreds of women of different ages and backgrounds and about thirty children of both sexes from infancy to eight years old. In the evenings, as if gushed out of a flooded ant hole, they poured out of their rooms into the hallway and walked, alone or in pairs, creating a cacophony in which words from different conversations intercepted one another. In their midst, the rusty voice of a woman, who repeatedly shouted curses, spoke the language of insanity.

Yet, the instant my eyes caught sight of Bahareh, all this noise withered away. I was captivated by the penetrating gaze of this little girl who, hanging tightly to her mother's neck and sucking on her pacifier, stared at me with a stunning fusion of innocence, curiosity, and a strange wisdom, so unusual at her age, immersed in her dark pupils. When I asked what her name was, she gently removed her pacifier and sounded, "ah-ah-ah." I must have looked puzzled for a petite woman, apparently her mother, who was holding her, intervened and said, "Bahareh. She says her name is Bahareh." Only then I recognized that ah-ah-ah, had the rhythmic sound of "bah-ha-reh." During the next year that I lived with Bahareh, I became used to her particular rhythmic language and was tamed by her bright dark eyes, though continued to be surprised by the way she looked at everything as if for the first time, yet also as if she had been around forever.

As the meaning of her name, Spring, suggested, Bahareh's presence enlivened every rotten thing around her. She had an amazing ear for music. You did not have to sing more than a few bars of a song for her before she hummed the rest of it for you. To put her to sleep, you had to sing her favorite song; she had favorite songs for different occasions. Yet, as if a bird, Bahareh sang and spoke without words. There was only one word that she uttered while in prison. The word was "amama," by which she called her mother, a distortion in which "mama" (ممم), in Farsi the children's word for breast, hunted the word "mama" (ماما), or mother.

According to the doctors, there was nothing wrong with Bahareh's vocal cords to prevent her from speaking. She however did not speak, at least not in the conventional sense of the term. Yet, she understood us perfectly and spoke, if not in words but by sounding their intonations. One could make sense of most of what she said, if one took time to become accustomed to the music of her otherwise silent words and the scope of her language, which was rather minimal. She rarely initiated a conversation, and when urged to respond, she did so reluctantly. Our attempts to encourage her to speak proved futile.

Cut from the Reed Bed

In the spring of 1983, the fifteen-days-old Bahareh had just been breast-fed by her mother and was about to fall asleep to the warm voice of her father, who, as he often did, was strolling around the room holding her in his arms and singing her favorite song, when the door was suddenly crashed wide open and several armed men raided their home. The father was shot dead while Bahareh and her mother were taken to prison. Bahareh must have sensed the drastic difference between home and this new place in which, caught from the loving arms of her father, she became privy to the nauseating odor of prisoners' injuriously infected and sweaty bodies and the eerie stench of death that swathed everything as if fog. What did she understand when she saw so many prisoners who were taken downstairs on their feet but returned on their buttocks, or those who came back still walking, but as if with artificial legs, and still others who were carried upstairs wrapped in stinky blankets? How was she affected by the fact that for the next two months, she could not see her mother's eyes for her mother and other prisoners around her were blindfolded? What did she see in the only eyes open around her, those of the guards and the interrogators? Indeed, Bahareh was not merely deprived of her mother's eyes but also of her milk, for her mother's breast were dried out after the second day of torture, along with her upright posture—for months, the mother was unable to move around except on her buttocks.

Due to massive arrests and lack of space, for the first couple of months following their arrest, Bahareh and her mother, and many other prisoners, had to live and sleep on the floor of the hallway under the watchful eyes of interrogators and guards, witnessing new waves of arrests, constant beatings, and deaths by torture. Bahareh's mother had no way of protecting her from seeing or hearing all that went on around her, except by holding her closer to her shivering and thinning body, and whispering songs in her ears. Prisoners were tortured by interrogators to speak and by the guards to remain silent. How confusing it must have been for Bahareh to fathom why speaking was sometimes so desirable while deemed dangerous other times, or why prisoners often refused to speak when ordered by the interrogators while grabbing any opportunity to communicate with one another in their absence.

***

Amama, Amama, this was how Bahareh called her mother. "Why don't you call her mama? Isn't it easier than amama?" we asked her. But she kept calling her mother amama. It was as though this deliberate or unconscious "distortion" abridged the gap between the signifier and the signified, between the saying and the seeing. For in Farsi, the last two letters, the two "a"s of "ma" (ﻣﺎ) and "ma" (ﻣﺎ) in "mama" (ﻣﺎﻣﺎ) are written vertically. Phonologically too one has to cut the air vertically while sounding the word "mama." But in "amama," except the first "a," the "a"s (ﺍﻣﺎﻣﺎ) are written and sounded horizontally.

I cannot help but think of the way Bahareh's mother was transformed from her upright posture to a horizontal position. I wonder if this may have shaped Bahareh's perception of her mother and the world around her, thus turning her mama (ماما) into amama (اماما). I also wonder whether the loss of milk becomes the haunting force in the term "amama," for in children's language in Farsi, the word "mama" (ماما) means breast. The distortion of "mamâ" to "amama" seems to recall not only the mother's breast, and hence the loss of the mother's milk, but also her descending from an upright posture to a horizontal one. May this also explain Bahareh's attachment to her pacifier, or *pestoonak* in Farsi, which indeed means little breast?

Although, with the exception of amama Bahareh never uttered any other word while in prison, words were not entirely absent from her language. But they rather had a ghostly presence. Neither did she lack language. Her mode of speech inhabited a peripheral position in relation to our language; she hummed the rhythm of the words and syntaxes of the major language, a relation that reminds me of Deleuze and Guattari's notion of major and minor languages. Yet our communication with Bahareh could not lead to a real dialogue. She sometimes hummed while still sucking on her pacifier, as if intentionally mocking the very communication she pretended to have with us, as if demanding that we understood her in her terms, without subjecting her to the rules of the authoritative language.

Without a visible body of its own, as if a ghost, her singular mode of speech borrowed the body of the major language, while turning it nearly against itself. It spoke without speaking while her silence frightened us, as if the "Silence of Sirens" in Kafka's story of Odysseus. Bahareh's ghostly language, with its simultaneously minimal and excessive expression, was unsettling to us. We were left in oblivion about the reason for the absent presence of words in her language. This anxiety was not merely due to the fact that her manner of speaking reflected and demarcated "the very limit of [our own] language" (Botting and Wilson 1998, 2). But it was also because the gaping silence created by this absence palpitated our imagination of her imagination about the malice of the world we inhabited. In Foucault's (1998, 24) words, Bahareh's minimal and wordless language also showed us "just how far speech may advance on the sands of silence."

Her mode of speech left us anxious, for without words the level of our communication remained at a basic level—I am not sure what the result would have been had we tried to learn and speak with her in a sign language. This minimality was agonizing for it denied us entry into Bahareh's world. We wondered about that which floated in the vast lacuna between her seeing and saying. We envisioned the dread she experienced at the horrifying scenes her eyes saw. Seeing what we had witnessed, now through her eyes, terrified us. What if the cruelty of this world took away her innocence—the innocence we often attribute to children? What if her refusal to speak the adult's language was a means of resistance to growing up, as and into an adult to whose cruelty or misery she had become an unwilling witness? All we knew of her world we read from her eyes, her bodily gestures, and our own imagination of her imagination.

A Flash of Lightning

It was the summer of 1984. The roar of the lashes was making the whole ward tremble as if from the shocks of a long-lasting earthquake. These were the sounds of lashes on a woman's body on the second floor, right above our ward, who was subjected to whipping five times a day during prayer times until she would either die or accept to pray. Every time the lashes roared, the children screamed and cried of fear. Unlike other children, Bahareh never cried nor did she ever scream. Sucking faster on her pacifier, she silently looked with her unusually enlarged pupils. In such moments, I shivered to my bones wondering what she knew of horror that even we, the adults, did not or could not recall. It was as if she had a vivid memory of sometime in the past, of all the times in the past, even of future; as if she knew of the imminent coming of a much more potent malice, as if she could see the future as already present, already past, yet still to come, of all the times that have been, are, and will be "out of joint" (Shakespeare).

In *Impasse of the Angels*, Stefania Pandolfo (1997, 248) writes about a young poet, "little more than a boy," who seems old while singing of "loss and sorrow," "for he is infused with the authority of what is spoken through him." Bahareh too sang, despite her limiting language. I see her, in retrospect, like a storyteller, a poet, who has not yet lost "the instinctive knowledge of dying," hence "does not speak death to the world" (Harrison 1992, 249).

In my mind, she still sings without words, for her experience is of the kind about which Botting and Wilson (1998, 3) write: "certain experiences disclose an 'unknowing' at the heart of experience that denotes the limit of language, discourse, culture." The only way to talk about such experiences is to be a poet, a painter, a singer, or a sheer existence. Bahareh reminds me of the palm trees, which stood upright and alive in the midst of the ruins in the ancient city of Bam after the disastrous 2003 earthquake.

The Return of Madeleine?

A few years ago, I had a dream of a beautiful sunny day and of myself in the ocean with my pants rolled up to my knees, while holding a friend's hand. The sunrays had a dazzling orange reflection in the blue water. Yet, I was saddened by a deep loss. Somehow I knew, as I assumed all others walking along in the ocean knew, that we were the only survivors of a disaster. I was torn between my joy of being present to this splendid beauty and the horror of inhabiting a world in the aftermath of a disaster. We kept walking deeper into the ocean but, all of a sudden, it began to roar and vomit, as if in anger. The waves were rising and pushing toward us as though to wash us all away or to swallow us in. As I paused indecisive about running away or giving into the waves, I suddenly saw Bahareh, far deeper in the ocean, playing with the waves. I awoke, bewildered!

Why would Bahareh inhabit this strange space in my dream? Why now, after so many years, should Bahareh, whose language lacked words, the essential element of any human language, come to speak through me, to me, or for me? What is it in her story that compels me to unearth it, as if an archaeologist, from under so many layers of memories? Why does she come to occupy such a significant space in my dreams?

In his discussion of voluntary and involuntary memory, Walter Benjamin writes, "Proust tells us how poorly, for many years, he remembered the town of Combray in which, after all, he spent part of his childhood." "One afternoon," Benjamin recounts, "the taste of a kind of pastry called madeleine (which he later mentions often) transported him (Proust) back to the past, where as before then he had been limited to the promptings of a memory which obeyed the call of attentiveness." Proust suggests that "it is the same with our own past. In vain we try to conjure it up again; the efforts of our intellect are futile." For Proust, Benjamin suggests, "the past is 'somewhere beyond the reach of the intellect, and unmistakably present in some material object (or in the sensation which such an object arouses in us), though we have no idea which one it is. As for the object, it depends entirely on chance whether we come upon it before we die or whether we never encounter it'" (Benjamin 1968, 158). Benjamin argues, however, that our memory can also be invoked voluntarily.

I am not sure what awakened Bahareh's memory in my mind; perhaps, I had in fact never forgotten about her. All I remember is that one cold winter night, while walking home, her image penetrated my skin, as if the wind. I immediately ceased it, as it ceased me and rekindled a series of other memories in my mind. Yet her appearance in my dream urged me to think about the ways in which her story relates to my life, both in the past and present.

Both Bahareh and I were survivors of disasters. Bahareh was born in 1981, in the midst of a bloody war with Iraq and the crackdown on political dissidence. Bahareh articulated herself in words only after she was released from prison. I, too, survived those disastrous years of the early 1980s, as well as the massacre of political prisoners in the summer of 1988, during which thousands of prisoners were summarily executed despite having been tried and already serving their time. My last real piece of writing in my native language,[1] for years to come, was a long letter to my husband, during the summer of 1988, without knowing whether he was alive or already killed. I unconsciously hoped the letter, as if it were a talisman, would protect him. It had not. Months later I would learn that he was executed. I found myself unable or reluctant to write, as if refusing to express myself in a language that was also spoken by his killers, resisting, like Bahareh, to deploy words that had spoken death to others. Only in exile I resumed writing, not in my mother tongue, but in a foreign language.

In 1984, nearly three years old at the time, Bahareh was given to her grandparents while her mother was still imprisoned. Less than an hour after joining with them, she was already conversing in complete sentences as if she had been speaking for years. The outside world was as foreign to Bahareh as was the United States for me. Prison had been the only place she knew, at least as far as her conscious memory went; who knows what she remembered of the fifteen days before she was taken to jail.

The Storyteller, the Poet

And now Bahareh has come to act as my interlocutor in the aftermath of disasters and massacres. Her presence reminds me that in a world after the massacre, one has no way of surviving except through an artful expression, through poetry, in a wide sense of the term. I think of Bahareh's playing with the waves in my dream as such poetry—a poetry that speaks life to the world rather than death. Yet, words seem to escape me. The fire of the images and memories makes them evaporate or melt away like small pieces of ice under the hot summer, while a burning sensation lingers on in my soul of the loss, of the losses, and the mourning for that which never came to be. I seek a way to tell these stories of injustices, those of Bahareh's and mine, in the only language possible for me, in elusive or even evasive words.

Compelled to reveal the injustices of our histories that have come to be repeated yet again since the postelection movement in Iran in June 2009, I am faced with a dilemma. How do I narrate Bahareh's story in words, while she so ardently refused to speak in words? How do I convey the power of silence that is often seen as muteness? Yet even though Bahareh's silence spoke louder than words, she articulated herself in words after leaving prison, perhaps because only then was she able to recognize herself as a mourner and a survivor and to speak in a language that could survive her and the dead. I, too, came to write after my release from prison and leaving my country of birth—it was, in fact, due to this separation from home and family that I reckoned with my losses and my survival, in their repetition, in the second time, as with every traumatic event, in an always already belated manner. Yet, to narrate a past that has seeped into present not merely in its impacts and memories, but in its uncanny repetition, one has to write of the past, as Benjamin suggests, at once as a present in transition, and as a past in which "time stands still and has come to a stop" (Benjamin 1968, 262). Perhaps it is this dialectic of transition standing still that Benjamin portrays in the very moment of one's death when "a sequence of images is set in motion inside" us as our lives "[come] to an end" (94). Through this dialectical poetic imagery of life and death, one may find a way of exploring bygone presents.

Like an enigmatic allegory, in my memory, Bahareh has stood at once still and vivacious, always a little girl, never growing old or dying, appearing and disappearing, never failing to appear again. She comes to speak to and through me, constantly there, as I move from one stage of my life to another, thorough my growing older, whenever I face the limitation of language and the need and desire to tell the story of new injustices; she is there to remind me of my survival, of my ethical responsibility as a witness of injustices. She is there to be a witness to my witnessing.

Bahareh teaches me how to live and converse with the ghosts, while remaining committed to life. In that space of abyss in which, as Victor Hugo (1862, 471) suggests, "what can be done . . . but to talk," Bahareh chooses not to speak, a silence that I read as a means of survival and a profound response to the responsibility to which she was born, a refusal to speak in the language of the killer. Her speaking after her release thus may be construed as an articulation of her defiance against the "crime of the other," a recognition that "one does not, for all that, bear any less responsibility, beginning at birth" (Derrida 1994, 21).

Blue Jays and Pigeons

There were pigeons in Evin Prison, the kind I used to see in New York City. Perhaps these pigeons were one of the reasons that in New York, more than anywhere else in the United States, I was reminded of my prison experience. In prison, pigeons would gather behind our bars and make sounds, especially in the spring, which to the ears of some torture-inflicted prisoners sounded as if saying, "Please do not beat. Do not beat hard!" For months, however, while living in New York, I woke to sounds that I assumed to be the cries of orgasmic pleasure of a couple living upstairs. Only months later did I learn that they were the sounds of pigeons. As I initially began to write about my story, I thought if my ears could hear such drastically different sounds from the pigeons of prison in Iran and those of New York City, I wondered how my voice would be heard in the United States.

NOTES

1 Farsi is not actually my native language either. My mother tongue is Azari. But Farsi is the language I have read and written in and the one with which I am more comfortable, and that is also another irony regarding our relationship to languages.

7

Voices of Silence

On Speaking from within the Void
(A RESPONSE TO SHAHLA TALEBI)

GABRIELE M. SCHWAB

The experience of my reader shall be between the phrases, in
the silence, communicated by the intervals, not the terms of
the statement.
—Samuel Beckett

The paradox of silence in literature has forever intrigued writers and
philosophers. Among the many different types of silence, Beckett refers
to the silence of what is being invoked indirectly, but not said explicitly,
that is, the silence between phrases that we can hear in the intervals
of a statement. This is a deeply literary silence not only because poetic
language is generated by modes of indirection but also because, almost
paradoxically, it is often this silence in the interstices of language that
breathes life into literature, endowing it with the ability to engage readers with the limits of what is sayable, namable if not knowable. This
type of silence is, in the words of Beckett's (1955, 414) the unnamable, "a
dream silence, full of murmurs."

Beckett was obsessed with silence. True silence in his work is more
than an absence of words; it is a resonating absence generative of meaning and affect. In his stage directions to *Endgame*, for example, Beckett
establishes a pointed difference between "pause" and "silence." While
"pause" marks mere intervals in dialogue, silence carries existential
weight and philosophical density. In a highly experimental staging of
Endgame at a small theater in the Swiss border town of Kreuzlingen, director Norman Elrod placed the generative power of silence at the play's
center. When Beckett's stage directions read "pause," Elrod had the ac-

tors pause for precisely ten seconds. By contrast, each time the stage directions read "silence," the director asked the actors to stop playing until complete silence fell upon the audience. Typically, after a while, tension mounted in the audience as people began to stir in confusion. The actors had been instructed to hold out until this tension gave way to absolute silence. Only then were they allowed to resume the play. In this way, the audience was compelled viscerally to experience the difference between pause and silence. In order truly to hear silence, Elrod's particular staging suggested, one needs to clear the mind from the mindless chatter of daily life. Or, in the words of the unnamable, silence resides in a "mind at peace, that is to say, empty."

It seems no coincidence that Elrod, the stage director, was also a psychoanalyst. Beckett's own use of silence is deeply influenced by his experience and engagement with psychoanalysis, and especially the role silence plays in the work of Bion, Beckett's own analyst of many years. Freud had discovered the analyst's silence as a powerful tool for the transference of unconscious memories and fantasies. In a similar vein, Beckett uses silence in his plays and texts as a tool to engage his audience and readers at an unconscious level. Yet, Beckett also explores the profound ambivalence of silence. While many of his characters dream of a silence able to stop the endless flow of words that routinely clutter mental space, the imagined peace of mind remains unattainable to them because the characters' logorrhea covers up another silence replete with the terror of abandonment, if not death.

I turn here to a different kind of silence, namely silence in the wake of violence and trauma, and specifically the relationship among violence, trauma, memory, language, and silence. I explore this relationship through the silence of Bahareh, a little girl whose story is told by anthropologist Shahla Talebi in the previous essay. Talebi met Bahareh during her time as a political prisoner in Iran's infamous Evin Prison. When Bahareh was fifteen days old, the police stormed her house, killed her father in front of her eyes, and took her with her mother to the Evin Prison, where they lived together in the women's section for the first three years of Bahareh's life. Bahareh routinely witnessed the beating and torture of her mother and the other women. During these three years, it appeared as if Bahareh never learned to speak. The only identifiable word she uttered was "amama," a word that in Farsi is a condensation of "mama" and "breast." Her other utterances remained cryptic and inaccessible, almost as if she had formed a private language from the shards of broken words around her. However, as Talebi illustrates in her account, Bahareh nonetheless communicated vividly. She used cryptic words and sounds, including the humming of songs, and she was able to signal her needs and desires. Otherwise she relied on the language of her body, and above all her dark eyes with their intent and probing gaze. At age three, she was released from prison and put in the care of her grandparents. In an astounding turn of events, she began to speak in well-articulated words and sentences only a few hours after her release.

How can we understand the silence of this child, and what may it tell us about silence more generally? What interests me is that Bahareh's silence falls into the first three years of her life, that is, the period in which children commonly enter the symbolic order of language and develop the first language-grounded memories as the basis for a rudimentary sense of self. What does it mean that for Bahareh this time coincides with her time in prison, and how can we interpret her silence within the traumatic space of her imprisonment? How are we to understand the fact that she communicated with great intensity through the language of her body and through sound and song, but refused the use of words? Did she have any way intuitively to understand that words could be dangerous? Did she have any sense of the ambivalent wavering between precarity and power that lies in withholding words? Shahla Talebi underscores the deep ambivalence of Bahareh's silence. She sees the mute cry of a child whose ability to speak was cut short by violence, but at the same time she also sees the poetic quality of the detours Bahareh takes through body and song in order nonetheless to speak and connect with those around her, albeit indirectly. What is this child withholding, and what is she protecting in her refusal to speak? How does she process the violent world around her, and what can we possibly guess about her "silent memories" from her prison time, before she began to speak?

Children who have not yet learned to speak experience the world, including the voices they hear, almost exclusively through the senses. They learn to read the surrounding world through impressions of light, warmth, sounds, shapes, colors, and smells. They begin to read the people who take care of them through mutual gazing and touching, and these people become the mirrors through which they develop a sense of self. Gradually, they learn to read the faces and voices of those who care for them. From the very beginning they know the difference between comfort and discomfort and thereby distinguish between a friendly and caring or hostile and dangerous environment. They viscerally experience the impact of their environment on their own well-being.

Children who witness parental trauma become avid readers of silences and memory traces hidden in a face that is contorted with pain, frozen in grief, a forced smile that does not feel quite right, an apparently unmotivated flare-up of rage, or chronic depression. Traumatized bodies reveal traces of trauma in the form of what Marianne Hirsch calls an "optical unconscious." Without being fully aware of it, child witnesses of parental trauma become skilled readers of their parents' unconscious as it is expressed in the embodied language of affects, and especially in traces of affects that remain unintegrated and inassimilable. It is in this vein that I imagine Bahareh's experience of her mother's and the other women's trauma. Something compels her to remain in her preverbal world of sensuous and affective experiences and modes of relating. At the same time, however, the women who cared for her also read stories, sang, and talked to her. They transmitted word-forming experiences that must have made a subliminal impact, even if Bahareh didn't use them at the time. While she refused their words, she absorbed their songs, their rhythms, and the affects they carried.

Meanwhile, her phonetic system seemed to remain minimally developed, almost as if she suffered from childhood aphasia. I'm comparing Bahareh's condition to aphasia because we know in hindsight that her language skills must have been more developed than her use of them. Describing the constitution of the phonetic system in infancy, Roman Jakobson argues that, in certain cases of aphasia, this phonetic edifice is destroyed in the reverse order of its acquisition.[1] The last word the aphasic can utter before sinking into the gurgling silence of complete aphasia, Jakobson says, is the earliest phonetic acquisition, namely "a kind of 'mmma-mmma, ma-ma.'"[2] Bahareh's only clearly identifiable word, we remember, is "amama." It may therefore seem as if she had never moved beyond this earliest phonic acquisition and was incapable, if not refusing, to enter the symbolic order of language. But we need to look more closely at the nature of this inability or refusal. The fact that Bahareh spoke a few hours after her release from prison suggests that she had tacitly acquired the symbolic order, yet refused the active use of it. Her speaking almost immediately upon release indicates that her silence was a traumatic silence. What made Bahareh swallow her words? Did she perceive language in prison as a dangerous, if not toxic object? Did her fear of facing the brutal world around her make her withdraw into silence?

We know of children who, under the impact of severe trauma, stop speaking, sometimes for years. We know of children who, during the war in Guatemala, for example, were kidnapped for ransom and returned a few months later, mute and withdrawn. People called them *los retornados*—the returned ones. Can a child who has never learned to speak already be held captive in a traumatic silence? Is this silence imposed by a violent world she viscerally experiences without being able to comprehend? And what is the effect of her silence on those at the receiving end?

Shahla Talebi speaks of Bahareh's "loud silence" and describes the powerful hold it has on the women in prison. In fact, the strong affective responses she elicits from the other women indicate that her silence operates creatively as an empty screen to elicit projection and transference. Talebi writes,

> Bahareh's ghostly language, with its simultaneously minimal and excessive expression, was unsettling to us. We were left in oblivion about the reason for the absent presence of words in her language. . . . But it was also because the gaping silence created by this absence palpitated our imagination of her imagination about the malice of the world we inhabited. . . . We envisioned the dread she experienced at the horrifying scenes her eyes saw. Seeing what we had witnessed, now through her eyes, terrified us. What if the cruelty of this world took away her innocence—the innocence we often attribute to children? What if her refusal to speak the adult's language was a means of resistance to growing up, as and into an adult to whose cruelty or misery she had become an unwilling witness?

Bahareh's silence thus becomes a mirror for the cruel world and the silenced affects of the adult prisoners. They don't know how Bahareh sees the world, but, in a way speech never could, her loud silence places her in a central place in their imagination. When it does not come from a peaceful place, silence creates anxiety and fear. "All we knew of her world we read from her eyes, her bodily gestures, and our own imagination of her imagination," says Talebi. The girl's silence becomes a catalyst that causes the adults to see the world and language through the eyes of a child, as if for the first time. It is as if her silence tells her story as a mute witness to their violent and cruel world. In this respect, her silence operates as a creative voice in its own right. In fact, Bahareh's use of a "voice of silence" resembles what Merleau-Ponty in "Indirect Language and the Voices of Silence" defines as the creative use of language in true speech. "True speech . . . speech which signifies . . . is only silence in respect to empirical usage," Merleau-Ponty insists and concludes that "we must consider speech before it is pronounced, the background of silence which does not cease to surround it and without which it would say nothing. Or to put it another way, we must uncover the threads of silence with which speech is mixed" (Merleau-Ponty 1964, 248). Similar to the intervals between phrases Beckett invokes in the quote I used as an epigraph, Bahareh's "threads of silence" open up a transitional space between purely sensorial preverbal experiences and a rudimentary story of mute witnessing, a story generated by the silent memories of a time before the formation of language.

Bahareh's cryptic words as well as her humming of songs seem to become interwoven with the silences of the women who witness her silence. In a complex transference, Bahareh seems to embody and thereby lay bare the threads of silence that weave together the adult prisoner's traumatic speech, including the cries and whispers not meant for Bahareh's ears. It is as if the child's silence shakes the adults' linguistic and narrative apparatus to the core in order to tear a new sound from it. I see a primordial mirroring at work in Bahareh's words that forces the women to *gaze* at her asemic words and, mediated through them, at their own language. This gaze resembles the gaze Merleau-Ponty invokes of deaf people who "look at those who are speaking, compare the art of language to the other arts of expression, and try to see it as one of these mute arts." "We must pretend never to have spoken," says Merleau-Ponty (1969, 248), "if we want to understand that there is a tacit language." Bahareh does not have to pretend: she has never spoken. It is precisely by inadvertently giving the adult women this gift of the mute art of a tacit language that Bahareh turns language from a tool into a living process and thereby opens the world of the female prisoners at Evin to a new kind of "being in language" as well as a new mode of listening. It is through the mirror of Bahareh's silence that the women learn to listen to each other in a way that engages the silenced traumatic core of their selves. Perhaps it is because of this gift that Shahla Talebi sees Bahareh in retrospect "like a storyteller, a poet." After all, isn't it the task of storytellers and poets to make us hear and see, as if for the first time?

Perhaps Bahareh's story is so deeply moving because her silence, rather than encapsulating, walling in, or encrypting trauma, embodies trauma in the voice of sounds. While refusing the order of speech, her sounds connect to trauma through rhythm, tone, pitch, and even melody. Bahareh's minimal word creations speak a song of silence that becomes a bridge to reach those around her. At the same time, her loud silence is also a silent scream. In this sense, Bahareh's story is rather exceptional since usually traumatic silences do not reach out but create a wall, if not a "double wall," between people (Bar-On 1989, 328). How does Bahareh negotiate the difference between the ways in which the women care for her and their simultaneous inability to shield her from the daily violence that marks their world? How did she hear *their* silences rather than inviting them to hear hers?

Trying to understand Bahareh's role as a silent witness reminds me of what silences felt like as I grew up during the traumatic postwar years in Germany. The stories told in my family were built upon an unfathomable silence. The words and images of adults had grown over their silenced wounds like a second skin. There was another type of silence, also. I grew up listening to war stories that I was completely unable to comprehend. Told in my presence as if I was not there, these stories were not addressed to me and left me stranded in a muted space outside. A silent witness, I was not allowed to ask questions or interrupt the flow of words. I became an empty vessel to hold a terror that remained untold, a silence covered by words, a history condemned to secrecy and handed down as shards of splintered affect. Without fully understanding, I felt that words could be split into what they said and did not say. It was as if they carried a secret that cast me outside. I had a vague sense of something deadly, of words filled with skeletons. My own words were stolen, and I became withdrawn and taciturn, a girl without words, as I used to think of myself.

Trying to grasp these tacit spaces of storytelling and writing and the silent witnessing of a child exposed to stories not meant for her ears, I see a resonance with Bahareh's story. She too was placed in the position of a silent witness to events not meant for her. Thinking on the deep impact my parents' war stories made on my psychic life, I wonder about the long-term effects of Bahareh's witnessing on language and psyche. While I could hardly understand the full horror of war behind my family's stories, they nonetheless conveyed a sense of this horror on an affective level. By contrast, Bahareh was a witness to brute facts. While she was too young to understand the violence of imprisonment and torture, she received at least some of its effects on a visceral level. What are the inscriptions and traces of such experiences, and how do they affect language and silence?

Shahla Talebi mentions in her story of Bahareh that the attack by the police happened during the time her father was singing to her while putting her to bed. His song was disrupted when the police shot him in front of Bahareh. Given that she was only fifteen days old, she could not understand what was happening. But she certainly took in the atmosphere of violence, fear, and tension that accompanied the attack. Her corporeal memory may have recorded the screams that disrupted her father's song. But she was too young to mourn him because her traumatic loss happened before she had acquired a cultural and symbolic sense of death and mourning. Traumatic loss, Abraham and Torok assert in *The Shell and the Kernel*, tends to be silenced and cut off from the world. Commonly, the lost person or object is taken into a crypt inside the self that remains sealed off from consciousness and the outside world. The very occurrence and devastating emotional consequences of trauma become entombed and consigned to internal silence by the sufferers. As a child witness to severe violence and trauma, Bahareh must have taken these events in viscerally and somatically by watching and reading the injured bodies of the adults around her, by seeing the pain on their faces, the scars and the blood on their bodies, by hearing their screams, but also by feeling the weight of their own traumatic silences.

I am tempted to make a link between Bahareh's silent memories of these events and her actual silence. I think of Bahareh as sealing off her own words, her emerging language, in a crypt inside her self. Since we know that after her release she was perfectly able to speak, we may assume that she shielded her words and stories from the outside world and others, burying them inside. Her words were cryptonymic sounds, reaching out to others, yet withholding at the same time. Buried with her language was the symbolic order to which it belonged, an order that for Bahareh spoke violence and trauma, an order that stood for the killing of her father and the continued violation of her mother.

But how are we to imagine Bahareh's silent memories? We know that even infants are able to "read" the world around them. Almost from birth, if not before, they are capable of deep empathy, able to read and feel what goes on in their environment. They are also capable to form rudimentary memories of these times. In *The Shadow of the Object*, Christopher Bollas analyzes a form of existential early remembering he terms the "unthought known." Experiences formed before the acquisition of the symbolic order of language, Bollas argues, will later be remembered as moods rather than memories proper. These experiential, sensorial, and existential memories continue to form a silent underpinning of actual memories in later life. Moods evoke early modes of receiving language through rhythms, sounds, tonalities, pitch, rhymes, or alliterations. These "semiotic" qualities become inscribed with traces of affect and henceforth constitute a particular subliminal mode of being in language.[3] The latter routinely accompanies verbal communication, often on an unconscious level. What Merleau-Ponty calls "the silence between languages" relies on semiotic resonances to such affective states of being in language. We retain these affective states as an "unthought known." Resembling what Derrida (1988, 115), in *The Ear of the Other*, calls "the unthought thinking," this visceral knowledge contains the things we know and (unconsciously) remember from the experiences we made before the acquisition of language. It is a knowledge inscribed in the body and its sensorial memories and recalled in the form of moods.

Such forms of "unthought knowledge" can also emerge collectively. Bahareh's silence may have had such a powerful hold on the women in the Evin Prison because it functioned as a catalyst for soliciting primordial, unthought forms of knowledge. Primordial forms of knowing may well characterize the corporeal memories inscribed in these women's bodies during the experiences of torture with its attacks on language and the world. Torture enforces regression to a state of catastrophic helplessness that resembles the experiences of early infancy before the acquisition of language proper. In *The Body in Pain*, Elaine Scarry (1985, 35) writes, "Intense pain is also language-destroying: as the content of one's world disintegrates, so the content of one's language disintegrates; as the self disintegrates, so that which would express and project the self is robbed of its source and its subject." We may assume that some of the ways in which the women at the Evin Prison processed the states of catastrophic helplessness during and after torture operated on such a primordial level of sounds, looks, and touch as well as on the level of a basic care for each other, like one takes care of infants or people in need. This primordial mode of caring also helps to rebuild the self that has been shattered, if not annihilated by torture. Like the formation of self in early infancy, the rebuilding of the self after catastrophic events is relational and requires the support of others through mirroring experiences. Just as the self needs the other's mirror for its formation, it needs a mirror to be rebuilt after a shattering experience. Bahareh's silence, as well as the resilience expressed in her songs, offered such a mirror experience to the women in Evin.

Human beings have always silenced violent histories. Some histories, collective and personal, are so violent we would not be able to live our daily lives if we did not at least temporarily silence them. A certain amount of silencing pain, of splitting or sealing it off from the daily world, is conducive to survival. Too much silence, however, becomes haunting. While silenced histories are the product of internal psychic splitting, they can be collectively deployed and shared by a people or a nation. The collective or communal silencing of violent histories leads to the transgenerational transmission of trauma and the phantomatic return of the past. I'm locating Bahareh's story in a transitional space between individual and collective trauma. Her individual history is not completely singular. There were many other children incarcerated with their mothers in the Evin Prison. Her way of processing the traumatic world of her early years, however, was unique. She created a silence interspersed with a cryptonymic language of her own that became a space for collective resonance. Talebi describes how the girl elicited a powerful transference: as Bahareh became a silent witness to the other women's pain, they in turn witnessed her pain through both her silence and her cryptic words and songs. Most importantly, the women were able to witness their own pain mediated through Bahareh's silence, seeing it through the eyes of a child, as if for the first time. It is in this way that I share Shahla Talebi's sense that Bahareh's role for the women resembled that of a poet and storyteller: she gave the other women their story back, seen through the mute cries and soothing songs of a silenced child.

Let me end with a note on literature and silence. Calling Bahareh a poet and storyteller, Talebi also points to mirroring and transference as rarely acknowledged functions of literature and storytelling. In "Words and Moods," I described the ways in which literature can become a transformational object that generates access to the silent memories of early childhood in the form of resonance. The sensorial dimension of language, or what is usually called the "poetic voice," uses rhythm, sound, tonalities, pitch, alliterations, and rhymes or, in short, the entire arsenal of poetic devices to evoke early modes of being in language and to tap into the traces of affect inscribed in them. In *Revolution in Poetic Language*, Julia Kristeva calls this dimension of language "the semiotic." Literature provides a space of resonance with our earliest modes of being in language. These are, at the same time, the modes in which our affects are formed and inscribed in our later ways of using language as a symbolic order.

Traumatic histories constitute an attack on memory, language, and the symbolic order. Traumatic silences can be accessed and transformed only via detours and indirections. Literature provides such detours to look into ourselves without the dangers of a direct, invasive confrontation. It also provides a space to access those unconscious modes of being in language that recall the dependency of early infancy and are reawakened in the vortex of trauma. It is in this vein that literature—just as Bahareh, the infant poet and storyteller—can assume a healing function in the wake of trauma.

NOTES

1 According to Jakobson, the acquisition of a quasi-universal order of a phonic edifice is composed of labials, dentals, posterior occlusives, fricatives, and an apical r (cited in Derrida 1988, 131).

2 Derrida (1988, 131).

3 I use "semiotic" in the sense defined by Julia Kristeva (1984).

8

Future's Past

A Conversation about the Holocaust with Gabriele M. Schwab

MARTIN BECK MATUŠTÍK

MARTIN BECK MATUŠTÍK: In Holocaust studies, "second generation" has come to describe children of the survivors. Among key formative impacts on this area would be, for example, Holocaust literature as well as memoir narrative (Helen Epstein, Primo Levi, Elie Wiesel), the Yale Video Archive Testimony project (Larry Langer, Geoffrey Hartman, Shoshana Felman, Dori Laub), and theoretical struggles with representation, meaning, and faith including the memorial, political, and clinical repair work of coming to terms with the past and open future. It took you many years of courage, thinking, listening, and personal working through to offer your testimony as a member of another second generation. Can you say something about that journey?

GABRIELE M. SCHWAB: One of the reasons why the term "second generation" commonly refers to children of survivors is that witnessing is, in most cases, linked to a position of victimhood. This raises crucial questions: Can the perpetrator speak? Can perpetrators or their descendants bear witness? Under what conditions and at what risk? For the children of perpetrators, these questions become complicated by the fact that they are neither witnesses nor perpetrators in the strict sense of the terms. However, they can speak from within and for a history of perpetration as witnesses of its impact on their own lives. The most important decision for children of perpetrators or children born in a nation of perpetrators (since not all Germans were perpetrators) is then *how* to claim a voice of their own if they choose to do so. Many of my generation were either frozen in guilt and shame or locked into a defensive position, rejecting collective responsibility by insisting that one cannot be blamed for something that happened before one was born. From what position then can descendants of perpetrators speak? It is too easy to feel like a victim of the guilt and shame handed down by the parental generation, and it all too often feeds into a politics of resentment. It is also tempting to invert the Manichean delirium that splits the world into good and evil, assuming that all Germans are intrinsically evil whereas all their victims, especially the Jews, Roma, and Sinti, are unfailingly good. All these positions are traps, of course. But it's hard to avoid them altogether.

In my essay "Identity Trouble" [in *Haunting Legacies*; Schwab 2010], I used Fanon to analyze this problem, looking at the "identification with the victim" by children of perpetrators. I argue that seeing such identification (including extremes such as philo-Semitism) merely as inverse racism is a simplification that overlooks the possibility of it being an early transitional phase of working through the parental legacy of racism. We have much to learn from theories of decolonization and critics of colonialism such as Fanon and Ngugi wa Thiong'o, who speak of the necessity to "decolonize the mind." During the entire period of de-Nazification, the German people have never fully engaged the problem of what it would take to "de-Nazify the mind." This problem does not end with the generation of actual perpetrators. After all, it is this very generation that raises the children. In my essays, I draw on theories that helped me think though this problem such as Frantz Fanon, Ngugi wa Thiong'o, and Ashis Nandy. But none of these theories provides a framework for addressing the fundamental question: "How can the perpetrator or their descendants speak?"

In this context, you asked about the journey that brought me to write *Haunting Legacies*. I have been compelled to write about what it meant to grow up in Germany in the wake of WWII and the Holocaust almost since I first was confronted with the facts of the concentration camps and the genocide. It started when we saw the film *Night and Fog* in high school, and I write about this deeply scarring, yet formative experience extensively in *Haunting Legacies*. Since there was no one to talk to at the time, writing was the only way to process what felt like toxic knowledge, if not like a foreign implant in my mind. My entire world had changed within a few hours. In shock, I looked with horror at my own people. But even more generally, the knowledge of the Holocaust made me lose faith in humans and in God (I had grown up Catholic). I remember drafting a letter to God in my diary in which I stated: "I have had many questions and doubts about the existence of Heaven and Hell. Now I don't care anymore about the question whether you exist or not, because even if you insist, knowing that you allowed the Germans to kill millions of innocent people and that you can tolerate such unfathomable cruelty in the world, I no longer want to have anything to do with you." (Later, I learned that I shared this loss of faith with many survivors and their children.)

The wish to write about my experience of growing up in postwar Germany returned full force when I first visited Israel in 1994. At the time I shared my thoughts with Zephyra Porat, a colleague who later became one of my closest friends. Yet, the talk I gave at the time at Tel Aviv University was a straightforward piece of literary criticism, safely removed from personal history. After my lecture, a group of women colleagues took me for lunch, and Hana Wirth-Nesher (author of *What Is Jewish Literature?*) brought up the recent wave of second-generation memoirs of children of survivors. Hana, a friend for whom I have the deepest respect, argued that these memoirs cheapened the true suffering of real victims. A controversial debate issued in which some of the other women countered that no generation should or can ever be deprived of a voice. I was completely silent, frozen once again in guilt and shame. What would people think if I wrote as a child of perpetrators? I threw out what I had written and put the project on hold.

The breakthrough finally came seven years later in the wake of September 11, 2001. My sons and I had returned from my mother's funeral when we learned about the attacks on the Twin Towers. I was horrified about the ensuing rhetoric of retaliation, the discourse of the axis of evil, and the almost instant preparations for war in my new country. When Bush invaded Iraq, for the first time I felt like a bystander. The fact that I took part in demonstrations against the invasion of Afghanistan and Iraq didn't seem enough to mitigate a crushing sense of guilt. Suddenly I understood how one could become guilty without *actively* participating in a violent history. I turned to what I had learned to do: writing. Soon, I realized I had to deal with the legacy of Germany's violent history before I could focus on the present war. As it happened, this time also coincided with the beginning of my training as a research psychoanalyst. During our first session, my training analyst asked: "If you were to name a goal of this analysis, what would it be?" Without thinking twice, I surprised myself by answering: "To be able to write about what it meant to grow up in postwar Germany." As I said in the preface of *Haunting Legacies*, after this answer I felt I owed it to my unconscious to follow up on what it made emerge by surprise. I put all my other projects on hold and began to write.

MATUŠTÍK: Alan L. and Naomi Berger brought children of survivors and perpetrators under one book cover, in their *Second Generation Voices* (2001). And they witnessed in their book the disagreement whether this should even be done. They even courted the danger that several contributors from the second generation of the Holocaust survivors would withdraw their essays from the company they did not expect to share under the same book covers or across the same bridge or in the same conversation. Here we are at the same symposium. Has something changed or have we just become more attuned to this transgenerational difficulty, for which there is no easy *pharmakon*?

SCHWAB: Some things might have changed, but I don't think the controversies about thinking the legacy of second-generation victims together with that of descendants of perpetrators will ever go away. There will always be victims who feel deeply offended by encounters with perpetrators or their descendents, and on a personal level this must be accepted. At a political level, however, we need to move beyond this divide. What has changed, I think, is that from within the community of victims, powerful voices have emerged that argue for the importance of encounters between second-generation victims and perpetrators. Dan Bar-On was in this respect the most important inspiration for me. Of course, he was severely criticized in Israel for his interviews with children of Nazis, but nonetheless his work has become very influential. (I am also thinking of the important work of Vamik Volkan and others on transgenerational trauma and reconciliation.)

Descendants of victims who do not want to see their voices in the same volume as those of descendants of perpetrators might fear that the latter are daring to claim something like an isomorphism of victimhood. Postcolonial theorist Ashis Nandy in *Intimate Enemy* calls this position "isomorphic oppression." I have tried though to move beyond this notion of isomorphism and a concomitant "trauma of children of perpetrators." My emphasis rather lies on the responsibility of descendants of perpetrators to account for the inevitable impact of their legacy of violence as well as their responsibility to take part in breaking the silence that has persisted on an emotional level. This includes acknowledging that the awareness that your own people, perhaps your own parents, were part of one of the most horrendous genocides in history is traumatic. But this trauma is different from the one suffered by descendants of victims. In my book, I am trying to emphasize and analyze those differences. I actually have come to prefer the term "transgenerational haunting" for descendants of perpetrators to that of "transgenerational trauma," because it emphasizes that you can be haunted by the ghosts of the past without being a victim in the strict sense of the term. My commitment to the task of voicing these issues, and preferably of voicing them across the divide of victims and perpetrators, stems from the conviction that any aspect of violence that is repressed will come back to haunt both victims and perpetrators with a vengeance.

MATUŠTÍK: We may not have a way of telling that we have been heard because words cannot always describe the bridges that go to nowhere, articulate sounds that are not meaningful or consoling, ask questions that have no "warum." What then draws the transgenerational witness into breaking silence in which the tone deaf and mute must learn to hear? Have you found survivors or members of their progeny who have listened to the testimony of your generation?

SCHWAB: Have I found survivors or their progeny who have listened to the testimony of *my* second generation? I want to answer this question with two concrete examples. The first time I presented from my project was in 2003 at the Postcolonial Institute in Melbourne. I lectured on what eventually became my second chapter, "Haunting Legacies: Trauma in Children of Perpetrators." My Australian colleagues put my presentation together with that of Esther Faye, a

second-generation Jewish Australian survivor of the Holocaust. As
our discussion deepened, we were struck by how many complemen-
tary challenges our different second generations face, not only the silence of our parents and the taboo placed on asking questions about
the war but also more subliminal forms of internalizing unmetabo-
lized parental affects such as grief, shame, rage, and also rejection.
Esther and I listened to each other and, given the strong feedback we
received, I think the audience listened not only to each of us, but also
to the dialogue between us. We also became aware of the complicated
transference that occurs in such an encounter and the necessity to
face and tolerate the emotions that emerge in the process.

Two years later, I presented from "Writing against Memory
and Forgetting" at a conference at Hebrew University in honor of
Shlomith Rimmon-Kenan. I was never as apprehensive about giving
a talk as I was that day in Jerusalem. My fear was not that my Israeli
colleagues would criticize my approach; I feared they might *reject*
it. The opposite was the case: their support was truly overwhelming. The long and engaged discussion went to the core of the most
difficult problems, concerning not only past legacies but also present
issues, including Israel's politics toward the Palestinian people today.
The many engaging letters I received after my return were testimony
that both survivors and their progeny had heard me. Yet, there is a
complicated twist to this story. There were three German colleagues
in the audience, all friends of mine. Sadly, I don't think they heard me.
Two of them reacted with outright hostility. They were particularly
offended by my claim that all Germans, whether actual perpetrators
or not, needed to bear responsibility for the legacy of the Holocaust.
They also took issue with the concept of haunting, let alone transgenerational haunting. It would have been one thing to disagree, but
the hostility pointed to something much deeper. I had become what
our parents and teachers used to call a *Nestbeschmutzer*, that is, a
bird who soils its own nest. My other friend was not hostile, but she
withdrew into a marked emotional distance, arguing that, since my
lecture contained autobiographical references, she could not engage it
from a scholarly perspective and therefore couldn't say anything about
it. Since I had taken great pains to emphasize the devastating effects
of the emotional silence in postwar Germany, my friend's response

ironically confirmed my argument; yet at the same time, I felt she could not hear me. I should, however, add a cautionary remark not to generalize these particular reactions, because in the meantime I have also received very positive feedback to *Haunting Legacies*, especially from the second and third generation of Germans. As I am thinking about translating *Haunting Legacies* into German, I wonder how controversial its reception will be among my own generation.

MATUŠTÍK: Erin McGlothlin's monograph *Second-Generation Holocaust Literature* (2006) opened a wider space for these conflicting legacies, although even the book cover shrouds its words and title with the counter-representation from Daniel Libeskind's architectural counter-memorial in the Berlin museum, which is void of history. If *Haunting Legacies* is not an explanation, a monument, a consolation, a sympathy or empathy for and from children who may not have found it, a forgiveness-giving or seeking, how would you describe being the witness from your generation? What are the difficulties in your telling, representing, thinking, and working through your story?

SCHWAB: How to describe the "witness of my generation"? I must begin by acknowledging that my generation has seen very diverse forms of both witnessing and nonwitnessing. The way of witnessing I chose is not a common one. First, I mix scholarly work with autobiographical pieces, which is in and of itself a controversial issue. Initially I conceived *Haunting Legacies* as a straightforward scholarly work. Soon, however, I realized that such a choice would once again silence any personal involvement and avoid the emotional challenge, dilemma, and work one must face in doing this kind of study. Second, I chose to analyze in the same book memoirs of both second-generation victims and perpetrators from the problematic position of a descendant of a perpetrator nation. Third, I am analyzing these texts in the context of a larger body of literature that deals with transgenerational trauma and haunting, concerning not only the Holocaust but other histories of violence such as colonialism and slavery as well as more recent forms of war and violence, including torture. I am in a sense following Michael Rothberg's call for studies that look at the Holocaust from the perspective of our age of decolonization.

In this respect I had to face another challenge: for nearly thirty years now I have been living in the United States, and recently I have

become a double citizen. I have written my book not in my native
German but in English and published it in the United States. The
United States, as we well know, is a country founded on the genocide
perpetrated against its indigenous peoples. It is also a country deeply
marked by the history of slavery and its continuation in the slave
labor of the prison-industrial complex. Finally, the violence of the
country's many more recent wars leaves a legacy of responsibility for
all those who live here. Yet, to this day the United States fails fully to
acknowledge and commemorate its own long history of atrocities . . .
as we could witness a few years ago with the attacks on the Smith-
sonian Institution for a WWII exhibit that tried to commemorate
the nuclear bombing of Hiroshima and Nagasaki. In other words,
the challenge consists in linking the process of working through the
violent legacy of my country of origin to new forms of violence in the
here and now, especially in my new country of residence. As I mentioned earlier, the invasion of Iraq made me painfully aware of how
easy it is to become an involuntary bystander to an illegitimate war.
It is these interconnections between different histories of violence
that required orienting my working through of past legacies toward
the present and future. When you are asking, "what are the difficulties of telling, representing, thinking, and working through your
story?" I am therefore also thinking about the third generation and,
at a personal level, my sons, one of whom was born in Germany and
the other in the United States. Both of them have inevitably inherited
Germany's legacy not only because of the historical responsibility
that continues to the next generation, but also because of the psychological effects of being raised by a mother who was herself deeply
marked by growing up in the wake of WWII and the Holocaust.
And yet, after the invasion of Iraq, my younger son surprised me by
saying, "These days I'm more ashamed to be American than to be
German."

MATUŠTÍK: Your work integrates critical and literary theory with the
first-person memoir genre, psychoanalytical reflection, and imaginative reading of fiction to assist one with representations and meanings for which one lacks generic frames. How do you write from
ruins and crypts that are working through the haunting legacies?
How do we read a work that performs the author at once as a theorist

and subject, dramaturge and actor, analyst and the one who must be seen and read through the lenses of transgenerational transference?

SCHWAB: Your question about transgenerational transference is very interesting and complicated. You are absolutely right in observing that I have chosen a mode of performative enactment of my own transference to the material. This enactment in fact supplements the more immediate autobiographically informed reflections in multiple ways. First of all, my critical readings of second-generation memoirs and other literary works that translate histories of violence into auto-biographical, narrative, or poetic form are simultaneously theoretical and personal. I emphasize my own engagement with or, if you wish, transference to the material. I have selected specific texts and films that have deeply affected me. In other words, in my selection of both creative and theoretical works I gave priority to personal consider-ations over systematic, let alone comprehensive choices. Some of the texts and films are those through which I acquired my knowledge of the Holocaust as a teenager (like *Night and Fog*); others have changed my thinking and emotional relationship at a later stage.

Even my engagement with theory in this particular case is marked by transference. Some of the theories I use—such as, for example, Al-exander and Margarete Mitscherlich's *The Inability to Mourn* or Dan Bar-On's *Legacy of Silence*—have helped me work through the lega-cies of the Holocaust. So the integration of critical theory with the first-person memoir genre not only comes quite naturally but also is methodologically justified. Here again I need to emphasize that the range of possibilities in the transference second-generation Germans may have to the persecuted Jews is quite large, and even the forms of identification may be drastically different. For example, I have always been taken aback by the slogan used by some of my comrades during the 1968 protest movements: "We are all German Jews." Apart from its problematic arrogation of the victims' position, however, the slogan can also be read as a symptom of the much more widespread desire to identify with the victim against the parental generation of perpetrators that I mentioned earlier.

MATUŠTÍK: The Mitscherlichs wrote in their clinical analysis of post-war Germany that the generation of perpetrators and bystanders was unable to mourn because it could not permit itself grief over love

lost. Just as Stalin and the Soviet Union of the gulags today, so also
the führer may have no space and time for a memorial. One must not
work through this trauma. Even at Berlin's Kollwitz Pieta dedicated
to all war dead, even at Bitburg cemetery where snow momentarily
covered our shame, one unmourns that sinister love in vain, as from
here to there, there opens no future. For me as your reader, there is a
moment that I identify as the never before told core of your telling.
The moment announces itself whether one listened or not. In chapter
five, you describe what you never experienced as your own memory,
but which has been acted out and inscribed into your life. "Late one
night, in a state of reverie, I was suddenly hit by a flash of insight: I
always felt guilty for owing my life to the death of my infant brother
who was killed during the war" (120). This is the story of your
ghost brother killed in an allied bombing. Did I hear you witness to
yourself as your baby brother's replacement child who may not be
mourned because *she* is an offspring of the perpetrator lineage? Did
I hear soundings of disconsolation in your testimony that grieves
without a memorial, yet alive, everywhere, every time? Is this then
the haunting legacy of your generation: inhabiting oneself as an
archive and afterlife of memory that may not die and so may not find
its dissident Antigone who would bury, mourn, or even replace the
ghost brother?

SCHWAB: The "inability to mourn" that Alexander and Margarete
Mitscherlich name as a particular pathology in postwar Germany
has many facets. In a sense, *Haunting Legacies* deals with both
the inability to mourn and the extremely difficult responsibility
to mourn. I ask myself whether this responsibility is one of the
legacies that has been passed down to the postwar generation. The
Mitscherlichs analyze the war generation's inability to mourn the
loss of the führer, that is, their supreme object of idealization. But I
think the inability to mourn goes much deeper: after the war many
German people had a hard time mourning their own losses because
of their unfathomable guilt and shame. How can you fully mourn
a son or brother who has been killed in the war or feel the pain of
seeing your family's centuries-old house destroyed during the air
raids, if you feel, perhaps even unconsciously, that this is the well-
deserved punishment for the German people? Of course, everybody

mourns these losses in some way, but guilt and shame interfere with this mourning in major ways. I am now speaking of the war generation. For the second generation, mourning is impeded in an entirely different way. First of all, how can you mourn something that you have not directly experienced? This is one of the central questions in *Haunting Legacies*. I am arguing that you can mourn secondhand, so to speak. Children unconsciously take in not only their parents' grief and pain but also their guilt and shame. And their psychic life is profoundly shaped by parental silences. I have so far spoken of the Germans' inability to properly mourn their own losses, but we should not forget that some Germans are also mourning the Jewish victims who died in the camps and the Jewish culture and life in their midst. I found the best analysis of this mourning in Robert Meister (2011, 187), who argues in *After Evil* that postwar Western Europe internalized its missing Jews and "rebuilt itself on the archeology of a cosmopolitan Jewish civilization that had been destroyed in the two great wars of nationalist excess." While the complex and problematic feature of this type of mourning has barely been recognized, I believe that the German postwar generation must bear responsibility for mourning the losses of their own people together with the victims' losses—which also includes the many non-Jewish victims that died in the camps.

It is interesting that you are connecting the inability to mourn with the problem of the "replacement child" because this is one of the most striking examples of a transgenerational legacy. "Replacement children" are children who unconsciously take over the task of replacing a child that has not been mourned properly. There is a particular inability fully to mourn children who die a violent death, such as the children who died in the camps or during the air raids. One way of reacting to the unbearable pain of their loss is unconsciously to deny it. In consequence, their death assumes a haunting quality. I focus on a growing body of research on replacement children that describes this unconscious denial of the loss of a child. The dead child is kept internally alive in a psychic tomb, like a living ghost. Such denial is often enhanced through the unconscious fantasy that a later born child becomes the replacement of the lost child. Hence, the term "replacement child."

In your question you refer to my own experience as a replacement child for the infant son my parents lost during the war. This brother has played a larger role in my life than many of the relatives I know, partly because he was an imaginary brother. It was as if he became part of my core self. It took me a long time to understand this role my "ghost brother" played in my life, even though I understood it at an affective level long before I came across the research on replacement children that helped me understand it intellectually as well. Yes, I think these things need to be said and heard. Strangely enough, they have been said for a long time, but it seems much harder to hear them. I was amazed how many literary texts on replacement children I found once I started paying attention to the phenomenon. However, the literary criticism that deals with these texts has so far not yet focused on replacement children. For me, doing this research on replacement children and writing about the brother I never knew created a form of displaced mourning for him that helped me work though a lifelong confusion. The fact that in response to my chapter I received quite a number of letters from readers who identified themselves as replacement children gives me hope that this work will help others as well.

MATUŠTÍK: Your narrative awakening opens chapter five with verses of your own poem: "Brother of mine, you were the war baby our mother never wanted . . . ," "A cold shadow of death falls upon the world I enter . . ." (118–19). Like you, I am an immigrant in this country, and with the new citizenship I have been inscribed into legacies of perpetrations that I never inherited with my Slavic Jewish memory. How far and how long does one have to journey in our times beyond the blindness of Oedipus, the deracination of Odysseus, and the homelessness of the wandering Jew? You call your ghost brother poem in chapter five "Baptism of Fire" and "Baptism of Water" (118–19). Have you been heard from the depth of the Native American genocide in your dialogue with Simon J. Ortiz? I would not dare to call any memory with these transgenerational and "multidirectional" (Michael Rothberg) pasts and presents as cheaply consoling and vicariously redemptive about our future. What testimony does the title that you and Simon J. Ortiz gave to your book speak with its "resonances" (a word Simon used when he described this dialogue)? Are *we*, what are *we*, how are *we* as *Children of Fire, Children of Water*?

SCHWAB: Your final question is about *Children of Fire, Children of Water*, the collaborative memoir pieces I am writing with indigenous author Simon J. Ortiz. You make the link to my own poems about my ghost brother that I titled "Baptism of Fire" and "Baptism of Water." These titles provide a wonderful example about the working of the unconscious, or more precisely about unconscious attunement between people. It was Simon who one day suggested the title *Children of Fire, Children of Water* for our collaborative book project. Yet, at the time I had already written the poems about my brother with the titles "Baptism of Fire"/"Baptism of Water." Simon's suggestion of our title has therefore instantly become very dear to me, especially since I see our collaborative project as another way to continue working on my "haunting legacy" by looking at it through the lens of the haunting legacy of an indigenous writer in my new country. Yes, these journeys are long and unpredictable. I see Simon's and my work on *Children of Fire, Children of Water* as a companion project of *Haunting Legacies*. Earlier, I argued for the necessity to work through the legacy of the Holocaust in the context of other histories of violence, including contemporary ones. The memory pieces Simon and I are writing perform a kind of dis-location of memories for the sake of a syncretistic re-membering. We are reflecting on the legacies of colonialism and WWII through the lens of our different life experiences, and in a sense we bring these legacies into a present that is marked by new violent wars and by an increasingly global intertwinement of people's lives. Often it is through the sharing of memories and stories that we connect with each other across cultural differences. But these exchanges leave their mark on the stories, changing the very fabric of memory by letting it be affected by another's memory. This is what intrigues us in working together and what inspires our memory collages. The feedback we've received after our readings during the past years moreover indicates that our interspersed stories inspire some of our listeners to connect them with their own stories. Isn't this one of the best responses one can hope for?

9

"No Other Tale to Tell"

Trauma and Acts of Forgetting in The Road

AMANDA WICKS

As a temporal disruption, trauma dislocates individuals from the integrated, narrative context of personal memory and collective history.[1] Thrust into the role of survivor, trauma victims often fail to understand and navigate their new position, since trauma initially exists as an absence in the mind.[2] Following the initial failure to remember, trauma comes to be situated on the margins of consciousness—implicit memory and dreams—as the brain takes on the work of comprehension and meaning making that cannot yet be faced when cognizant.[3] Those who emerge into trauma's *after* find themselves confronting endless repetitions of their experience, an experience that continues to elude explicit memory, and whose power over the subconscious persists in haunting the survivor. Overcoming such a disturbance requires an act of recuperation, wherein traumatized individuals attempt to recover into language those memories that exist outside the boundaries of active recollection, thereby structuring the event into their narrative memory systems (Payne et al. 2008).[4] Working through trauma, therefore, ultimately becomes a narrativizing act, because the act of remembering and recounting structures *through* language what has occurred *beyond* language. Given language's primary place in working through trauma, reading the intersections between literature and trauma studies becomes increasingly important, for each speaks to the other's "silences" (Whitehead 2004, 4).

Trauma narratives tend to reference real, historical events configured as traumatic, including, but not limited to, slavery, the Holocaust, wars, colonization, and sexual abuse. Given the prevalence of apocalyptic language and imagery used throughout such accounts, it seems increasingly beneficial to turn the tables and read the escalating number of post-apocalypse narratives published since the late twentieth century through the lens of trauma studies. While this is not to suggest that all post-apocalypse narratives are traumatic or that all trauma narratives register in the apocalyptic vein, the two overlap in ways that could expand the interdisciplinary field of trauma studies. Contemporary post-apocalypse narratives challenge memory and, subsequently, narration as a pathway to recovery.[5] The act of working through trauma by means of memory and testimony—what psychoanalysis traditionally views as a constructive means to recovery—instead becomes a violent act within post-apocalyptic space (van der Kolk and van der Hart 1995, 167).[6] Traumatic memories (both personal and collective) act as a conduit to the historical destruction inherent to the original traumatic event, thereby threatening continual damage to both the self and others (Caruth 1996).[7] Although it would appear that apocalyptic trauma must be recalled, reconstructed, and placed within narrative memory in order to help individuals regain a sense of identity and order, many post-apocalypse narratives resist such actions in light of disaster, which according to Maurice Blanchot (1995, 3) "is related to forgetfulness."[8]

Cormac McCarthy's 2006 post-apocalyptic novel *The Road* follows a man and his young son as they journey south through the charred ruins of the United States. The pair attempt to survive increasingly brutal elements, the ever-present threat of starvation, and danger emerging as a result of the previous two: cannibalistic tribes. The novel and, to a lesser extent, the film produced some three years later reject memory as a means to recuperate and work through past trauma(s); instead, characters must concentrate on surviving, an act requiring myriad acts of forgetting, oftentimes a physical *and* mental process within the bounds of post-apocalyptic space.[9] As not only a traumatic event, but a disaster in the fashion of Blanchot, the apocalypse signifies an impossible history, one not worth recuperating—*or perhaps not capable of being recuperated*—in the space of the text. By considering traumatic memory as a dangerous connection to a damaged and damaging past that must be discarded, *The Road* portrays a controversial outlook concerning traumatic memory. Yet, while this outlook differs quite sharply with traditional viewpoints regarding recovery from trauma, it has been progressively echoed in contemporary post-apocalypse narratives.

The Road presents a country that has been "looted, ransacked, ravaged" (McCarthy 2006, 129). Nature and culture alike have been devastated: ash coats the land, affecting breathing quality to the point that survivors must wear masks, and the cities are "mostly burned" (12). Early in the novel, the reader comes face-to-face with the disfigured landscape (8):

> On the far side of the river valley the road passed through a stark black burn. Charred and limbless trunks of trees stretching away on every side. Ash moving over the road and the sagging hands of blind wire strung from the blackened lightpoles whining thinly in the wind. A burned house in a clearing and beyond that a reach of meadowlands stark and gray and a raw red mudbank where a roadworks lay abandoned. Farther along were billboards advertising motels. Everything as it once had been save faded and weathered.

The landscape itself—the space of post-apocalypse—exhibits a physical trauma that comes to be mirrored in the survivors; the "charred and limbless" trees here stand for the traumatic experience that cannot be named and worked through in the narrative. In the midst of this slowly decaying world the man and boy move south from their northern hideout, for the winters have grown increasingly harsh and he worries they will not endure another one.[10] They travel by way of a sparsely populated state road or "what used to be called the states," using the old infrastructure to navigate their way through the unforgiving terrain (McCarthy 2006, 43).[11] The main task required by the post-apocalyptic world in *The Road* is survival. What animal and crop life may have survived in the early years following the event are no more, and, as previously mentioned, cannibals roam the countryside seeking sustenance from fellow survivors. As such, the man and boy remain continually on the defensive while they work their way south; they have no time to pause and work through their memories of the apocalyptic event and the subsequent traumas it entailed. Although the son was born after the apocalypse and contains no knowledge of a world different from the ash-covered, barren landscape through which he and his father slowly make their way, the father remembers life before *the end*, and quickly realizes how memories serve only to keep him from his primary task: protecting his son.

Why does *The Road* reject memory as a way to work through the past? My argument is twofold and hinges around first considering the ways in which *The Road*, as a post-apocalypse narrative in both the textual and visual sense, speaks to and augments trauma studies. Unlike other fictional accounts of trauma, *The Road* does not utilize fragmented descriptions or testimony regarding "the end"; rather, its sparse language and bare plot serve to keep the details at bay, for, in this particular instance of narration, sharing too much of the past threatens characters and readers with the damage inherent to the original apocalyptic event.[12] By grasping McCarthy's unique vision of the future, a future where forgetting is of primary importance, readers reach a new understanding of how history transmits trauma. In order to protect his son and usher in the future, forgetting becomes essential and occurs in a dual manner: First, the unique space of the imagined, post-apocalyptic world—a space outside any temporal or historical mode once used to measure preceding centuries—fails to permit a traditional relationship with memory, be it traumatic or otherwise. Second, what memories do survive encompass the violence inherent to the original traumatic event, a violence appropriated through spectatorship, and cannot be shared at the risk of also sharing that violence.[13] Those who witness the end of the world internalize the destruction they see; sight, therefore, comes to signify appropriation—of the apocalypse and in turn violence—so much so that seeing becomes as much a threat as memory. Necessary to surviving in *The Road* is forgetting, a task set forth for both characters and readers, and a challenge to both trauma studies as well as traditional apocalypse narratives.

Post-apocalyptic and Traumatic Narratives

Once considered unimaginable because it denotes a time when all existence has been eliminated, the post-apocalypse instead constitutes life *after* the apocalyptic moment and the difficulty in navigating that *after*. James Berger notes in *After the End: Representations of Post-apocalypse*, "The end is never the end. The apocalyptic text announces and describes the end of the world, but then the text does not end, nor does the world represented in the text, and neither does the world itself" (Berger 1999, 5). This particular genre resists a concrete ending, because the act of narrating "the end" extends time beyond a linear, historical frame, so that there can never be a true end. As a form dating back to ancient Greece and Egypt, the apocalypse has never signified *the end*; rather, the term designates a transition from one mode of consciousness to another, or the ending of one way of life and the beginning of another.[14] Even though media outlets continue utilizing the term "apocalypse," in addition to apocalyptic rhetoric, to describe catastrophes resembling the end of the world, the term still retains the transitory quality inherent in its original meaning when viewed alongside trauma studies.[15] The post-apocalypse and trauma echo one another in myriad ways, for a traumatic event is never an end, as much as it may seem like one; concerning representations of each, something always *exceeds* the initial experience, something always *remains* in the wake of the event. Post-apocalyptic and traumatic events signal transitions in modes of consciousness and "refer to shatterings of existing structures of identity and language" that must then be restructured through narrative (Berger 1999, 19).

It seems fitting to read fictional post-apocalypse narratives in light of trauma studies, for, as with other traumatic events, the imagined apocalyptic moment precludes immediate representation and understanding "and must be reconstructed by means of [its] traces, remains, survivors, and ghosts" (Berger 1999, 19). In fact, the mounting number of contemporary post-apocalypse narratives speaks to a fascination surrounding what life might comprise after the apocalyptic moment, which in turn points to an increasing social identification regarding notions of *the end*. Elizabeth Rosen (2008) explains, "The story of apocalypse has become a part of our social consciousness, part of a mythology about endings that hovers in the cultural background and is just as real and influential as our myths of origins." More than just a mythology, however, the preoccupation with the end of the world is actually, I argue, a residual trauma from the past that has ingrained itself in the cultural consciousness.[16] Historical events that once seemed to be the end of the world— and in many cases were the end of the world for those who experienced them—transmitted lingering questions regarding *the end* to cultural memory, so that now the apocalypse registers in Western cultural consciousness in a way that continues to haunt the present.[17] According to Berger (1999, 23), each disaster "invokes and transforms memories of other catastrophes, so that history becomes a complex entanglement of crimes inflicted and suffered, with each catastrophe understood—that is, misunderstood—in the context of repressed memories of the previous ones."

As both "an impossible history" and that which continually references past catastrophes, trauma exists as a moment or memory the traumatized cannot entirely possess (Caruth 1996, 5). Trauma narratives attempt to assert a narrative order where none originally existed in order to make sense of a moment beyond the immediate recall of memory. Working through trauma cannot be accomplished alone, and so community and culture must assist in the task of recovery. The relationship is twofold, however, for trauma narratives are important to cultural consciousness; they "reshape cultural memory" by providing testimonies and details concerning traumatic events that might not otherwise surface (Vickroy 2002, 5). Besides providing a structured narrative and temporal order, the trauma narrative also emerges out of "the need to tell and retell the story of the traumatic experience," which materializes from a desire "to make it 'real' both to the victim and to the community" (Tal 1996, 21). The community often operates as listener to the traumatized, thereby acting as "the blank screen on which the event comes to be inscribed for the first time" (Laub 1992, 57). However, the community's position with regard to the traumatic experience does not end with listening; an instinct to "tell and retell" what remains beyond their comprehension emerges within a communal sense, and makes up an important part of trauma narratives: those written by second- and third-generation survivors, as well as by those in the community who were not directly involved in the event.[18] Such a need becomes apparent, I maintain, with authors who imagine a post-apocalyptic future. Their narratives demonstrate a structuring impulse—albeit a creative one—to make sense out of what has remained and continues to remain unintelligible by imagining the end of the world, as well as its *after*.

The function or purpose of the post-apocalypse narrative shifts in degree with each telling, but at the heart of the genre exists the inclination to comfort, criticize existing social and political structures, and make sense of the seemingly incomprehensible. Traditionally, authors attempt to assert a narrative order where none yet exists by envisioning an ending that has not yet occurred; in so doing they construct a "reorientation in the midst of a bewildering historical moment" (Rosen 2008, xiii). Post-apocalypse narratives are fictional, though, so the work of sense making is an imaginative one that attempts to envision order where none exists in real life. The shock associated with apocalypse—like any trauma—must be remembered, narratively structured, and shared in order to help characters regain a sense of identity and order.[19] Apocalypse survivors—those who have witnessed communal tragedy on a global scale—negotiate and work through this *after* in order to process the psychic wound that continues to impact individual consciousness. Yet, post-apocalyptic narratives of the past forty years differ from their predecessors precisely in *how* memory functions within the imagined post-apocalyptic space. Unlike other trauma survivors, apocalypse survivors in contemporary literature eschew attempts to work through and overcome their shattered pasts. In *The Road*, the man remembers his past through implicit memory and dreams, but these connections to life before the end only frustrate his attempts to survive, for, within post-apocalyptic space, memory serves as a dangerous link to a destructive past. Furthermore, positioned as a spectator or witness of the end, he risks passing what violence he saw to his son, representative of the future, and chooses not to consciously engage with his memories concerning the apocalyptic event.

The Road's sparsely narrated form reflects the razed post-apocalyptic world, which the film starring Viggo Mortensen also demonstrates. McCarthy's other novels, such as *Blood Meridian* and *Suttree*, are verbose and expansive, with no end to the lengthy sentences that describe in enormous detail every aspect of the world he wishes to paint. *The Road* differs quite sharply from this style, and its divergence speaks to the trauma situated at the novel's core. McCarthy's language is stripped bare from description to dialogue, indicating in its starkness the difficulty with language often seen after a traumatic experience. Often the boy and his father communicate in short questions and even shorter answers, because language appears to have shifted in the post-apocalyptic world and does not require the same level of lengthy meaning making it did before *the end*. In one particularly telling scene, a snowstorm forces them to stop moving for the night and find shelter (94):

> We have to stop, he said.
>> It's really cold.
>> I know.

> Where are we?
> Where are we?
> Yes.
> I dont know.
> If we were going to die would you tell me?
> I dont know. We're not going to die.

Their exchange has been paired down to the bare necessities, because language, as a primary social tool, falls short without a cultural context in which to place it. Facts such as "It's really cold" and questions regarding their survival take precedence over unrestrained descriptions and insight into the characters' emotional state. In this way, McCarthy's style reflects a traumatized sensibility, one that continues to work against memory and recuperation, since post-apocalyptic space affords no such place for recovery.

Regarding what actually caused "the end," McCarthy provides little in the way of explanation, leaving both the event and what occurred in its wake a mystery. Both the novel and the film explain that "the clocks stopped at 1:17. A long shear of light and then a series of low concussions," but actual specifics concerning the apocalypse remain outside the text (52). Whereas other trauma narratives attempt to make sense of the traumatic experience by way of explaining and narrating what fragments remain and return, *The Road* does not explain.[20] Even while it reveals slivers of life immediately following the apocalypse, it goes no further in providing a *why* or *how*:

> In those first years the roads were peopled with refugees shrouded up in their clothing. Wearing masks and goggles, sitting in their rags by the side of the road like ruined aviators. Their barrows heaped with shoddy. Towing wagons or carts. Their eyes bright in their skulls. Creedless shells of men tottering down the causeways like migrants in a feverland. The frailty of everything revealed at last. Old and troubling issues resolved into nothingness and night. The last instance of a thing takes the class with it. Turns out the light is gone. (28)

Again, McCarthy's style reflects the paltry post-apocalyptic landscape. The staccato sentences provide no more than what is needed to ascertain the events occurring shortly after the end of the world. Profuse descriptions would distract from the effort of survival, because such language connects survivors to a world that no longer exists, and risks transmitting the destruction inherent to that world. Instead, knowledge becomes restricted in order to aid in the act of surviving. Just as knowledge regarding the catastrophic event is not important to the man and boy in their mission to survive, so, too, are they unnecessary for the reader.

Writing on the nature of naming and meaning in the novel, Ashley Kunsa (2009, 64) argues, "By divesting the post-apocalyptic landscape of those names that signify the now ruined world, *The Road* frees both character and reader from the chains of the old language." The "chain of old language" affixes survivor and reader to a past where language acts as a meaning-making structure, in turn imparting the destruction ingrained to a historically oriented use of language. As such, language as explanation and/or narrative has no place in the space of *The Road*, because meaning-making structures (which also include memory and dreams) are no longer privileged forms of working through trauma. By moving beyond language as it was utilized in the past and keeping the apocalypse outside the space of the text, *The Road* creates a new relationship with meaning making, one bound up in forgetting.

Outside Time and Space

Within both the novel and the film, *The Road* depicts a world cut loose from any measurable time or spatial context, such as country, state, or city. The temporal and spatial boundaries that once defined life before the apocalyptic event (e.g., seasons) no longer exist, further confusing the individual's place within such a time/space. Spring, summer, fall, and winter do not exhibit definitive beginnings and endings, and, in fact, life seems to hang between fall and winter since the "dull sun" can barely be seen "beyond the murk" (14). This continually experienced middle signifies post-apocalyptic space in *The Road*, which is never quite *after*, a point I will return to momentarily (Rambo 2008).[21] A landscape once bright with color now exudes varying shades of gray, growing darker with each passing day, so that midnight becomes indistinguishable from noon. The man has no idea of time, because he has not "kept a calendar for years" (4), and throughout the novel he continues to wonder what month it might be. Shelly Rambo (2008, 108), who briefly explores McCarthy's novel and trauma in her article "Beyond Redemption? Reading Cormac McCarthy's *The Road* after the End of the World," contends, "The quest McCarthy sends us on in *The Road* is one in which temporal markers of past, present and future no longer hold." As such, the odd time/space of the post-apocalyptic world does not permit the same relationship with memory; remembering the past fails to offer the same redeeming qualities for apocalypse survivors that it potentially contains for other trauma survivors.

The traumatized, post-apocalyptic space in *The Road* exhibits temporality in terms of duration, as opposed to a linear structure, suggesting Henri Bergson's theory of time. For Bergson, linear time requires thought, that is, pause, because it is nearly impossible to think analytically in the midst of duration. Speaking of numerical sequencing, an analogy Bergson often turns to throughout his first work, *Time and Freewill*, he explains, "It is certainly possible to perceive in time, and in time only, a succession which is nothing but a succession, but not an addition, i.e. a succession which culminates in a sum" (Bergson 2001, 78–79). Linear time—or measured time—allows individuals to consider a series of perceptions, so that they add up to a sum or conclusion, an analytical process for Bergson requiring evaluative thought. However, duration does not permit such thought. Bergson explains, "real duration is what we have always called time, but time perceived as indivisible" (80). In other words, duration exists as time without a consciousness beyond the immediate moment, without a bigger picture. Gilles Deleuze (1990, 37) further expounds upon Bergson's definition, writing, "It is a case of . . . a becoming, but it is a becoming that endures, a change that is substance itself." With regard to trauma, duration suggests the transitory period that occurs between first experiencing the event and eventually processing it into a narrative structure. The "change" Deleuze suggests manifests as a change in consciousness that "endures" long past the traumatic experience (the apocalyptic event in this instance) has ended.

Time, as understood through duration, cannot be completely grasped by the human mind; once individuals attempt to transform pure experience into thought or language in order to comprehend a larger picture, they no longer interact with time at the level of duration. Suzanne Guerlac (2009, 2), who has written extensively on Bergson's concept of time, explains how critical thought "presents an immobile world for us to master, projecting our thought through a grid of space, thrown out ... like a net to collect and organize the heterogeneous and dynamic real, so that we can better act upon it and take control of it." While Bergson in no way condemns the act of analyzing, he admits its unnaturalness in the face of pure duration, which connects the mind/body to consciousness in a way thinking and processing cannot. By pausing in time, an act that spatializes temporality, Bergson (1946, 149) argues, the individual moves away from pure duration, explaining, "it is in spatialized time that we ordinarily place ourselves. We have no interest in listening to the uninterrupted humming of life's depths. And yet, that is where real duration is." Thought—the intent to explain, analyze, and master that which cannot be made sense of—removes the individual from real duration into measured time. Post-apocalyptic space denies such thought, though, because the apocalyptic event has left the survivor in a space that does not guarantee them an *after*, so that characters must continually fight for survival. Duration, therefore, becomes the privileged mode of grasping consciousness in the post-apocalyptic world, because it is concerned with experience as it occurs, as opposed to measurement and analysis.

Kunsa (2009, 57) argues that *The Road* "gives us a vision of after: after the world has come to disaster, after any tangible social order has been destroyed by fire or hunger or despair." Yet, the *post* of *The Road*'s post-apocalyptic space through which the man and his son travel is never a space of *after* or at least not a full *after*, unlike other post-apocalyptic narratives. Instead, it is a traumatic space where the disaster persists, and survival has not yet been ensured thanks to the presence of cannibals, the lack of sustenance, and inhospitable natural conditions. As a result, the man never gains the distance necessary to begin processing both the larger traumatic event of the apocalypse, as well as the more personal traumatic events, such as his wife's suicide. His memories serve as distractions that shift his focus from protecting the boy, further frustrating the man's struggle. In terms of duration, the man cannot pause to attend to his thoughts about the events that have taken place, but must continue moving forward, existing in space bound up in movement *and* time required by existence on the road.

Yet the past does resurface for the man as a result of the trauma he has experienced. As a result of his movement through the post-apocalyptic space the man comes face-to-face with his past trauma, which includes both a sense of loss concerning the known world as well as a more personal loss pertaining to his dead wife and friends. Even though, as the novel opens, his losses are not new to him, it is only when he proceeds through the post-apocalyptic landscape that the man encounters nightmares and memories, momentarily returning him to the trauma surrounding the apocalypse. McCarthy describes the landscape as a "cauterized terrain," bespeaking the nature of a physical wound. As the man moves throughout the countryside, the land's "cauterized" nature affects him, often returning him to moments before the apocalypse. Awaking one morning, the man discovers a forest fire whose color freezes him in his tracks (31):

> He woke toward the morning with the fire down to coals and walked out to the road. Everything was alight. As if the lost sun were returning at last. The snow orange and quivering. A forest fire was making its way along the tinderbox ridges above them, flaring and shimmering against the overcast like the northern lights. Cold as it was he stood there a long time. The color of it moved something in him long forgotten. Make a list. Recite a litany. Remember.

In the pause he allows himself, his memory flares up and brings to light a moment from the past; the color, so vivid against the gray and black terrain he has become accustomed to since the apocalypse, arouses old emotions. The wounded land draws him away from his task and distracts him with memories that awaken a desire to "remember" and repeat, but such repetition only transmits the trauma and desecration ingrained in the past.

Instead of working through these memories and "repetitions," however, the man discards them—both physically and mentally—in order to concentrate on the business of surviving. Meaning making, be it through dreams or memory, cannot offer redemption from a past that has not yet passed. What the man remembers of his own life cannot help him, and he refuses to consciously engage with it because he recognizes the barrier it creates for the present. When his son asks him if he ever had any friends, he refuses to elaborate and provide details regarding his life before the apocalypse (59–60):

Yes. I did.
Lots of them?
Yes.
Do you remember them?
Yes. I remember them.
What happened to them?
They died.
All of them?
Yes. All of them.
Do you miss them?
Yes. I do.
Where are we going?
We're going south.

Just as it is not important for the reader or the boy to know what brought about the end of the world, so, too, do details surrounding the man's life before the end not matter because thinking requires a pause that the post-apocalyptic space cannot offer (54): "Sometimes the child would ask him questions about the world that for him was not even a memory. He thought hard how to answer. There is no past. What would you like? But he stopped making things up because those things were not true either and the telling made him feel bad." The past is not even situated as a memory in his mind, because the magnitude of the event he experienced has erased it from explicit memory. Therefore, rather than spend time and energy recalling his past, the man instead chooses to keep moving—to literally advance south away from his past.

Interestingly, the man also exhibits an awareness concerning the ways in which remembering enacts violence against the original experience: "He thought each memory recalled must do some violence to its origins. As in a party game. Say the word and pass it on. So be sparing. What you alter in the remembering has yet a reality, known or not" (131). Memory attempts meaning making by structuring the past where no structure originally existed, and imparts meaning in a way significant to the present, *not* the original experience. Memory changes with each recollection and is reconstructed with each remembering, and the man understands how sieving through events and memories fails to offer salvation from what has already transpired; no final meaning will ever be achieved from such an endeavor, and even were it possible it would contribute nothing to his present-day focus on survival. Rather than actively remember in order to forget, he finds it better to forget entirely, to sever himself, at times physically, from his history so that he can concentrate on surviving the present. Both he and the boy must slowly unlatch their memories from the things they carry in order to survive. These moments of shedding can be seen both metaphorically as well as literally throughout the novel. In one particular moment, the man examines the contents of his wallets, finding identification from before the end; he acknowledges its insignificance in the present moment by refusing to engage it for any kind of meaning (51):

> He'd carried his billfold about till it wore a cornershaped hole in his trousers. Then one day he sat by the roadside and took it out and went through the contents. Some money, credit cards. His driver's license. A picture of his wife. He spread everything out on the blacktop. . . . He pitched the sweatblackened piece of leather into the woods and sat holding the photograph. Then he laid it down in the road also and then he stood and they went on.

Within *The Road*, the man's personal memory predominantly stems from life before the apocalypse, and so must be discarded in order to concentrate on survival. This movement appears to be easy for the man, because the space of post-apocalypse requires focus on the present, but the reality of such a move poses great difficulty in actuality. The man recognizes that living in the past—parsing through memories in order to gain some sense of understanding or comfort—becomes a futile gesture in duration. Since past traumas return through memory, it cannot offer a redeeming connection to the past.

The film opens with a dream memory, and brings to light the nightmares, flashbacks, and vivid recollections often experienced by trauma survivors. While the novel initially locates the man in the post-apocalypse, the film wishes to situate the viewer in the *before*, and does so by presenting brief snippets of the world before the apocalypse. The audience sees vibrant colors in the green tree leaves, hanging yellow flowers, and bright pink blooms, which juxtapose the gloomy gray and dismal landscape the man wakes up to moments later. When it comes to the traumatized, dreams and implicit memory reveal the ways in which "the experience cannot be organized on a linguistic level," in turn leading to an "organiz[ation] on a somatosensory or iconic level: as somatic sensations, behavior reenactments, nightmares and flashbacks."[22] The man's brain takes over the work of what he daily ignores and will not face. Still, as with memory, dreams serve only to draw the man's focus away from his present situation. The man awakens from a particularly disturbing dream where his son has died, and he finds "what he could bear in the waking world he could not by night and he saw awake for fear the dream would return" (130).

In the film's opening scenes, the man lies beside a waterfall, dreaming of the apocalyptic event. In his dream, he is in bed with his wife when he is awakened by loud bangs and screaming. Even though the man peers outside and seems to quickly understand the severity of what is taking place, the audience never sees anything more than the couple's bedroom and their reactions to the events outside. The apocalypse is shrouded in mystery; all the viewer can see are glowing lights—presumably from fires—in the curtained windows. Once he discovers that they no longer have electricity, the man rushes to the bathroom, stoppers the tub, and begins running water, his instincts for survival already starting. Presumably the waterfall by which he sleeps has triggered the sound of running water, and so the man returns to the night of the apocalypse in his mind. In this way, pausing in the post-apocalyptic space, as he and the boy must do each night to sleep, affects his mind and risks overwhelming it with past visions.

The novel also first works with memory only to eventually move against it. The land's wound surfaces in the man's mind, but he can make no meaning from what has transpired. Instead, the man prefers nightmares to nice dreams about his past (18):

> He mistrusted all of that. He said the right dreams for a man in peril were dreams of peril and all else was the call of languor and of death. He slept little and he slept poorly. He dreams of walking in a flowering wood where birds flew before them and he and the child and the sky was arching blue but he was learning how to wake himself from just such siren worlds. Lying there in the dark with the uncanny taste of a peach from some phantom orchard fading in his mouth. He thought if he lived long

enough the world at last would all be lost. Like the dying world the newly
blind inhabit, all of it slowly fading from memory.

The post-apocalyptic space is one in which memories and dreams about
the past return, although they eventually slip away, "slowly fading from
memory," because the future cannot sustain a link to the past without
also assuming the past's destructive nature. As such, forgetting comes to
take precedence over working through past traumas.

Seeing and Destruction: Spectatorship and Appropriation

Besides impeding a position of *pause* that allows trauma survivors to
work through the past, and in turn offering a new relationship with
memory, the post-apocalyptic world in *The Road* raises questions about
spectatorship when it comes both to trauma and traumatic memory. The
man, who witnessed the apocalyptic event (his son was not yet born),
internalizes and in some ways appropriates the destruction inherent to
that moment by means of spectatorship. Whereas Caruth (1996) reads
sight as a form of erasure, which in turn leads to forgetting, I view it as
appropriation, which can readily become a crippling act in the post-
apocalypse world for both character and reader.[23] While it would seem
that working through traumatic memories helps individuals overcome
trauma, with regard to spectatorship, memory proves to be a problematic connection to an already unstable and destructive past. Memory
entraps the witness in the past, because as spectator, the individual is at
once complicit with destruction and hostage to it. The land itself even
rejects sight; McCarthy (2006, 3, my emphasis) describes the "nights
dark beyond darkness and the days more gray each one than what had
gone before. Like the onset of some cold *glaucoma* dimming away the
world." In the word "glaucoma," McCarthy figures the world as one
incapable of sight—toward the past, toward the present—as means to
recovery.

Sight and, more importantly, erasure become major themes throughout the novel, as the past continues to be whited out (127–28): "They
passed through towns that warned people away with messages scrawled
on billboards. The billboards had been whited out with thin coats of
paint in order to write on them and through the paint could be seen a

pale palimpsest of advertisements for goods which no longer existed." Looking too often to the past only enshrouds the man in a life that no longer exists and serves to distract him from his purpose. Therefore, he refuses to share details about the apocalypse with his son, for to pass on such a sight would surely damage the boy. Similarly, by not sharing specifics about the apocalypse in the space of the text, *The Road* denies the reader a chance to appropriate the violence associated with history. Denying the boy answers regarding the past may seem strange given the fact that the boy, as a survivor on the road, daily encounters the disaster through its remains, but it is the traumatic event that must be forgotten and not the aftereffects. The boy admits that he views things much differently from his father; he exudes a natural goodness toward survivors on the road that his father cannot because he has been turned by the violence of the past. The two encounter an old man named Ely on the road and share a meal with him. Upon parting with Ely, the boy wishes to leave him some food, recent provisions they discovered in an abandoned fallout shelter, but the man does not want to share. He tells the boy, "When we're out of food you'll have more time to think about it. The boy didn't answer. . . . He looked back up the road. After a while he said: I know. But I won't remember it the way you do" (174).

The man and boy's meeting with Ely goes differently in the film than in the novel, however, and the sense of erasure so important to McCarthy's post-apocalyptic space takes a different turn. Sight offers no definitive answers in the film, where visibility does not and cannot equal meaning making for either the characters or the audience. As the man and boy part with Ely, the boy asks his father to give him a portion of the cans of food they recently found. When the father refuses, the son, referring to their nomenclature of "good guys," questions the man's ability to intuit survivors' true nature. *The Road* posits sight as something beyond physical visibility—an act undertaken with the eyes—and more in keeping with an inner sight, a sensibility intrinsic to the new way of being in the world. The boy complains, "You always say watch out for bad guys. That old man wasn't even a bad guy. You can't even tell anymore."[24] Having witnessed the end of the world, the man has internalized the damage associated with that past, and he has trouble seeing people as anything other than "bad guys." The son, however, as representative of the future, understands that physical sight does not offer the answers it once did.

Rather, an inner sensibility, one that is not restricted by the eyes, comes to offer understanding in a way that physicality cannot.

The term "destructive spectatorship" first appears in Martin Harries's book *Forgetting Lot's Wife*, which examines how modern acts of self-destructive viewing mirror the biblical tale of Lot's wife, who turned into a pillar of salt upon looking back at the burning cities of Sodom and Gomorrah. The *destruction* implicit to the concept of *destructive spectatorship* emanates from the act of witnessing: the observer witnesses a catastrophic event, and is in turn physically undone by such witnessing. Unlike the immediate destruction of Lot's wife, however, destructive spectatorship for the modern viewer is not an instant annihilation. It is only later, through memory, I argue, that the event returns and disrupts the individual. In keeping with other traumatic experiences, modern-day destructive spectatorship occurs not at the moment of viewing, but rather *after* in the space of the mind. Caruth aptly summarizes when trauma manifests, writing, "trauma is not locatable in the simple violent or original event in an individual's past, but rather in the way that its very unassimilated nature—the way it was precisely not known in the first instance—returns to haunt the survivor later on" (Caruth 1996, 4). So, too, does the trauma associated with destructive spectatorship return to damage the individual through memory after the initial event.

Despite briefly turning to trauma studies before disregarding its use for the purpose of his work, Harries (2007, 21) does raise a compelling question: "What happens when retrospection begins to look like, and to feel like, masochism, a choice to damage the self? We tell ourselves we have the responsibility to remember and to look back; we think less often about what it means that such looking back may simply cause pain." Although Harries frames his question as a choice over which the individual seemingly has control, a problematic maneuver no doubt, he does make a valid point: when do traumatic, seemingly destructive, memories threaten to overwhelm the subject rather than help her recover? Memory is innately enveloped in the development of identity, so when trauma affects memory it naturally affects identity as well. Susan Brison (1999, 41), who studies trauma's lasting effect and has herself survived severe trauma, explains, "Trauma undoes the self by breaking the ongoing narrative, severing the connections among remembered past, lived present, and anticipated future." Individuals who have come through a traumatic event oftentimes feel alienated from their former life as a result of memory. Indeed, "Certain memories become obstacles that [keep] people from going on with their lives" (van der Kolk and van der Hart 1995, 158). Should the man transmit the destruction inherent to his memories to his son, the boy's identity—something that is still forming—stands to assume that very destruction. Remembering, therefore, can represent a destructive act, especially if the memories continually position the viewer as a spectator.

There is significant evidence that trauma damages an individual's memory systems. Russell Meares (2000, 49) notes, "Moderate trauma will eliminate autobiographical and episodic memories, leaving the semantic and other systems intact. Severe and/or chronic trauma leaves only the earliest, most primitive, preverbal memory systems functional." Neurobiology reveals physical evidence that trauma damages the brain, specifically those areas related to the more developed systems of memory. The hippocampus plays an integral part in the regulation of stress, and has also been connected to long-term, episodic memory. Severe trauma has been found to "impair the neuronal structure and function of the hippocampus" (Payne et al. 2008, 77). On a metaphorical level, psychologists have come to view trauma as "equivalent to a blow on the head, leaving a lacuna in the psychic system, an interruption in a personal existence" (Meares 2000, 49). Reconstructing trauma into the narrative of self becomes imperative in order for the individual to heal and move on, yet narrating that event after having undergone both physical and mental disruptions in the cognitive memory systems becomes increasingly difficult. As much as memory is imperative in developing and maintaining identity, there is something to be said about the benefits of forgetting; cognitive psychologists often warn of the dangers associated with relying too heavily on memory as a fact-based source. Richard Thompson and Stephen Madigan (2005, 24), who have studied memory, argue, "The problem is not so much being able to remember . . . traumas but instead being able to forget them."

Conclusion

In light of both the theoretical and practical nature of trauma studies this collection speaks to, how does forgetting work outside of a literary context? Forgetting is often considered a weakness when it comes to memory. Early on in his examination into the nature of forgetting, Paul Ricoeur (2004, 412) contends that "forgetting indeed remains the disturbing threat that lurks in the background of the phenomenology of memory and of the epistemology of history." To forget is to not only fail the self, but to fail the past in some way. With regard to trauma, forgetting becomes the ultimate failure since the act of recovery depends on recuperating memory and restructuring it into a temporal, linear narrative. Practitioners would argue that forgetting is incredibly detrimental to those who have undergone a traumatic event or experience. Indeed, trauma survivors may not be able to consciously remember their trauma, but they do not entirely forget it either. Can forgetting offer freedom from trauma that has not yet been fully explored in trauma studies? Such an act may work theoretically, but poses numerous problems with enacted, say, in the safe space of a social worker's office. Post-apocalypse narratives of the past thirty years unsettle the long-held belief that working through trauma by recuperating memory offers the best means to survival. As a form of trauma narratives, they work against memory by exhibiting the dangers inherent to holding on too tightly to a violent past. The problems they pose, however, must continue to be investigated in light of trauma studies, which can, at times, overlook what forgetting provides when it speaks of memory and trauma.

NOTES

1 By "collective history," I refer to an amalgamation of collective memory and narrative history that structures one's place in larger contexts such as community and nation.

2 Cathy Caruth explains in her introduction to the collection of essays *Trauma: Explorations in Memory* how "the historical power of trauma is not just that the experience is repeated after its forgetting, but that it is only in and through its inherent forgetting that it is first experienced at all" (1995, 8).

3 The link between memory and identity has been well established within cognitive psychology and neurobiology. Suzanne Nalbantian's (2011) collection of essays in particular offers fresh perspective regarding how memory functions and its purpose in life. Explicit memory or declarative memory refers to episodic or semantic memory, which can be actively recalled by the brain at will and also retains the consciousness of being a memory. Implicit memory, on the other hand, pertains to the unconscious nature of memory, that which "we do not know we know" (14). See also van der Kolk, McFarlane, and Weisaeth (1996).

4 I here speak of multiple memory systems, because neurobiology has revealed that memory exists not as one large system, but rather as a complex combination of systems, each focused on a different aspect of memory. Memory acts as a narrative along which individuals can place themselves and gain a sense of development over time. Trauma physically damages memory systems, a point I will return to later in this essay, which makes it far more difficult to control memory. For more information, see LeDoux (1996).

5 For other examples, see Johnson (1985), Atwood (2003), and Kunstler (2008). While not every text challenges memory to the same extent, each questions how useful memory is as a connection to a past that has been utterly devastated.

6 The authors explain how "psychodynamic psychiatry has always attached crucial importance to the capacity to reproduce memories in words and to integrate them in the totality of experience, i.e., to narrative memory" (167).

7 Caruth, writing on Freud's notion of the death drive, reads a seemingly endless cycle of violence emerging in survivors' future decisions, which continues to lead them toward similarly destructive situations as their initial trauma.

8 Blanchot does not structure his study as a typical analysis, but instead uses his form to mirror the subject matter and in this way gets at the heart of disaster. Rather than outline a clear argument, Blanchot literally examines the task of writing the disaster; bullet points take precedence over complete paragraphs, thereby reflecting the fragmented nature of disaster and the ways in which language cannot begin to convey it.

9 The novel and film do not suggest that forgetting is a simple task for survivors, but characters continue to choose it as a means to survival.

10 The man's wife and the boy's mother committed suicide sometime (the novel never reveals specifics like *when*) before the pair set out on the road, because she was unable to deal with the annihilation of any normative way of life.

11 While the mysterious apocalyptic event that exists on the novel's horizon does not initially eradicate humanity, the population quickly diminishes over time between the growing food scarcity and the appearance of cannibals who hunt the road for "provisions."

12 For more information on trauma literature, see Tal (1996), Whitehead (2004), and Vickroy (2002).

13 Dori Laub (1992) explores the difficulty of speaking about a traumatic experience. He explains how survivors are often afraid to begin the work of remembering traumatic experiences in case those events should happen again. He writes, "The fear that fate will strike again is crucial to the memory of trauma, and to the inability to talk about it" (67). While the man does not convey an inability to discuss the past, he does appear to recognize the dangers in putting the experience into language, and transmitting that language to his son, lest he also transmit the violence and destruction inherent to the event.

14 For a comprehensive history of the apocalypse, see Collins (2000).

15 Besides using apocalyptic language, the actual term "apocalypse" has been employed in print to signify both 9/11 and natural disasters. For example, the *London*

Daily Mail's headline following 9/11 read "APOCALYPSE!" and *Newsweek*'s cover for the March 21, 2011, issue states "Apocalypse Now," in reference to the recent string of natural disasters that affected Japan and the southern United States, the economic recession, and the unrest in the Middle East.

16 By a residual trauma, I here mean either the possibility of a primordial trauma that has ingrained itself in the human psyche, or the traces of trauma from an actual historical event that have been transmitted and transferred via collective memory.

17 This haunting, I argue, can readily be seen in the escalating use of apocalyptic rhetoric to describe varying degrees of tragedy. Jacques Derrida noted in 1984, "The worldwide organization of the human *socius* today hangs by the thread of nuclear rhetoric." See Derrida (1984, 20).

18 I here refer to cultural traumas that may not have been experienced firsthand, but were still felt in such a way that authors, artists, musicians, etc. needed to make sense of the event by generating a creative project that structures both the historical event as well as the residual trauma.

19 Historical events that register in the traumatic vein, such as the Holocaust, Hurricane Katrina, etc., have often been considered apocalyptic in nature. By "shock" I here mean the traumatic experience apocalypse survivors undergo. The shock associated with these real-life occurrences can have long-lasting effects on survivors, as well as those outside the affected community.

20 See Morrison (1987), O'Brien (1995), and Michaels (1996).

21 Rambo explains how "the experience of *living on* in the aftermath of trauma as in *The Road*, is often described as a tenuous middle, in which both what is behind and what is ahead are unsettled and threatening and unknown" (2008, 109).

22 Van der Kolk and van der Hart (1995, 172).

23 See especially Caruth's second chapter, "Literature and the Enactment of Memory."

24 *The Road*, directed by John Hillcoat, 111 minutes (Dimension Films, 2009, DVD).

10

Body Animations (or, Lullaby for Fallujah)

A Performance

JACKIE ORR

Editors' note: At the conference on which this chapter is based, the author performed the work via a montage of spoken words, recorded sound, and images. *Lullaby for Fallujah* was stunning, and while the written text may not fully recapture the lived experience of "being there," it does something else: it brings text and images directly to the reader in the "privacy" of her own reading/viewing space. How do we think about the circulation, across different media and contexts, of trauma and its representations?

Preface

What can live performance become when reinscribed for the page? How does a writing voice (without breath) generate the embodied animations, and invite the intimate architextures, of the timespace of performance? Torn from the "real time" of its never fully real staging, performance struggles to reenact on the page its peculiar obsession: to inhabit the magical, archaic economies of possession and dispossession. Hands empty. Hands full. Empty. Repeat. If trauma often vibrates at the collective edge of live performance, then where does trauma dwell when the performative text is held in your hands, alone? How does trauma's body transform when there is no body exactly performing its animate transmissions?

1. Exhibiting Corpses

"Fiat ars—pereat mundus" [Let there be art, and may it conquer the world] says Fascism, and . . . expects war to supply the artistic gratification of a sense perception that has been changed by technology.
—Walter Benjamin (1968, 242)

Figure 10.1

"Bodies: The Exhibition" reads the large black-and-white sign at the entrance leading up to the second-story exhibition hall. On the first floor of the building, in a display window running the length of the store, are six bright white mannequins lined in a row, each one headless, with brief arms ending just above the elbow. "Bodies: The Exhibition," a semipermanent museum display housed above a Gap store in a Manhattan shopping mall, enters the crowded field of commodity visions with the promise of a new aesthetic: "corpse art" as some critics call it; or "anatomical art works" in the words of Gunther von Hagens. Von Hagens is the German anatomist, entrepreneur, performance artist, and hemophiliac who launches "corpse art" in 1995 with his traveling Body Worlds exhibits, displays of plastinated human body parts and whole-body specimens that splice together family entertainment and a popularized anatomical gaze into a hybrid commercial theater of the perpetually animate dead. The plastination process, which von Hagens develops and patents in the late 1970s, produces "anatomical art works" out of human corpses that are frozen, flayed, dissected, cured, and chemically saturated with polymers (or plastic compounds) in place of the body's own water and blood.[1] The "plastinates" are then sculpted into a range of life-like poses such as playing chess or riding a flayed, vaulting horse. To date, over thirty-seven million people worldwide have visited the Body Worlds exhibits; hundreds of those viewers have agreed, upon their deaths, to become "body donors" in future exhibitions.

The invention of the corpse, writes Robert Romanyshyn (1989), is the historical and epistemological correlate of the invention of linear perspective in early modern Europe. An aesthetic technology founded on newly mathematicized grids of perception, where the simulation of depth on a two-dimensional surface creates a three-dimensional visual experience, linear perspective also marks the contours of a new experience of embodiment: that of an individualized spectator, separate from while observing the world through an increasingly abstract, geometric perception of space. It is this body of linear perspective, grounding an everyday modern aesthetics of "realism," that also provides the first glimpse, hallucinatory and real, of the corpse. The sixteenth-century anatomical gaze that produces as well as maps the new corpse and its "anonymous muscles," abandons a ritual symbolics of the dead body for a cultural reformatting of the body-as-specimen.[2] As a technology for seeing, for knowing, for cutting into and cutting up bodies, linear perspective helps perform the psychic and social enclosures necessary for biopolitical practices of autopsy and death statistics on which the modern state builds its expansive forms of governance.[3]

Figure 10.2

More elusively, the historically specific perceptual fonts of linear perspective help create the sanctioned delirium of an individualized subject, captivated by an ever-receding horizon point that paints the fiction of singular perception even as it constructs a new aesthetic form for "realist" representation. Death, for such a subject, is simultaneously interiorized and dispersed into a despatialized void of abstract equivalences. The new psychogeography of individualized consciousness displaces an older, proliferate social imaginary of death and finitude.

Perhaps the "corporeal turn in the museum" today, where "historical memory as a consumer product is increasingly centered on violence and the body,"[4] marks a popular return of the repressed, a refusal of the accumulated abstractions of the artifactual body and its deferral of death, its perspectival corpse always already an art form. Perhaps the new "body museum"—where I swear, I smelled meat as I entered the lobby of Bodies: The Exhibition—perhaps the body museum rematerializes the insistent empiricity of embodiment against an Enlightenment deanimation of living being.

Figure 10.3

But in today's Body Worlds something far more hyperreal than the repressed returned seems to be enacted. Something more on the order of another twist in the mis en abyme of abstractions, another swerve in the nonrandom precession of simulacra. As one observer of Body Worlds notes, "These plastinated bodies are both corpses and illustrations, representations and maps . . . [they] resemble the effect . . . [of] the digital imaging techniques in the Visible Human Project . . . a virtual, three-dimensional anatomical atlas of entire human bodies where visualization grinds the flesh into nothingness."[5] Composed of 70 percent plastics, 30 percent dead matter, the sculpted bodies in von Hagens's worlds often themselves simulate the figures rendered in sixteenth-century anatomical paintings, or the visual conventions of twenty-first-century medical imaging techniques like MRI: several of the specimens are cut into dozens of thin slices and arranged in empty space for close viewing from all angles.

Figure 10.4

Archive without memory, death outside time, perhaps the body-as-museum today memorializes the serial acts of forgetting, the sustained emergency of affective triage, that compose a contemporary militarized zone of psychic and political violence. And its simulation. What new forms of embodiment today walk through the exhibition halls of the relentlessly unburied dead? What nonlinear perspectives are emerging at the digital crossroads of technohuman perceptions and binary plasticities? Zoom out. Zoom in. And how, really, to continue talking with the dead when they're now chattering through so many distributed networks?

2. Killing the Dead

It is not the object of the story to convey a happening *per se*,
which is the purpose of information; rather, it embeds it in
the life of the storyteller in order to pass it on as experience
to those listening.
—Walter Benjamin (1968, 159)

Daddy died while watching TV. You'd think we would have thought to turn it off (the scented candles, the clouded mirror) but it's funny the things you forget as the clock ticks down on the inning. As the storm moves in. As effects superseded all cause, we were caught in the cancer ward with the tellie on and that ticker tape of breaking stories crawling fast along the bottom of the screen. All those broken stories streaming across the screen.

The dreams started a few months later. Always the same story, with a touch of difference—Daddy wandering into the scene, through what opening I could never exactly see. "But Daddy," I'd say, "what are you doing here? You're dead, Daddy. You're dead." It's funny the things you forget "as grief stuck, stuck on the trauma, on the scratch in the war record, where one starts over, over and over again."[6] The last time I saw Daddy in my dreams was March 23, 2001. That night, after I told him he was dead, Daddy laid down under the table, next to a wood-paneled wall. Kneeling down, but never touching him, I watched as he turned to bone and disappeared into the wall. It was the sound of chanting that woke me up. Though I could never exactly hear through what crack it was coming.

> *People often ask . . . what prompts someone to donate their body for Plastination. We would therefore like to know your own personal motivation (please check all that apply):*
>
> *a) As there is no need for a burial service, my relatives will not have to worry about tending my grave.*
>
> (Body Donor's Consent Form)[7]

On March 25, 2001, I stopped sleeping (the electric sunrise, the relentless alarm). The doctor said this was normal. The psychiatrist said .5 milligrams of Klonopin. The television said the stock market was on the rise and archeologists discovered a three-million-year-old fossil linked to our human ancestors. The massage therapist said grief is stored in your pelvis if you want we can spend a whole session just working on that.

> *b) I have no relatives to tend my grave once I'm gone*

In July 2001 I took the train to Chicago and drove the rental car to northern Wisconsin and found Daddy's remains in the corner of the living room in a see-through plastic bag that Mama had driven up from Florida in the trunk of her car so we could all gather at the summer cabin to bury Daddy under the birch tree. In the photograph, my brother is holding the shovel and my nephews are smiling brightly. Then there's a thin, middle-aged woman, looking stricken. I remember we put the plastic bag of ashes and bone in a brown plastic chest that Mama bought from the neighborhood vet for the remains of large dogs. She thought it would be cheaper than the urns from the funeral home.

> *c) I wish to save on the costs of a funeral*
> *d) I am fascinated by the thought of being preserved*
>   *forever* (Body Donor's Consent Form)

3. Necromancy

His eyes are staring, his mouth is open, his wings are
spread. . . . But a storm is blowing. . . . It has got caught in
his wings with such violence that [he] . . . can no longer close
them. . . . The thoughts which we are developing here origi-
nate from similar considerations.
—Walter Benjamin (1968, 257–58)

Little girl: Sing me a lullaby . . . sing me "Lullaby and Good
Night."
Daddy: I don't know that one.
Little girl: Sing me "Hush-A-Bye Mountain"?
Daddy: I don't know that one either.
—*War of the Worlds* (Spielberg 2005)

Figure 10.5

"At 0330 on the chilly and damp morning of 10 November 2004, I sat
in the troop commander's hatch of my assault amphibious vehicle in an
assembly area just north of Fallujah. In 30 minutes our company would
push over a mile into the heart of the city."[8] *Through the night vision
goggles the desert dust shimmered an eerie green in the moonlight. Behind
me, our line of advancing vehicles stretched for 15 to 20 miles. In front,*

Fallujah was already on fire, under sustained aerial attack, flaming green in the night vision we gained in exchange for giving up an accurate perception of depth. A loss to which we are learning to adapt.[9]

"Suddenly I had a sinking feeling in my stomach. Had we trained the right way? Historically, urban assaults have proven bloody and oftentimes disastrous. It suddenly seemed preposterous to think that we had cracked the code on urban warfare and that we would not pay the same price as our predecessors." *We had assembled 15,000 Marines and soldiers for the attack, tank battalions, aircraft gunships, unmanned drones, Navy carriers, bulldozers. We were ready to conduct a flexible fight on a fluid, nonlinear battlefield. But could we prevail in the end?*

Apache. Basher. Black Watch. Cobra. Dragon Eye. Gun Smoke. Hornet. Lava Dogs. Predator. Raven. Scan Eagle. SuperCobra. War Hammer. Wolfpack.

"It would only be after a month of hard fighting in Fallujah that I . . . began to look for historical parallels for the type of fighting we experienced. Where did men first see engagements at extremely close quarters, in a confined battlespace, where they had to reduce numerous strongpoints? One can see that many of the same tactical challenges posed in urban warfare [in Fallujah] were faced for the first time in the stagnant trench fighting during World War One." *Fallujah was a densely packed desert city, with 50,000 buildings crowded into five square kilometers. We digitally mapped and numbered thousands of those buildings based on months of drone surveillance. Every pilot, every tank commander, every ground warrior was equipped with the same map, the same informatic imagery to coordinate our assault as it unfolded in real time. But we couldn't see inside each building during the course of battle; we couldn't know which interior space would become our trench warfare. We can't foresee all the encounters with intimate combat that await us.*

"The Germans found a solution to [their] tactical problems with the introduction of their stosstruppen (storm troop) units . . . the assault troops whose mission was to overcome the enemy through speed, surprise, and overwhelming firepower.

". . . The storm troopers' use of light artillery was particularly innovative . . . especially the storm troops' use of the flamethrower. The flamethrower was a useful weapon for clearing structures . . . [but it] was also a psychologically devastating weapon. . . . 'A man who thinks nothing of a shell or a bullet may not like the prospect of being . . . roasted by fire.'

Figure 10.6

". . . A flame weapon at the platoon level in the Marine Corps would enhance our urban capabilities." *The enemy's knowledge of the interior terrain was a match even for our most advanced intelligence technologies.* "The insurgents we fought in Fallujah were fanatical and willing to die in most cases. However, it takes a higher level of commitment to burn to death at the hands of a flamethrower as opposed to dying nearly instantaneously when the building you are in collapses. Although some may argue that the use of flame weapons is excessively brutal, we must remember the extremely violent nature of urban warfare." *The enemy knows this violent reality; the enemy knows* "that *even the dead* will not be safe . . . if he wins."[10] "Marines who fight in this environment should be given the tools to win."

"One month after the battle for Fallujah began, our company pulled out of the city. I sat in the troop commander's hatch looking out over the destruction the battle had left behind. . . . In the parts of the city where the fighting had been the most intense, the devastation was total. Bulldozers and tanks had turned entire square kilometers into rubble." *Almost all of Fallujah's 50,000 structures were damaged in the offensive; 70 percent of all buildings were completely annihilated or rendered uninhabitable.* "We came to the city to destroy every insurgent, and in so doing destroyed most of the city." *"Remember Fallujah!" had been a battle cry of insurgents throughout Iraq. But after Operation Phantom Fury it became the rallying cry of the US Marines.*

Memory is and remains our battlespace. The defeated not only struggle to remember what has been lost, but to remind the future that a battle once took place.

Remember Fallujah.

"The veterans of Stalingrad [or] Hue [City] would have felt at home [in Fallujah]. In addition, they would have found their tactics little changed. The great tactical innovators of the past cannot be forgotten." *"Every image . . . that is not in some way recognized by the present as one of its own concerns threatens to disappear entirely."*[11] "In the future I will pay greater respect to the tactical innovators of the past."

  —From "Relearning Storm Troop Tactics: The Battle for Fallujah," *Marine Corps Gazette* (September 2006)

Figure 10.7

Little girl (singing softly):

"A gentle breeze on hush-a-bye
  mountain
Softly blows o'er lullaby bay
It fills the sails of boats that are waiting
Waiting to sail your worries away
So close your eyes on hush-a-bye
  mountain
Wave good-bye to cares of the day
And watch your boat from hush-a-bye
  mountain
Sail far away
from lullaby bay"
—"Hush-A-Bye Mountain" lyrics, *War
  of the Worlds* soundtrack (Spiel-
  berg 2005)

4. In Memoriam to Remembrance

We are invited into a space in which we are not one, cannot be, and yet we are not without the capacity to see. We see here, as a child . . . perhaps . . . whose body is given as the remnants of another's trauma and desires. What is it we seek to recognize here? . . . It is to suggest that trauma stages

its encounters, has its own illuminations . . . [when] trauma
finds its rare encounter with appearance itself.
   The dead did not obey the prohibition on life upon them,
and they return, partial, scattered, and animated.
—Judith Butler (2004: 99–100, 98)

> We are the ones left standing
>   after the roadside bombs
>   after the latest pandemic
>   after the swelling rains raise the water toward apocalypse
>   after the burning rigs at sea, after the shattered ice shelf
>   heaving
>   after the white skullbones bloom in the spring desert
>   after the 4 a.m. drone attack
>   after the latest siege in
>   the latest city
>
> We are the ones left and with a limited quota of life boats
>   without compass or solace except perhaps the strict injunction to
>   never look too hard at the horizon for imminent signs of the
>   shore.
>
> (*And everything shivered, and everything shook, and just because I
>   left you by the roadside burning never meant I don't still wear your
>   ring.*)
>
> Down in the valley
> Valley so low
> Hang your head over
> Hear the wind blow
>
> Watch the child dreaming
>   Wrapped in dark sleep
>   Flames in the doorway—
>   (Be fearless, my sweet)

Hear the wind blow, love
Hear the wind blow
Hang your head   over
    Hear   the wind   blow

Postscriptings

"Half the art of storytelling [is] to keep a story free from explanation," Walter Benjamin once wrote.[12] So what I want to offer here in this brief afterword is not at all an explanation. And what you have just read may not really be a story. In 1936, Walter Benjamin wrote that the storyteller had vanished, disappeared by the rise of industrial time and fractured memory, and by the withering of experience through the constant, daily, senseless mediations of information.

But perhaps Benjamin is wrong. Perhaps the story as craft and the storyteller as figure disappear only to reappear in different forms and formats. Forms not entirely human. For Benjamin, the fate of the story is tied tightly in modern capitalist cultures to the fate of death. "Death is the sanction of everything that the storyteller can tell," he writes. The authority of the dying, lying on a deathbed of unforgettable images, is the very figure and force of the authority "at the very source of the story."[13] In a modernizing society where death, too, is dissolving or disappearing, "pushed further and further out of the perceptual world of the living," Benjamin senses that the authoritative, animating source of the story is fading away.[14]

But perhaps death is not disappearing from perception today. Perhaps, today, death is being disassembled and reassembled in different, still insistently storied forms.

Figure 10.8

What I want to offer here is a brief meditation, however fractured, on trauma as it connects to my performance work, and my methods for making it. Let me begin, again, with a story about storytelling told by the novelist Maxine Hong Kingston. The story goes something like this:

Once upon a time there's a kingdom in ancient China, ruled by a very cruel king. The king hires women workers from the kingdom to be knot makers, and the women knot makers learn how to make amazingly intricate knots. The knots they learn to tie are so intimately entangled that eventually the women knot makers go blind from the making of the knots.[15] And that story from Maxine Hong Kingston is like a dreamscene of how it feels to work, of how I sometimes feel as I write. It's like a dreamscene where I am the woman knot maker, and I am the cruel king, and I am the knot being made. And by the time the knot is tied, I can't see it. Because the making of it has made me blind. So there's nothing I really can tell you about this lullaby for Fallujah except that by the time it is made I can't clearly perceive it anymore and that—I think—is partly a story about trauma.

I want to write about three questions or preoccupations that run through my work when I think about it in relation to the language of trauma. First, is the question of the real. What comes to count as the real within particular cultural and disciplinary formations? And how does what we call "trauma" compel us toward a different accounting of what's real, a different kind of reckoning with the demands of "realism" as a genre of social knowledge?

You could say that, historically, the "real" has been the currency in which the social sciences exchange disciplined knowledge for disciplinary power; the real is what the social sciences promise to deliver up in one empirical form or another to our interlocutors and ongoing patrons, including the State and the philanthropic agencies of Capital. "Realism" is the representational style or epistemological aesthetic of the empirically driven social sciences. The reality of "social structure"—that theoretical fiction at the heart of the sociological imagination—is repeatedly secured through the aggregate data of statistical patterns or the qualitative analysis of ethnographically observed individual or collective experiences. The signs of trauma can be re-presented through this realist empirical aesthetic, capturing sometimes significant features of the social structuring of traumatic vulnerabilities and uneven insecurities: the racialized, class-stratified, gendered, or sexualized precarities structured historically in relation to power, disease, immiseration, violence.

But the temporalities and the elusive materialities of trauma also present a haunting excess to what can count, and be counted, within a realist social scientific empiricism. Avery Gordon's *Ghostly Matters: Haunting and the Sociological Imagination* (1997) is an eloquent, fiercely intelligent analysis of the need for constructing an "other" kind of realism, a different practice of materialism that gives notice to "the hinges that open and close what is apparent and what is disappeared; what can be seen and what is in the shadows; what can be said and what is whispering inaudibly; what is true and what is a lie, what is rational and what is magical; what is real and what is surreal."[16] The hauntings that are central to any adequate representation of the real or, Gordon argues, to any adequate knowledge that might really move us toward social transformation, touch closely on the social body of trauma. The historical material force of lived experiences of violence or trauma is what makes haunting really present as a dis-ease or a demand to be reckoned with. It's what makes the ghosts really dance.

Yet as the social sciences struggle to reckon with an "other" genre of realism, one not guaranteed by a data-driven empirical aesthetic, something seems to be happening to the reality of data itself, as everyday life goes informatic. Digital mediations, the design and transmission of digital images and information, are rapidly restructuring perception and politics, memory and bodies, the circulation of capital and the production of war and counter/terrors. Simulation, Patricia Clough teaches us, has become the new realism of digital media.[17] The digital image does not re-present so much as in-form, as reality is increasingly rendered via informatic codes and digitized, electronic networks of information circulation and exchange. Here, in the contemporary implosions of information technologies, simulation, and the social production of the real, I begin to play seriously with "PSYCHOpolitics." PSYCHOpolitics tries to suggestively evoke the screenings of reality via powerful electronic circuits of images and information in a postindustrial, perhaps post-fascist, society of the spectacle and the speculative.[18] And while PSYCHOpolitics is a crazy concept for trying to notice how the real and the unreal, the digital and the traumatic, fact and phantasm are strategically recomposed via new technologies of perception, it also names the deadly serious perceptual space I try to conjure in my performance work and writing. Performing social science fictions is a PSYCHOpolitical strategy, deploying digital image and sound to design an experience of the "real" that might account for what is systematically discounted by an aesthetics of empirical realism.

A second question running through my work asks how we might engage trauma as method. How is trauma incorporated in the production of social and historical knowledges? Here, I'm not thinking about trauma as a symptomatic rupture that needs to be healed or a psychic content that needs to be recovered or resolved. Instead, trauma appears here as a form of transmission that pursues its own—repetitious—performance. As an impossible language with which to, failingly, try to speak. As a breach in the public defenses blown open in the elusive name of a sociality whose powers of communication, of contagious contact, remain secret even to itself. Trauma, here, becomes a kind of tactic, never precisely chosen, but a tactic that situates me as one node in a mobile network of underground broadcast, of pirate radio, through which trauma seeks over and over again to signal its presence by amplifying all of the volatile, vital signs of its failed erasure.

In her essay "The Trauma of Dada Montage," Brigid Doherty situates the anti-art practices of early twentieth-century Dada, particularly its techniques of photomontage, and aural and visual collage, in the context of shell shock and an emergent post–World War I sensibility that things have been blown apart.[19] Bodies, borders, landscapes, habits of perception, ideologies of progress—all exploded in the psychic and material trenches of newly mechanized warfare. For viewers of Dada's photomontages, the "traumatic experience is . . . already embodied in the composite image of a figure whose parts do not match."[20] Collage artists have pursued a contemporary politics of form that leans on joining parts that do not match, making cuts into saturated image landscapes that mimic the aggressive disarticulations of meaning and dismemberments of sense that became an everyday feature of televisual and informatic cultures.[21] Much of my own commitment, as a performance sociologist, to collage techniques emerged out of my encounter with the history of Dada and my desire to experiment with aesthetically, analytically juxtaposing thoughts and images as an explicit refusal of the epistemological, professional demands for a seamless, styleless style of social science writing.[22]

But with the proliferation of digital media and the dis-re-assembly of image-information downloaded into everyday perceptions, the force of collage and its juxtapositions atrophies into routinized, preformatted perceptual experiences. I stopped knowing how to engage visual media once the "cut" that gives collage its affective energy, its force as a cut 'n paste punk politics, became normalized in everyday digital cultures. So I started working exclusively with sound and text, without visuals, for several years. *(Lullaby for Fallujah)* is the first time I returned to working with visual surfaces again. The plasticity of digital, binary images makes it much harder to create visual effects that affect, that surprise or shock. It's much harder to decompose visual surfaces that are already in so much motion, that don't hold still, that are always already open to manipulation and fragmentation. It's confusing to work across juxtaposing scales when "zooming in" and "zooming out" become algorithmically accessible visual options, and not the jagged materiality of collage storytelling. It's a different kind of challenge to find the cutting edges of perception when the cut is incorporated in advance into digital design practices and perceptual experience.[23]

(Lullaby for Fallujah) became, then, an uncertain attempt to find a politics of form that can perform the relations between the digital and the traumatic as an (anti)aesthetic political practice. And this piece that you hold in your hands is an experiment in how to translate that multidimensional space of digital performance into the pages of a book—that beleaguered media format itself in so much motion today as it becomes modulated through multiply-scaled interfaces with other media platforms and digital practices.

If the aestheticization of destruction was, for Benjamin in 1930s Germany, a sign of the fascistic mobilization of war as an art form, then what to make of the emergence today of complexly distributed, digitally circulated, visibilities and invisibilities of war's casualties? How to think about a politics of aesthetic form today, when wars are given names like TV miniseries or video games, and when the so-called "enemy" is also using digital forms of aestheticized communication to mobilize memories and counter/violence?[24] Are there algorithms of redistributed perception that can render sensible the particular sensations—some of them aestheticized, some of them not—of participating as a spectacularized player in the digital gaming of war? How might trauma perform its methods today when shell shock is a faded psychiatric artifact, and posttraumatic stress disorder in US military personnel is treated via digital simulations produced by a military-entertainment-academic complex targeting both the psychic wounds of soldiers and the expanding consumer market for violently realist digital war games?[25]

In thinking today how trauma can be engaged tactically, I turn to Grace M. Cho's stunning book, *Haunting the Korean Diaspora: Shame, Secrecy, and the Forgotten War* (2008). Cho deploys trauma as an explicit methodo-logic for performing "diasporic vision"—part unconscious thought, part "seeing feeling," part sustained hallucination—that enables her sustained rememory of "The Forgotten War."[26] Working to invent the contours of a traumatized scholarly text, Cho describes how, still today, Koreans reportedly witness *bon hul*, ghost flames, rising from the earth at the site of a massacre conducted a half century earlier during the Korean-American war. "This book is a study of what cannot be known with certainty," she writes as she moves through the spectral fields of social research elaborated out of the embodied secrets of Korean diaspora and a traumatized transmission of displacement and desire.[27] *Bon hul*. Ghost flames, burning through the text. A desire that a "violently repressed history of violence"[28] can still burn like the bone-ash of undead bodies, giving off a ghostly light. A desire for other methods that perform trauma as one tactic for transforming it. A desire for an other form of scholarship that transgresses the tremulous scholarly boundaries built between reason and dream, the empirical and the elegiac. Between trauma and the transmission of longing.

A third question that troubles and shapes my work is how trauma, today, is not only a site of radical suffering or psychic shattering, but also a site of production. Trauma produces value through proliferating public and private discourses and therapeutic forms of expertise. And trauma produces violence as the state bears compulsive and unreliable witness to its own traumatic injury as the rationale for sanctioned violence against its terrorizing "others." In a post–September 11 United States, the necessary question becomes how trauma circulates simultaneously as a symptomatic marker of violence committed, and as a form of political reason—what Michel Foucault called "governmentality"—that mobilizes the exercise of systematic, state-sponsored violence. We might call this "traumatic governmentality," or the capacity to govern, through trauma, both individual bodies and entire populations.

My thoughts here are indebted in part to Maurice Steven's work, including his essay in this volume which thinks carefully about *what trauma makes possible*. In constituting the "traumatized" subject as a subject of harm and of treatment, trauma discourse generates at the same time a "recuperative fantasy" of the nontraumatized subject, an isolated, integrated self that appears secure despite the everyday precarity and insufficiency of the social world in which it moves. This recuperative fantasy of a "whole" citizen-subject works then as a kind of alibi for everything the social fails to give, repeatedly, in the face of our needs and our own yearning:

> The proliferation of affect and informational economies, the society of control and surveillance . . . and the precariousness of existence inherent to this stage of globalization, almost necessitate a very powerful recuperative fantasy. What better time for the ascendancy of a way of knowing injury that presents individual, whole, coherent bodies as its object of analysis; discrete and spectacular injuries that can be identified and healed, while at the same time providing technologies for managing large pools of affect and the populations understood to be defined by them.[29]

The production of traumatized populations helps to mobilize the state's own capacity to act, to effect action by channeling affective flows of insecurity, or fear, or grief. Such flows then congeal into state-sponsored memory management and cultural productions that feed back into the building of particular forms of community, of race, of national identification, of sanctioned violence. Craig Willse and Greg Goldberg extend this insight to the biopolitics of war, where biopolitical regulation "does not require a reduction of traumatic interference; the management of trauma is itself an end for biopolitics."[30] The trauma of the wars in Iraq and Afghanistan for US soldier populations produces unexpected opportunities for governance, such as "the financialization of health, illness, and injury," and new rehabilitative techniques that "modify and extend governmental management and administration of mutations of life."[31]

If the management of trauma becomes a productive goal for a bio-politics of war, my performance work tries to make palpable a PSYCHO-politics of war that productively manages trauma through the sustained con/fusions of entertainment and militarization, pleasure and violence, deadly aesthetics and vital corpses. The impossibility of making a lullaby for Fallujah—an impossibility this performance text spins on as it tries to conjure a public memory of what it feels like to live in a culture that buries only some of the dead, a culture that doubly kills the many dead whom it never intends to mourn—is built around the public secret that "we" are part of the systematic, sanctioned production of militarized trauma as a PSYCHOpolitical response to the attacks of September 2001. Trauma is mobilized and memorialized in the United States in order to produce unremembered, traumatic massacres in places like Fallujah. That the US attacks on Fallujah in April and November 2004 were mobi-lized, in part, by digitally circulated images of the charred, dismembered corpses of two US mercenaries (employees of Blackwater) hanging from a Fallujah bridge is part of a the psychotic imagescape that saturates my own relationship to a remembrance of Fallujah.[32]

With all this in mind, then, let me end with the reminder that trauma may also produce unexpected openings, the effects of which will also circulate. The queer and unlikely intimacies of a gathering of scholars, artists, lawyers, activists, psychologists, social workers, yoga instructors, and teachers under the banner of critical trauma studies at Arizona State University, may intensify the collective, embodied possibilities for liv-ing elsewhere, and otherwise, than in the traumatized stories we also choose to tell. As for how this text-based version of a performance of trauma might open toward other forms of knowing and remembrance, that story rests, gently and urgently, in your hands.

Images

All images in the text were designed and produced in collaboration with digital artist Dovar Chen. Thanks to Jacob Frank for research assistance with wartime images of Fallujah, Iraq.

Figures 10.1–4. Pixelated series of human corpse in Fallujah, reportedly killed by white phosphorous bombs used by the US military during the siege of November 2004.

Image sourced from the documentary *Fallujah—The Hidden Massacre*, broadcast on Italy's state TV network in November 2005. Available for viewing at http://www.infor-mationclearinghouse.info/article10907.htm.

Figure 10.5. Re-assemblage1, *War of the Worlds* 3.0 (Dovar Chen, 2012).

Figure 10.6. Re-assemblage2, *War of the Worlds* 3.0 (Dovar Chen, 2012).

Figure 10.7. Re-assemblage3, *War of the Worlds* 3.0 (Dovar Chen, 2012).

Figure 10.8. *Works of Body Art in the Age of Digital Reproduction* (Dovar Chen, 2012).

NOTES

1 See von Hagens (2006); see also Hirschauer (2006).

2 Romanyshyn (1989, 114).

3 Romanyshyn's genealogy of the corpse can be read alongside Michel Foucault's *Birth of the Clinic* and Foucault's lyrical history of the emergence of the clinical gaze through the "opening up a few corpses." Human anatomical insides become system-atically visible at the same moment that the contours of an individualized subject— patient or doctor—become the epistemological space of seeing and knowing.

4 Linke (2005, 13).

5 Kuppers (2004, 128).

6 Rickels (2002, 42).

7 All phrases in italics in this section are quotations from the donor questionnaire in the Body Donor's Consent Form, aimed at body donors to von Hagens's Institute for Plastination. See the Body Worlds website at http://www.koerperspende.de/en/down-loads.html.

8 All nonitalicized texts in this section are quotes from Ackerman (2006).

9 All text in italics was written by the author, except where otherwise cited, based on reports of the battle of Fallujah, November 2004. Sources used include Camp (2009), Grant (2005), Sattler (2005), Peterson (2005), Anderson (2004, 52).

10 Benjamin (1968, 255).

11 Ibid.

12 Benjamin (1968, 89).

13 Ibid., 94.

14 Ibid.

15 Kingston (1989).

16 Gordon (1997, 69).

17 Clough (2009).

18 See Orr (2006, 11–17).

19 Doherty (1997).

20 Ibid., 84. See also Biro (2009). Biro traces the cyborg's disassembled/reassem-bled architectures back to Dada's collage body-in-pieces.

21 For a nuanced history and analysis of collage-making practices and contempo-rary cultures of consumption, see Banash (2013).

22 See Pfohl (1992).

23 And so in the live version of the piece, the "cuts" I try to compose are not so much via the juxtaposition of texts as via a jagged composition, or layering, of digital image, digital sound, and text. In part 1 the text describes the Body Worlds exhibit while digital images zoom in and zoom out on corpses and battle scenes in Fallujah, Iraq. In part 3 the digital images are disassembled images and sound (including a lullaby scene) from Steven Spielberg's *War of the Worlds* (2005) while the text describes the US siege of Fallujah in 2004.

24 The live performance of *Body Animations (or, Lullaby for Fallujah)* remixes a digitally decomposed copy of a video produced by "Thunderbolts of Al-Fallujah," downloaded February 10, 2008, from archive.org. The video is one of dozens produced and circulated by Iraqi insurgents during the US occupation, showing attacks on US forces and the Iraqi police, accompanied by a musical soundtrack.

25 See Dyer-Witheford and de Peuter (2009, 97–122).

26 Cho (2008, 162–67).

27 Ibid., 17.

28 Ibid., 90.

29 Stevens (2010).

30 Willse and Goldberg (2008, 281).

31 Ibid.

32 See Scahill (2007, 155–79).

III

Praxis

11

First Responders

A Pedagogy for Writing and Reading Trauma

AMY HODGES HAMILTON

What ultimately matters in all processes of witnessing, spas-
modic and continuous, conscious and unconscious, is not
simply the information, the establishment of the facts, but
the experience itself of living through testimony, of giving
testimony.
—Dori Laub (in Caruth 1995, 70)

As I write this, my three-year-old naps upstairs, unaware that she is fighting for her life. She was diagnosed with acute lymphoblastic leukemia
(ALL) in March, and my research questions have become terrifyingly
and personally vital. I wonder anew: how does the writing classroom
link with trauma studies, and does writing really have the power to heal?

My toddler's cancer diagnosis did not bring me to this research interest; my students did, fourteen years ago. It was my first semester as a
college-level writing teacher, and Bill was the last student to turn in a
narrative essay. He was two weeks behind, and I was concerned with
how I might respond to my first "late" paper. By the time I sat down
to read Bill's essay, it was getting late, and I was ready to move on to
another task. As I began to read his opening, however, I recognized the
grief Bill narrated in his essay. I stopped rushing and began to read his
essay slowly; as I read, I shared his trauma. Bill wrote,

> Cursing my father and life in general, I didn't notice Jewels standing on
> the roof watching me. . . . Whirling around, I directed my anger at her
> and yelled for her to get off of the roof and go back inside. As I stepped
> toward her, she involuntarily stepped back into an empty space. Those

blue eyes widened in surprise as I dashed forward, hand out stretched, but it was too late. When I finally rushed down the ladder, she lay motionless on the ground. I held her in my arms and rocked her just like I had when she was a little girl, humming that song she liked so well, until those blue eyes closed one last time. I try not to blame myself for my sister's death, but not a day goes by that I don't ask—what if I had held my temper in check? (Bill, college freshman, 1999, used with permission)

I wanted to encourage Bill to continue writing, but I was unable to formulate the right words of response. I was trained to discourage too much emotion in my students' writing, but I felt the depth of his emotional experience.

I could share countless other stories from students who have written and researched powerfully out of deeply personal issues, regardless of the course or assignment focus. In a required first-year writing class on cultural analysis, for example, I received essays on the following: about a student watching his father try to kill his mother, about a student's father abandoning her over and over again throughout her life, about living with liver disease, and about being gang-raped.

Adam opened his essay with the following: "I was born in Lowell, Massachusetts; a cute little town full of gangs and crack heads. . . . Other than Steve, the bully, my stepdad's car getting robbed, and a few of my female babysitters molesting me, I had a nice childhood in Lowell." Students were invited to investigate a community, so how did Adam make the decision to investigate this tumultuous one?

In one student's process narrative, she explained her decision to write about being raped by her stepfather as a way to continue living: "I chose to write about this because I want to survive."

So if there really is power in writing about the personal, why is it undervalued and underinvestigated in the academy? In fact, if we examine current scholarship, it might seem as though we have moved further away from the idea of connecting our students' writing and our teaching through narratives and other personal accounts, like these from the classroom, and instead have focused on *theoretical* discussions of such issues. In this essay, I introduce the theory and practice of writing and healing through both primary and secondary research. It is an exploration of how to respond to trauma in any classroom.

Writing and Healing: History, Theory, Debate

In ancient Greece and Rome, scholar-teachers like Quintilian and Cicero taught students how to argue and orate on objective *topoi*. In fact, Robert Connors (1987) reminds us that no attention was given to personal writing or speaking within educational frameworks in antiquity. It was not until the seventeenth and eighteenth centuries that personal writing was viewed as an acceptable form of writing, and nineteenth-century romanticism encouraged writing about personal experience and writing in one's own voice, rather than with the voice of an orator. Connors also notes that Alexander Bain introduced the modes of discourse in 1866, and two of the modes—narration and description—became the foundation for many writing assignments within those modal directives.

In uncovering this long history of rhetoric, especially since the 1980s, scholars have noted a vast, uncharted history of women rhetoricians who helped define and redefine rhetoric as a discipline and argue for the validity of personal writing in the classroom, especially for female students. In *A Room of One's Own* (1929), Virginia Woolf focuses on conditions of education and economics that hinder women and their writing. She also focuses on literary language and its maleness, and she calls for a "woman's sentence." She encourages women to find new audiences, whether male or female, who will encourage their writing. Woolf is now regarded as an important foremother in women's rhetoric, and writers have cited and followed her feminist stand against the social and political forces that quiet women's voices.

Later women rhetoricians, such as Hélène Cixous, developed arguments that follow Woolf's rhetoric. A contemporary rhetorician, Cixous's body-rhetoric introduced feminism to *ecriture feminine*, which articulates the connections between women's physical bodies and their experiences. In "The Laugh of the Medusa," Cixous (1976) both calls for and demonstrates a new way of using language, particularly female language. As these rhetoricians remind us, women have had to argue for the right to use language throughout history, so why would we silence their voices in the modern classroom?

Within twentieth- and twenty-first-century education, personal writing is more widely taught, at least within the modes of discourse. But to this day, scholars grapple to define personal and academic writing. In his conclusion, Connors (1987, 180–81) makes clear his support for moving the personal into the college classroom as an acceptable genre: "The question persists as to what place personal stories and citing personal observations should have in the process of teaching students to write . . . but as teachers, we always have to encourage, even demand attempts at the next step—to go beyond merely personal accounts, either outside into encompassing the world in discourse, or inside into shaping our personal observations into the touching, deeply empathetic and finally metapersonal stuff of which the greatest writing is made." Because of this ongoing search for what constitutes acceptable academic discourse, personal writing assignments are often criticized for their lack of attention to intellectual or macro sociopolitical issues. The impact of personal writing on students' growth remains underinvestigated because of this opposition. For example, critics claim the focus on the personal is nonacademic and even dangerous, particularly in required courses. Lester Faigley (1992, 121) questions the authenticity of personal writing: "Why is writing about potentially embarrassing and painful aspects of one's life considered more honest than, say . . . [the] student who tries to figure out what Thucydides was up to in writing about the Peloponnesian War?" David Bartholomae (1995, 488) also discounts the emphasis of personal writing as "sentimental realism," and he finds the genre "corrupt." He believes composition classes should teach students to become critical, academic writers, and argues this cannot happen through a focus on personal writing: "I don't want my students to celebrate what would then become the natural and inevitable details of their lives."

Why would opponents of personal writing suggest that we encourage students to investigate the community and culture they live in, but not their own lives? According to opponents of personal writing, we should teach about the public, not the private, what students think, not what they feel. The result of such divisions, evocative of previous centuries' separation of the public sphere (defined as male) and the private sphere (defined as female), is dangerous. My research investigates the fruitful merging of these two binaries—the academic and the personal. Charles Anderson and Marian MacCurdy (2000, 17) support this dichotomy as false with their definition of writing as "an ongoing, recursive process in which self and community challenge, affirm, serve, and extend each other in the drama of personal and public history." Students come to our classrooms with many literacies or discourses—personal, cultural, global. Why should the academy value one over the other?

While the subgenre of writing and healing has historically been viewed as the most sentimental or inappropriately therapeutic genre of personal writing, in the past decade we have seen scholars draw from this form as a way to respond to national and personal trauma. Three of the most widely read publications to address the importance of writing and healing in the college-level writing classroom include Anderson and MacCurdy's (2000) collection, *Writing and Healing: Toward an Informed Practice*, which focuses on writing and healing in composition studies; the September 2001 special issue of *College English*, "Personal Writing: Storying Our Lives Against the Grain"; and Borrowman's (2005) *Trauma and the Teaching of Writing*. The area of writing and healing remains complex and contradictory for many scholars, but the call for attention to writing and healing is now being supported as a response to cultural events by a number of teachers and theorists. In fact, in what has been called a "traumatic turn" over the past few decades, some scholars argue that we are all teaching in a time of trauma, indeed in a "post-traumatic century," perhaps more so now based on our immediate access to trauma through the Internet and news journalism, as well as the popularity of reality and talk shows that glorify personal pain. Combine these collective traumas (or testimonies) with more immediate personal traumas like abuse and hate crimes, and it becomes clear why there is a need for more scholarly work addressing the subject of writing and healing.

In my exploration of ways to connect writing and healing, I was faced with terminology that focuses on personal writing or writing therapy, but I found little research on how the two fields intersect in the academy. Many scholars in my field, composition, have historically discredited the relationship between writing and therapy. For example, Kathleen Pfeiffer (1993, 670), in a response to Carole Delentiner's essay "Crossing Lines," questions the role of pain and trauma in the classroom. She discounts the "alleged" benefits of personal writing: "How does engaging in true confessions help students become better writers or thinkers?" Pfeiffer's final criticism represents the opposition facing any pedagogy that allows students to explore personal and traumatic issues: "This weepy world of confessions and revelations is a fundamentally egocentric sort of self absorption. Such teeth-gnashing and soul-baring might help a student recover from his or her lost inner child, but it will do little in the way of developing a sophisticated communicative ability, analytical skills, or a clear-sighted understanding of the world. . . . None of this can be accomplished when a student is taught to look inward and cry" (671). Because of this type of opposition, I was often faced with negative implications that writing teachers who focus on personal writing must assume the role of counselor; however, many psychological and composition studies are beginning to prove the importance of writing as healing. Wendy Bishop (1997, 144) addresses the terminology of writing and therapy, and we are reminded through her essay that writing "processes can be therapeutic; they can make you feel healthy and facilitate change, but the processes themselves are not 'therapy.' Thus, 'therapeutic process' seems to be the most appropriate term for what happens in writing or in a writing class."

While there are many ways for a person to work through trauma (or not), quantitative studies like Alice Brand's (1989) and James Pennebaker's (1990), as well as more qualitative studies like Michelle Payne's (2000) research of student compositions about sexual abuse, physical abuse, anorexia, and bulimia, have found writing to be an effective means for survivors to share their stories. Furthermore, the classroom can serve as a site where the most powerful healing can take place, because it is "a site at which the social and discursive practices of the individual, the community, and the larger culture are interrogated and from which they may be effectively altered" (Anderson and MacCurdy 2000, 7). Unfortunately, most writing classrooms still operate under a patriarchal model; however, if the writing classroom really does hold this much power, why aren't more classrooms focused on the pedagogical model of writing and healing?

Welcome to Class: Introducing a Pedagogy of Trauma

In order to analyze what E. Ann Kaplan (2005) describes as the "impact of trauma on individuals and on entire cultures," I developed and then researched a pedagogy focused on writing and healing in a first-year composition course titled "Writing about Life, Loss, and Experience" (Kaplan 2005, 1). The course is designed as a writing workshop, where students are invited to write, reflect, and learn together as they become stronger writers and thinkers.

I based much of my theoretical framework on Alice Brand's (1989) and James Pennebaker's (1990) research. Working in the underdeveloped interdisciplinary fields of social psychology and composition studies, Brand creates a speculative frame for including emotional factors within rhetorical and cognitive analyses, and she undertakes and encourages further linking of emotion and writing. Brand (1989, 4) includes extensive case studies that all support further development of her key question: "Why then is inquiry into emotion without place in contemporary studies of writing?" Psychologist Pennebaker's study on expressing emotion reports the effects on the body of expressing trauma in writing, which remains the most conclusive evidence yet supporting the need for writing about trauma. Through his collection of experimental studies, Pennebaker found that the writers involved in his study were able to organize facts about overwhelming experiences and demonstrated improved emotional and physical health through the writing process.

When I first designed the research study course, I wanted to ensure a pedagogical focus on writing and healing, while engaging both personal and academic discourse. The first part of the course invited students to write about the subject they think they know best, themselves. During this unit, students completed writing exercises focused on life writing, such as childhood experiences, sketches, and career dreams. Students were also invited to remember people and events through a writing workshop that provided prompts such as these: "At what time were you the most content? How long did this contentment last? Where were you? Who do you see?" The emotion expressed throughout this first writing project is always notable, and one of my main goals is to invite students to discover how the personal is also public and political. For example, one student, Kassie, wrote about her adolescent experience as a partier—or "bad girl" as she describes herself—which culminated in police brutality. She concluded her personal essay with the following emotions: "I'm having trouble getting past the flashbacks of the dirt, the slamming of the door on my skull, the infuriating laugh that one of the cops made, the raunchy smell of the jail, my fear that made me vomit and urinate on myself, and the emergency room bathrooms, where I washed my bloody hands and face for the first time that night." Kassie moved from word to sentence to draft.

Figure 11.1. Before

The focus on the personal often centers on loss or trauma. In this section of the course, students also completed a number of "before and after the loss" picture collage assignments, which invited student-writers to consider who they were before the experience and how the experiences of loss changed/shaped them. Lauren recorded a table of words to describe herself before and after her rape. Notice how these emotions are visually represented on the page. Lauren then took the visual power of the collages and moved them into her writing.

Before Loss	After Loss
confident	skeptical
invincible	depressed
trusting	stressed
fearless	self-conscious
happy	vulnerable

In the academic section of the course, student-writers were introduced to the importance of merging their personal and academic lives by writing an analytical research project that examined the broader issue surrounding one of their most significant lived experiences. This unit moved beyond the inward focus for which personal writing is often criticized, and encouraged writers to merge their personal interests and passions into academic writing.

Figure 11.2. After

In one of the course texts, *Writing as a Way of Healing*, Louise De-salvo (1999) encourages writers to move from silence to testimony by connecting, in writing, the personal, the community of writers, and the larger culture in order to reach "healing"—and that is exactly what took place during this research essay project. For example, Alicia wrote about her experience with childhood sexual abuse by a stepfather, and the power of her essay led to social action within the classroom community. There was a legislative session on the topic of child abuse a few weeks after the half-class workshop, and, because of her essay, four of the twenty-one class members attended the legislative session with Alicia where the bill was passed.

How can we encourage experiences like Alicia's to happen in all classrooms? I have found, through my research, that one of the most effective ways to connect students to the larger realities of their topics is through writing workshops or collaboration. I divide students into groups to brainstorm ideas and research questions, as well as to workshop each other's full drafts as they moved toward the completion of each project. Not only did the writing collaborations help students gain confidence as writers and researchers, but as Judith Herman's (1997, 214) research supports, the third stage in the overall healing or growth process occurs only when the survivor shares the experience with a community and begins to rebuild social ties: "Traumatic events destroy the sustaining bonds between individual and community. . . . Trauma isolates; the group recreates a sense of belonging. Trauma dehumanizes the victim; the group restores her humanity."

Kelli, another research study student, repeatedly mentioned the importance of the peer response workshops in her overall writing growth: "The classroom felt so comfortable, and everyone was so friendly. The peer response experience made it easier for me to write openly because they were writing about their experiences and passions, too. The entire-class workshop felt like a conversation with other scholars, and it was my favorite part of the class." She also noted the community's response to her writing focus on foster care, both personally and as a research topic, as one of the most powerful experiences of her *life*: "After four months of describing Mariah and sharing our bond with my classmates, they finally realized that Mariah was not just a foster child in my home, she was my sister. Being able to have a room full of strangers realize that this beautiful child shared the same bond with me as they did with their biological siblings was incomparable to any other moment in my life."

To continue the community focus throughout the course, students composed a radical revision project at the end of the semester. The radical revision project, first introduced by Wendy Bishop (1997), invites students to shift their essay's style, perspective, or genre. Through this final project, writers were able to reflect on their growth throughout the writing process by finding an alternate way to share their essay's focus. For example, Danielle created a mosaic of her research essay on women's rights from her home country, Afghanistan, and Ola composed a poem and painting in response to her sister's sudden death, which she wrote about in Essay I.

Overall, through this extensive research study, I found the necessary support for writing students and teachers alike to write critically about what they are most passionate about, even when it seems risky. Endorsing Borrowman's (2005) *Trauma and the Teaching of Writing* on the book's back cover, Jeffrey Berman argues for teacher-scholars to begin paying attention to personal and even traumatic writing as valid discourses: "[S]o many people, especially college students, suffer from psychological conflicts, including clinical depression, suicidal ideation, eating disorders, and drug and alcohol addiction—all of which contribute to a traumatic culture. This is one of the first books on what might be called the *pedagogy of trauma.*" Most of all, I hope that a writing and healing pedagogy invites both students and teachers to decide what experiences, both positive and negative, personal and public, shape their personal and academic lives through the writing and revision processes.

Responding 101: What to Do When Students Write about Trauma

Not all scholars will be interested in designing a course around what Berman (2001) termed *a pedagogy of trauma.* But as writing teachers, we will all receive essays or journals focused on loss and trauma, regardless of whether or not we invite personal reflection in our courses. Stories about painful, traumatic events do appear in academic classrooms, they have always appeared, and they will continue to appear. Each time I present or publish something on this topic, I'm met with the following questions: How do we most effectively respond to a student's story of rape or physical abuse? What are the risks of assigning *or not assigning* personal writing? How can we respond as humans and evaluators when students do write about their lives and losses? What does this mean in terms of the social and political constructs surrounding students' essays, experiences, and ideas?

We must begin by asking ourselves, *what are the risks of not allowing personal reflection and writing in the classroom*? Peter Goggin and Maureen Daly Goggin (2005, 40) remind all teachers of writing that "while it is crucial that we do not mandate writing and healing, it is equally crucial that we also do not silence it." Lad Tobin (2004, 113) echoes this with another question: "Do we make our classrooms safer by prohibiting confessional writing when there are people suffering and starving inside?"

Even if we are open to assigning personal writing or would at least appreciate some concrete ideas on how to best respond when we do receive essays on trauma or loss, there are risks here, too. Berman (2001, 35) reminds us that we must respond very carefully to a student's personal text: "Dead authors cannot be harmed by critics labeling their works as 'sentimental' or 'melodramatic'; by contrast, most students will be harmed—and silenced—if their personal writings are criticized in these ways." Herman (1997) studies commonalities between writing and grief, and her study finds that survivors can restore connections through three stages of recovery: (1) establishing safety, (2) reconstructing the trauma story, and (3) reestablishing the connections between the survivor and the community. In the second stage of recovery, the survivor writes her or his story of trauma. And when the action of telling the experience is concluded, the experience belongs to the past (Herman 1997, 195). However, if we, as teachers, respond in inappropriate ways, we can further emphasize the trauma. Michelle Payne (2000, 128) reiterates this risk: "Writing teachers don't need to be therapists to renew humanity in our classrooms, and we don't need to reinforce the violence that has destroyed someone else's humanity by banning that person's story from the classroom. . . . These students have much to teach us if we would only listen to what they're saying."

It is important to remember that trauma silences, and therefore we, as responders, don't want to further that by refusing to respond critically to personal and even traumatic texts. I understand the fear that focusing on issues like style and organization in our response to an essay on leukemia or incest might be viewed as inappropriate or insensitive. However, the larger concern should be that by *not* responding, we risk reiterating the truth that this experience has distanced the student from being normalized or heard in every community, even the academic one. Payne's (2000, 127) research supports this paradox: "To not be part of revictimizing them, I think we need to encourage their self-direction while helping them meet the expectations of the course."

Responding to student writing gained national attention following the massacre at Virginia Tech in April 2007, when Seung-Hui Cho, an English major, shot and killed thirty-two students and then turned the gun on himself. Some critics argue that professors and administrators should have responded more quickly and proactively to Cho's writing, but others claim that Cho's violence was not caused by what he wrote. According to a CNN report the day after the deadly shootings, Cho never wrote about killing people. However, one of his writing teachers, Lucinda Roy, was concerned enough by his dark writing style that she went to police and other university officials to seek help, yet was met with no official guidelines on how to intervene. "The threats seemed to be underneath the surface," Roy said. "They were not explicit, and that was the difficulty the police had" ("Professor: Shooter's Writing Dripped with Anger" 2007). Therefore I would ask, in cases in which students pose a serious threat to themselves or others, shouldn't there be a standard academic protocol set up for responding to trauma in colleges and universities across the country?

Once we receive the information, whether traumatic, disturbing, or argumentative, how do we approach the responding process? Anderson and MacCurdy (2000, 13) present four possibilities for responding to students' personal texts. They include rejecting the essays as nonacademic; engaging with the stories in inappropriate ways by becoming overly sympathetic; taking on the story as our own; or, as their research recommends, helping students create texts that "embody their lived experience, the clearest expression of it, and whatever understanding of that experience is available to the student and community within which the student lives and writes." Because we must always remain aware of the power our responses hold, Michelle Payne (2000, 120) proposes, "If we want to be ethical about the ways we respond to these essays, then we need to do what many of us ask our students to do: reflect critically . . . and assume responsibility for the responses we offer." Even when we respond thoughtfully and ethically, we are sometimes still unsure of when a student's writing is a cry for help or too traumatic to respond to solely as text. We are not all trained counselors, and therefore should keep the university's counseling center information close by. I decided to seek outside assistance when an advanced writing student, Lilly, explored her drug addiction and loneliness in one of her weekly journals:

> As far back as I can remember, I never really had as many friends as everyone else, and I got left out of slumber parties. I remember one party in particular. I was in 4th grade, and I thought the girls were my best friends. They invited almost every girl but me. I thought something was wrong with me. This is happening again. I ended up in the hospital after hallucinating/overdosing over the weekend. Apparently in the ER, I screamed at all of my friends that they raped me, so none of them want anything to do with me now.

Although I knew, just from this journal, that Lilly was wary of people in power, I called the director of counseling services and confidentially, without mentioning any names or specifics, discussed possible ways I might respond. I then emailed Lilly and acknowledged the strength of her journal and let her know I was available if she needed to talk. She responded with a tentative yes, if she could talk with me "confidentially." I think Lilly's initial concern of confidentiality brings up an important point for us all: it is crucial for students to be able to trust us, because we hold great power in the classroom community. Through our conversations, however, Lilly decided to seek help. As of this writing, she remains in counseling and attends AA meetings regularly. I'm not suggesting that my interactions with Lilly healed her, but I do think it was important that I was willing to listen.

We should also begin acknowledging the importance of responding to the personal in our pedagogical conversations, department meetings, and national conferences in order to facilitate discourse and change in the classroom. For example, Anderson and MacCurdy (2000, 13) argue, "Writing teachers find themselves more and more alienated from students who seem less and less attentive and more and more resistant to the increasingly abstract benefits of academic literacy, which students experience as increasingly removed from the circumstances of their particular histories. In the end, if teachers are not careful, they become the very thing they most despise, agents not of change but of dominance, personal glorification, and hegemony." These discussions often take place via email, in the hallway, even in whispers because many of us are afraid to come across as soft, antiacademic, subjective. A number of my colleagues email and stop by my office each semester to discuss students who have disclosed something personal or traumatic; they are unsure of how to respond, largely because we have been discouraged from addressing the personal in our study of pedagogy. Cynthia Caywood and Gillian Overing (1987, xii) argue in the introduction to their anthology *Teaching Writing: Pedagogy, Gender, and Equity* that "the model of writing as product is inherently authoritarian." They continue, "Certain forms of discourse and language are privileged: the expository essay is valued over the exploratory; the argumentative essay set above the auto-biographical; the clear evocation of a thesis preferred to a more organic exploration of a topic; the impersonal, rational voice ranked more highly than the intimate, subjective one." As research on writing and healing has shown us, it is dangerous and ineffective to *discourage* personal writing from the writing classroom and from our conversations as teachers.

Our Roles as Humans and Evaluators

Each time I present or publish my research findings on writing and healing pedagogy, I meet with some form of the following question: Do you really think it's ethical to respond to personal writing when we are not trained counselors? As I've become more familiar with the literature and research findings surrounding writing and healing, I've begun to respond with questions of my own: Are our concerns with how to respond to the personal really more of a question of how to respond to emotional ways of knowing? In other words, when writers describe painful or traumatic experiences, is it fair to assume that they are necessarily depressed or at risk? I then often remind my colleagues that we are not trained in many areas students research and write about, from sociology to nursing to physics. But would those areas be off-limits for us as responders? And should our responding styles be different based on the topic?

The answer to all of these questions, for me, is no, and emphatically so.

In responding to personal writing, or any rhetorical model, we should begin by responding as readers. Berman's (2001) research on risky writing supports the need for writing teachers to first respond as advocates, empathizing with the student while encouraging her to challenge herself as a writer and thinker. Payne (2000, xv) agrees: "My first concern was for the student—how she felt, why she wrote about this, how she wanted me to respond, and what if anything I could do to help her writing."

One research study student I introduced, Lauren, best illustrates the challenge of finding a balance between the roles of reader and evaluator. Lauren was one of two first-year writing students to share the story of her rape in her first online discussion response, but that's only where Lauren's writing focus on her rape began. She stayed after class the day that I introduced the personal experience essay to tell me that she was not ready to write about her rape, and I, of course, told her that was completely fine. In fact, I discouraged her from choosing as a topic anything that she wasn't yet ready to share publicly. However, somewhere in the drafting of her topic, without talking with me, she decided to write the story of her rape. In a postterm interview, Lauren explained, "I tried really hard to come up with different topic ideas, but then I thought,

'I've already opened the can of worms so why not tear the lid off and get going.'" However, Lauren encountered blocking and difficulty recounting the details throughout the drafting process. In a late-night email, she wrote,

> ms. Hodges-hamilton:
> im having a really hard time with this loss essay. I'm writing about what happened to me, but I tried to change my topic because it was so hard. Now i've changed it back, but im not done with the draft. I only have about a page and a half or two pages. If I have more time to concentrate on it this weekend, I might be able to tackle it a little better, I just didn't want to get in trouble for not having a completed draft tomorrow for in class. Please let me know if it's ok. . . . i promise it will get done this weekend, i'm just not in a strong enough emotional state to tackle it right this second. Thanx.
> lauren

I responded:

> Hi Lauren,
> Of course, you can bring a 1 or 1 ½ page draft of your loss essay tomorrow. I just wanted you to begin the writing process, which you have done. I completely understand that writing about your rape is hard (and remember this is exactly what Desalvo writes about). It hurts to bring up loss or trauma, but it ultimately helps us regain power—I, along with many of my past students, have found this to be true. And I think you will, too. We are going to work on a letter writing assignment tomorrow, which might help you express emotions and continue writing. Also, we can continue to work together next week during your individual conference.
> I hope this helps,
> Amy

Lauren was able to overcome her writer's block, and although she struggled in her individual conference and the peer workshop to share her essay with me and some of the classroom community members, she produced one of the strongest, most powerful essays across the term. Here is an example of that power from the fifth page:

His hands resumed their roaming and ended up on my breasts. He pinched and manipulated them like an artist without clay. They had marks on them for weeks afterward. He bit them, lightly at first and then harder until I was screaming in pain. He whispered, "Shut up, you know you like it." But my breasts were throbbing from the torture inflicted upon them. I couldn't stop crying. He was becoming more impatient with me. He picked up one of the smaller speakers and told me, "If you don't shut up, I'm gonna hit you with this." I tried to stop. I really did. But my attempts were not enough to satisfy him. He hit me over the head with the speaker, and I temporarily blacked out.

Throughout the entire essay, as in this description, Lauren takes the reader with her into the panic and trauma of the rape. In her final portfolio letter, she explains what she gained from writing this essay in a college course: "I think Essay two opened the door to healing, but more importantly being listened to and understood was one of the most powerful, affirming experiences of my life as both a student and person."

Why do students like Lauren choose the classroom as the space to explore their lives and losses? As a beginning teacher researcher, I assumed that students, particularly female students, would begin to write more openly as the semester progressed, as they became part of the community. And that did happen. For example, Brittani shared the story of her rape in her research essay on dance therapy. But Lauren and Rachel are examples of students who chose a relatively unknown space as the safest place to share their stories.

Perhaps this is a result of the way I organize my classroom community. I base much of my pedagogical framework around Virginia Woolf's idea of creating a space in which students are invited to share their stories—*A Room of One's Own*. My room happens to be a classroom. As rhetoricians like Woolf and Cixous have argued, the practice of writing can lead to the reclaiming of the female voice. I'm not arguing that all writing needs to be feminine or only writing by women can lead to healing; in fact, Hélène Cixous (1976, 893) supports this as an impossibility in the conclusion of her essay: "It is impossible to *define* a feminine practice of writing, and this is an impossibility that will remain, for this practice can never be theorized, enclosed, coded—which doesn't mean that it doesn't exist. But it will always surpass the discourse that regulates the phallocentric system; it does and will take place in areas other than those subordinated to philosophic domination. It will be conceived of only by subjects who are breakers of automatism, by peripheral figures that no authority can ever subjugate." I am arguing, however, that the feminist classroom and the space it creates can lead to powerful healing for all students—racially, politically, sexually. Students like Lauren, Rachel, and Brittani who practiced "writing the body" support this argument.

Peter Stearns (1994) provides further explanation for these students' decisions—his research suggests that Lauren and Rachel decided the classroom was the perfect place to share their writing because they had control over how the story was told and, to a certain extent, how readers interpreted their stories. The research of both Payne and Stearns supports the belief that strangers in a new community, in this case my classroom, are less dangerous than intimates. Because of the shift of power the new community creates, close people in their lives like family and partners don't have to witness the emotions, struggle, and truth of the loss or trauma again (Payne 2000, 17).

Perhaps we could begin all of our responses and evaluation by reflecting on Maya Angelou's (1969) focus in *I Know Why the Caged Bird Sings*—reclaiming voice after trauma. It is important to remember as we move from the role of reader to that of evaluator that the writer chose to draft an essay on the personal in an academic setting. Therefore it is our responsibility to respond to it as we would *any* other text. I have found students appreciate my responses to their writing as an academic text, as well as appreciate the chance to discuss those rhetorical choices in individual conferences and peer writing workshops. Therefore, I always ask hard questions and push all student-writers to further develop their arguments, ideas, and style. Alicia's postterm interview response supports this need for "normalization": "I realized through your written evaluations and peer workshops that there are other people in this world closer to me than I think, who have suffered from misfortunes much like my own, like when I read and responded to Natalie's paper on child abuse. Most of all, from all of the responses I received, I learned that I have an important story to share, even if traumatic, and I plan to take that power with me to law school where I, one day, will help support laws against child abuse." Alicia's response provides enough support for teachers of writing to always respond as humans *and* evaluators, regardless of topic.

Connecting to Cultural and Historical Contexts of Experience

As responders, we should always consider the cultural and historical implications of the topic. Personal writing is not an alternative cultural discourse or analysis, just as it is not an alternative to critical thinking. Carol Witherell and Nel Noddings (1991, 4) further support this argument: "Through telling, writing, reading, and listening to life stories—one's own and others'—those engaged in this work can penetrate cultural barriers, discover the power of the self and integrity of the other, and deepen their understanding of their respective histories and possibilities."

Tobin (2004, 106) reminds us that when students choose to write essays on subjects like rape or eating disorders, their stories are automatically tied to a historical or political reality. This was certainly true for my "Writing in the Community" class members. I designed the course around this very idea—of moving from the inside out—and students partnered with community members from local communities like Magdalene House, a halfway house for recovering drug addicts and prostitutes, an assisted-living facility, an inner-city school, as well as global communities like the Eating Disorder International Coalition.

Across the semester, we also studied the idea of place and displacement within communities through a range of lenses: memoirs and other forms of life writing, psychological analysis, as well as our own and our community partners' writing processes. All students worked in powerful ways to restore agency in their own lives and their community partner's lives, and I was struck by students' and community members' decisions to share and write out of times of deep loss—for example, one student, Bethany, wrote alongside an international student from an inner-city high school, and they both found tumultuous familial relationships as their focus. Bethany opens her memoir with the following: "Reverend Charlie T. Kittrell. His name still sends chills down my spine. He was a bastard. This man raped my mom. This man was her dad." Another student, Katy, collaborated with Jewel, an eighty-two-year-old resident at Morningside, an assisted-living facility adjacent to campus. Although Katy invited Jewel to share stories from across her life, every week Jewel recounted stories from her early childhood, including the deaths of her two sisters. The details of her sister Pearl's death when she was just four years old are moving: "I can still see her little frame lying static in our bed. Mama put copper nickels over her eyelids to keep them closed. When it came time for her funeral, I didn't own any socks that didn't have holes in them; Mama had to borrow a pair from our neighbor, Maria Rice." Other community members focused on issues ranging from marriages and relationships to moving from Iran, struggling with eating disorders, and addiction.

One oral history project that remains clear in my mind is the story of Beverly, a "sister" of Magdalene House. Mackenzie worked with Beverly to recount her life story, and they chose abuse as the focus of the project. Beverly explained at the end of the semester that although she certainly could have shared stories solely from her addiction or her life as a sex worker, the abuse that runs throughout her life seems clearest still. Mackenzie demonstrates that abuse in palpable ways:

> I woke up on the floor. I couldn't see anything. Were my eyes really open? Was I dreaming? What happened; who did this to me? My stream of conscious ran wild. I took deep breaths; calm down, get yourself together. I tried to get myself up and could barely see that he was lying on the couch watching TV.
>
> "I think . . . I need to go to the hospital, I think I need help." I thought. I struggled to mumble these words but it hurt. I was half way sobbing, not knowing what was happening.
>
> "F*** you. I'm not taking you anywhere. You'll jus' turn me in." He barked.
>
> I got up and stumbled my way up the stairs, feeling very disoriented and dizzy. I made it up to the bathroom and when I caught a glimpse in the mirror my heart stopped and my whole body was seized. My own reflection sent me into shock and I passed out only to wake up once more in a state of confusion. I called a cab to take me to the hospital; I didn't want an ambulance, nor to make a scene. As the cab driver pulled up to the house, I stammered out the front lawn and spilled myself into the backseat.
>
> "H, Hah, Hos-al, Pla . . ." I uttered, I couldn't move my face; my jaw was broken. The cab driver was horrified at the sight of me.
>
> "Who did this to you! Who did this to you!" He screamed.
>
> He drove as fast as he could to the hospital and must have warned them on the way, because they were waiting for me.

When I walked in the lady behind the wide desk gasped in awe.
"Don't blow your nose, don't blow your nose, it could be brain matter.
Here, here sit down," she cried. Then darkness.

Since the conclusion of that course, a majority of the students have remained actively engaged in both local and global communities. For example, Bethany is now a pediatric intensive care unit nurse, and she explained that many of the children she cares for have been abused and it's one way for her to heal that pain; Katy is studying history in graduate school, which she became interested in while recording Jewel's oral history project; and Mackenzie and Bethany still meet monthly for coffee, and Mackenzie volunteers at Magdalene House.

It is also powerful for students to see their experiences as socially constituted; therefore, as responders, we should invite students to engage in the social and political constructs surrounding their experiences. Perhaps we could recommend an outside text on their subject, ask them to research a particular idea presented in the essay, or tell them about community and cultural events connected to their topics. For example, this semester I have a student, Robby, researching homelessness because he once lived on the streets. As part of his research process, I invited him to investigate a new outreach program on campus, "Mobile Loaves and Fishes," which provides food and clothing to the homeless on a daily basis. This organization and his experience giving back to his community form the center of his dynamic research project. As evidenced throughout these various students' experiences, our writing classrooms can be important sites for recognizing otherness and initiating social change. The more we move students away from introspection, the more we can shift away from our fears of moving into the role of therapist and instead focus our responses on issues of writing growth.

When the Pedagogical Becomes Personal

Although I always try to write and workshop with my students, when my daughter Grace was diagnosed with leukemia during spring break, I didn't know that I could ever teach *or* write again. I was teaching a "Creative Nonfiction" course that semester, and students were in the process of composing memoirs on topics ranging from abuse to alcoholism, and I felt inadequate and inept as both a teacher and a responder. My personal identity and my academic one as a professor were merging in unsettling and frightening ways. But as we were quickly swept into the world of childhood cancer, I realized I had to write my story or the years of research I poured into trying to prove the validity of writing and healing would be lost on me. So when I asked my creative nonfiction students the question, "When did you know true love?," I responded with them. Here's a draft of what I composed:

> I just tucked Grace into bed after her third birthday party, but I'm not standing in the kitchen cleaning the cake stand or on a ladder taking down her birthday banner. Instead, I'm sitting on a small couch in the dark next to Grace's hospital bed where she is receiving high-dose chemotherapy for Acute Lymphoblastic Leukemia.
>
> But let me back up to the beginning of the story. Grace was our miracle baby—after years of infertility treatments, the miscarriage of twins, and a lot of tears and prayers, we became parents to a beautiful, healthy baby girl. So on March 13th, when the doctors diagnosed that same beautiful, healthy two-and-a-half-year-old with leukemia, my world stopped. I couldn't breathe. Not our Grace. We waited too long and tried too hard. Not our baby.
>
> Beyond the miracle of her birth, Grace was a dream child. She was the toddler who would walk up to babies in the mall and start cooing and singing them lullabies. She never cried or threw tantrums, and my friends always looked on in a state of awe when I asked Grace to start cleaning up her toys when it was time to leave a play date and she actually did it without a fight.
>
> Once she was diagnosed and our days filled with transfusions and surgeries and steroids, she stopped talking, interacting, singing. It was like she went away. Except one morning at 4 a.m. after a grueling day and night of tests and meetings with doctors to discuss her prognosis, Grace asked the nurses checking her vitals to hold hands. So we did. We all gathered around her bed holding our hands and our breath in anticipation of what she might say. She began, "Let's pray. God is good, God is great, ummm, please make Gracie to feel better. Aaaammmeeennn." And then she giggled, closed her eyes, and went back to sleep.

My memories come in blows, short and sharp, but the love shared by strangers—nurses, doctors, other patients' families—remains clearest still. When I awoke the first morning after Grace's diagnosis to the sound of her IV pump, I panicked. I wanted to grab her out of the hospital bed and escape back to our normal life filled with birthday parties and music classes. Grace's nurse Kayla must have noticed the fear in my eyes, because after administering Grace's medications, she walked over and sat down on the couch beside me. She didn't speak. She just sat down, put her hand on mine, and we stared off together. My breathing slowed, and I eventually started asking questions about the surgery Grace would undergo that afternoon to place a port-a-catheter in her chest. Hours later, when I squeezed into Grace's hospital bed to ride down to the OR with her, Kayla was still with us. As we stepped onto the elevator and tears splattered both our cheeks, Kayla distracted Grace. "Does the duck on the ceiling of this special elevator say meow?"

Grace laughed, "No! A kitty cat says meow!"

Kayla continued as we slowed toward the operating room, "Well then, what does that silly duck say?"

Grace's tears stopped, "Quack, quack."

"You are so smart. Here we go!" And off the elevator and into the OR Grace went without any fear.

After 13 days in the hospital, they let us take Grace home. It was a Thursday—the kind of perfect spring day that encourages everyone to find some way to be outside—but I shielded my eyes as we pulled out of the hospital parking garage. Why was the sun shining so bright? I noticed Grace's head turn as we passed her favorite park, felt myself cringe as people laughingly walked into our local coffee shop, fought back tears as I watched Grace unable to lift her legs to climb the stairs to her room. After we unpacked and settled in, we couldn't get Grace to respond to us. In desperation, I turned my questions to her baby doll.

"Grace, does Sleeping Beauty hurt?"

She answered, "Well, just her knees, back, tummy, and head hurt. But I'm Grace Bishop Hamilton Doctor and Spiderman and I'm going to take her to Clinic and make her all better."

We talked a lot about Clinic, the outpatient facility where Grace would receive her weekly chemotherapy treatments, to help normalize the process. I'm not sure anything could have prepared me to take my two-year-old into an open room filled with children sitting in recliners receiving chemotherapy, blood transfusions, and platelet infusions.

Grace was excited to see other children, though, and she immediately walked up to a four-year-old girl named Lilly and introduced herself. "I'm Grace, and I'm on a crazy adventure. Are you, too?" As the two little girls sat side-by-side receiving their chemotherapies, Lilly's mom comforted me. She reminded me that I would smile again, that Grace would run again, and most importantly, that we wouldn't always feel alone.

After a few minutes, another little boy sat down in the chair next to Lilly, and his mom told us his story—he was diagnosed at four-years old and relapsed at seven. His nickname is Bug, and he quickly started telling Grace stories. This is the one I remember most: "What do you want to be when you grow up?" He didn't give Grace time to respond. "Well, I just want to work for a rodeo, maybe even just as the guy who lets opens the gate for the sheep during 4-H competitions. After all, all I need to be happy is a pork chop and a potato." I smiled for the first time that day.

Then a gorgeous seventeen-year-old girl sat down across from us and caught my eye—her name is Natalie and she's fighting T-Cell Leukemia. She was set to go to Auburn University on a tennis scholarship but now she tells people that she chose Vanderbilt instead. "They don't have to know it's Vanderbilt Children's Hospital, do they?" she joked.

The last little girl we met was Alli. She's Grace's age and has the same type of cancer. Her smile was contagious and she wiggled and played with her feeding tube as her mother told me of her high-risk diagnosis and the month they spent in the Pediatric Intensive Care Unit. What struck me most was the parents and children weren't just discussing different side effects or prognoses for the hours we sat together. Instead, they talked about what they might want for lunch, how siblings were doing with their new soccer leagues, and movies we couldn't miss. As I listened, I caught a glimpse of Lilly and Grace dancing out of the corner of my eye, twirling while balancing their IV poles, and I realized these families would soon become our own.

Cancer and doctors and treatment protocols are now routine for us. We play doctor every day. Grace knows how to take her doll's blood pressure and temperature, and she knows how to insert a port. She knows the word "stethoscope" and how to use one. She even knows how to comfort like Kayla now. She rocks her doll and whispers, "It's okay. It'll be over soon. You're so brave," while her Daddy or I give the doll a shot. Grace shared some sad news with her stuffed lion last week: "I'm so sorry, Mr. Lion, but you have leukemia like me." Then she turned and asked, "Mommy, did you have leukemia as a child?"

Over the last six months of her cancer treatment, I have learned the true meaning of love. My new definition reads like a list poem. Love is Grace's nurse Dara singing silly songs while putting a needle into her chest every week for her to receive her chemotherapy. Love is our eight-year-old neighbor cutting ten inches of her hair for Grace to twirl like she used to do with her own hair. Love is the little girl Emma with an inoperable brain tumor dancing and spinning in the halls of the sterile Oncology floor at Vanderbilt Children's Hospital. Love is the twelve-year-old boy who did not know Grace but asked for donations for her medical expenses in lieu of gifts for his birthday. Love is 100 people coming to a tea party while Grace's immune system was strong just to catch a glimpse of her blue eyes and celebrate the gift of her life.

Please don't misunderstand me. I would do anything—anything—to take this pain away from Grace, but her joy in the midst of suffering has taught me what true love is. Grace.

What Now?

As Cynthia Gannett (1995, 126) reminds us, we along with student-writers can help end oppression through the writing and responding processes: "Child abuse, and incest, and other forms of violence against women will not disappear just because they can't be written about, nor will these experiences stop having profound effects on students and learners. Indeed, writing about the events that silence and fragment (female or male, minority or white) can help them heal sufficiently to see themselves as knowers once again." As members of the academy, we need to stop thinking of personal and even traumatic writing as threatening and anti-intellectual. Instead we must ask, as do many feminist theorists, philosophers, and psychologists, how we might begin to recognize emotional appeals as ways of knowing. For example, feminist theorists posit, "when the more powerful are trying to control the emotions of the less powerful, what is at issue is not the basis for the emotion (any woman would feel this way, it's in the genes) but the cultural interpretation of it" (Payne 2000, 5). This is demonstrated in the field of composition when an academic analysis of spousal abuse is considered more scholarly and appropriate within the university than one written from the perspective of an abused spouse. Bishop (1997, 320) addresses this paradox: "A writer who in discussing a paper also discloses childhood abuse is not simply 'burdening' us with more than we're trained to handle—rather this student has connected to us, made our day more whole, more human, more important."

The importance of writing and healing has become very real for me as we fight Grace's cancer. I am more convinced than ever that writing holds power. Paying attention to both the personal and the academic in students' writing can emphasize individuality in the context of the community, and the dialectical relationship among rhetoric, emotion, ideology, and lived experiences.

12

Answering the Call

Crisis Intervention and Rape Survivor Advocacy as Witnessing Trauma

DEBRA JACKSON

These really separate strands of academia, of theory, of philosophy, and of practice, and of experience . . . are not things that go together easily, or dove-tail in any way that we can explain. We are sometimes adversaries, competitors, claiming this territory. . . . It leads us nowhere useful. . . . And, we need to be useful.
—Dorothy Allison (2010)

After years of struggle with their disconnection, in 1999 I found a touchpoint between my activism and academic life.[1] I had been a Crisis Center volunteer for two years when I was introduced to the concept of witnessing trauma at the Feminist Visions of the Future symposium at Purdue University. Feminist philosopher Kelly Oliver's presentation on witnessing ethics resonated with my experiences of answering crisis calls and advocating on behalf of rape survivors. I was immediately struck by the fact that the central skills of crisis intervention enacted the process of valuing experiential truth over empirical truth and the double meaning of witnessing described by Oliver. I also found that the description of the role of witnessing trauma in the survivor's recovery captured my motivations for doing this work.

In this essay, I reflect on connections between the concept of witnessing articulated in trauma theory and my work in crisis intervention and rape survivor advocacy. I argue that crisis intervention and rape survivor advocacy are forms of witnessing, and that these forms of witnessing assist in the recovery of the victim's embodied, autonomous, and narrative self. I weave together the threads of practice and theory: my lived experiences—both my volunteer experiences answering calls and advocating for rape survivors at the Crisis Center and my personal experiences with loved ones who have been touched by violence and its aftermath—interrupting my conceptual understanding of trauma and witnessing.[2] In doing so, I show both how my encounters with survivors of trauma help me develop a richer understanding in my academic work and how my research in trauma studies helps me encounter and respond to trauma.

Trauma's Wounds

Psychological trauma is a normal response to acute or ongoing dangerous and/or life-threatening events. Whereas ordinary experiences are easily integrated into one's experiential landscape, traumatic experiences are not. Instead, they are experienced in fragmentary ways. The disaster or violence overwhelms the person's ability to understand and cope with the events. Helpless in the face of death or serious bodily injury, one's ordinary adaptive human responses to danger are insufficient, stretched, overwhelmed, disorganized. A person experiences traumatic events not in a direct, unmediated manner, but indirectly, through its subsequent aftershocks.

A few months after I started volunteering at the Crisis Center, my former partner, Kerri, was robbed at gunpoint while working alone at a video store. A masked man walked into the store, fired his weapon, and demanded that she place money from the register into a bag he had thrown down behind the counter. After he left the store, Kerri locked the door behind him and called the police. Shortly afterward, a few minutes after midnight, I arrived at the video store to pick her up, and saw the police cars and lights surrounding the building. I panicked, ran inside, and searched her face to understand what was happening. Almost instantly, I was sobbing. Kerri, on the other hand, appeared calm—so calm, in fact, that the officer suspected that she had conspired in the robbery despite the fact that the robber had taken less than sixty dollars (she had already made the night's deposit).

When a traumatic event occurs, the full realization of its impact is not immediately accessible. Instead, there is a period of latency between the time of the traumatizing event and the full emotional impact of the event. This belatedness can last anywhere from a few hours to decades, and traps the survivor in a cycle of repetitions and reenactments that makes the traumatic event contemporaneous with the present. Survivors of trauma experience a variety of cognitive, affective, and physical symptoms, characterized in the psychological literature as *posttraumatic stress disorder*, which interrupt their daily lives: feelings of helplessness, loss of control, anger, dissociation, numbing, denial, insomnia, nausea, heightened startle response, and hypervigilance, as well as revisiting the experience through nightmares, flashbacks, and/or hallucinations (Herman 1997). These symptoms are effects of both the traumatic event and the psyche's attempt to understand the event through a compulsive repetition of the experience. What returns to haunt the victim, explains trauma theorist Cathy Caruth, is not only the reality of the event, but the fact that its violence is not yet fully known. Although trauma survivors are firsthand witnesses and hence may be the most reliable source of testimony about what occurred, the nature of trauma disrupts the survivor's ability to understand the full extent of the experience. Caruth (1997, 208) describes the paradox of trauma: "... that the most direct seeing of a violent event may occur as an absolute inability to know it; that immediacy, paradoxically, may take the form of a belatedness. The repetitions of the traumatic event—which remain unavailable to consciousness but intrude repeatedly on sight—thus suggest a larger relation to the event that extends beyond what can simply be seen or what can be known, and is inextricably tied up with the belatedness and incomprehensibility that remain at the heart of this repetitive seeing." Through involuntary repetitions such as nightmares, flashbacks, and/or hallucinations, the survivor's reexperiencing of the traumatic event generates a voice that is released from the wound, which bears witness to the trauma.

Like many other trauma victims, Kerri experiences the impact of the robbery in a belated and debilitating manner. At the time of the robbery, Kerri appeared calm, and recalls that when she first saw the robber, she laughed. He had a pink bandana pulled across his face, which she thought made him look ridiculous. But, weeks later, she was anything but calm. Kerri had developed panic/anxiety disorder, which disrupted her ability to work, sleep, and complete other common life activities for over two years. She would have panic attacks while driving to work, she could not sleep without all the lights on in the apartment, she would check and recheck that the doors and windows were locked, and so on. With each panic attack, she believed that she was having a heart attack, and if not that, she was surely going crazy. Only after extensive cognitive therapy did her anxiety and panic attacks subside.

Trauma's impact on the self can be profound. Many survivors describe the trauma as splitting them into two distinct selves. Terri Jentz (2006, 9–10), survivor of a brutal attempted murder, describes herself as simultaneously an "official" self and "scarecrow" self: one bright, independent, confident, and ambitious, the other "an unacknowledged, angry, aggrieved shadow . . . plotting from the beginning to sabotage the other self." Many other survivors describe their experience as a kind of death, not only in terms of facing a life-threatening event, but also in the annihilation of their sense of personhood. A cofounder of the rape survivor support group I helped facilitate describes her rape as a kind of death. She often explained during the support group meetings, "The person I was before the rape is gone. She died that night. I had to mourn her death. I am not the same person, and I will never get her back." Similarly, rape survivor and feminist philosopher Susan Brison (1998, 17; 2002, 8–9) describes her dissociation during the forensic examination following her rape: "This was just one of many incidents in which I felt as if I was experiencing things posthumously. . . . Perhaps I'm not really here, I thought, perhaps I did die in that ravine. The line between life and death, once so clear and sustaining, now seemed carelessly drawn and easily erased. For the first several months after my attack, I led a spectral existence, not quite sure whether I had died and the world went on without me, or whether I was alive but in a totally alien world." One way of understanding this splitting of the self, according to Caruth, is that trauma is not simply an effect of destruction, but an enigma of survival. One's identity becomes bound up with, or founded in, the death one survives.

Shattered Selves

In "Outliving Oneself" (1997), Brison explores the effects of this crisis of death and survival on the self. She argues that an examination of the experiences of rape victims, Holocaust survivors, and war veterans advances a feminist ontology of the relational self as simultaneously embodied, autonomous, and narrative. Trauma disrupts a person's relationship to her body, destroys the victim's sense of control over herself and environment, and obstructs her ability to develop an ongoing narrative of herself. Such a formulation reveals both the essential vulnerability and resiliency of the self, as well as its fundamental dependency on others.

Many traumas resulting from human inflicted violence and natural disasters involve immediate physical injuries to oneself or others or the threat of such injury. The acts of human inflicted violence degrade the victim from the status of a subject to that of an object, while the pain resulting from such injuries reduces her to flesh. But even when the wounds of the body heal, the long-term impact of trauma produces physiological, cognitive, and affective wounds. For some, traumatic memory binds them more closely to their physical self, while for others dissociation generates a splitting of mind from body. The vulnerability of the embodied self is glaring, and trauma often motivates a victim to alter her relationship to her body. Although Kerri was not physically injured in the robbery, the event had severe, long-term effects on her embodied self. Any slight elevation in her heartbeat could trigger a panic attack, even something as simple as climbing a single flight of stairs to our apartment. Sensory flashbacks like the ones Kerri experienced are common in trauma survivors. They are physiological manifestations of emotional damage, memories lodged into the physical body.

Extreme disaster or violence involves the loss of control over what happens during the traumatic event, but the subsequent posttraumatic effects also deprive the survivor of control. Through compulsory repetitions, "the experience of a trauma repeats itself, exactly and unremittingly, through the unknowing acts of the survivor and against his very will" (Caruth 1997, 2). What were previously voluntary responses, such as recalling events of one's past to conscious awareness, become, through nightmares and flashbacks, the involuntary reexperiencing of the traumatic event. As a result, Brison (1997, 28; 2002, 60) points out, not only does trauma alter what one can do, but it also alters what one *wants* to do. "If a rape victim is unable to walk outside without the fear of being assaulted again, she quickly loses the desire to go for a walk." Similarly, in an attempt to stave off panic attacks, Kerri avoided many activities she had previously enjoyed, including driving, exercise, and sexual intimacy. Her agency was increasingly inhibited, and her self-esteem diminished.

Trauma studies scholarship often emphasizes trauma's damage to the narrative self. Traumatic experience, particularly human inflicted trauma, produces a victim as the object of a story, not the subject of it. Feminist philosopher Seyla Benhabib (1992, 198), for example, builds on Hannah Arendt's description of the self as the product of a "web of narratives": "The self is both the teller of tales and that about whom tales are told. The individual with a coherent sense of self-identity is the one who succeeds in integrating these tales and perspectives into a meaningful life history. When the story of a life can only be told from the perspective of the others, then the self is a victim and sufferer who has lost control over her existence." Because traumatic events are experienced in fragmentary ways, memory is disrupted and the events are not assimilated into a coherent narrative. But, even as survivors begin to reconstruct the fragments of memory into a story, trauma resists representation.[3] The ways we typically use words interfere with the use of those words for representing harrowing experiences. In narrating more ordinary life events, I may describe an aggressive colleague barging into my office without permission as making me feel "violated." Next to this use of language, characterizing one's experience of rape as a "violation" is trivializing. Language also fails because traumatic experiences are incredible. That is, the events are so horrible that they elicit disbelief. At best, we say that they are indescribable, unspeakable, or inexpressible. These terms indicate language's inability to accurately represent traumatic events. Moreover, a person's psychological responses to life-threatening events are often unintelligible. She may experience feelings that have no corresponding words, not only for conveying to another but even for understanding herself.

A dramatic example of the impact of trauma on one's embodied, autonomous, and narrative self was conveyed to me by a friend and fellow anti-rape activist, who survived being raped and stabbed with a knife. Following a severe flashback, Kim lost the ability to speak for several months. Although there was nothing medically wrong with her vocal chords, she experienced a physical manifestation of the trauma through the loss of her voice. Subjectivity and voice are often considered synonymous; and without the ability to speak, Kim's sense of herself as the

author and agent of her own life was constrained. Her temporary muteness signaled how her encounter with violence threatened her status as
a subject in the world.

Recovering one's subjectivity requires, then, the reestablishment of
one's embodied agency, including the ability to authoritatively tell one's
own story. Many survivors compulsively tell and retell their stories as
part of the process of healing. Brison (1997, 24; 2002, 54) explains how
constructing such narratives can result in "mastering the trauma":

> Whereas traumatic memories (especially perceptual and emotional flash-
> backs) feel as though they are passively endured, narratives are the result
> of certain obvious choices (e.g., how much to tell to whom, in what order,
> etc.). This is not to say that the narrator is not subject to the constraints of
> memory or that the story will ring true however it is told. And the telling
> itself may be out of control, compulsively repeated. But one can control
> certain aspects of the narrative and that control, repeatedly exercised,
> leads to greater control over the memories themselves, making them less
> intrusive and giving them the kind of meaning that enables them to be
> integrated into the rest of life.

But, this cannot be done alone. As Brison (1997, 29; 2002, 62) argues,
the embodied, autonomous, and narrative self is relational. She writes,
"It is not sufficient for mastering the trauma to construct a narrative
of it: One must (physically, publicly) say or write (or paint or film) the
narrative, and others must see or hear it, in order for one's survival as an
autonomous self to be complete." Constructing a self-narrative, particularly after experiencing traumatic events, is an essential component of
resubjectivation, and it is an intersubjective process involving dialogue
with an empathetic other, a witness to trauma. But, who is this empathetic other? How does one become a witness to trauma?

Witnessing trauma is not like our usual, everyday ways of listening
to the stories told by others. In ordinary conversation, our interlocutors have a relatively easy time relaying their experiences and we have
an equally easy time understanding the experiences conveyed. While
there are, of course, better and worse listeners as well as better and worse
storytellers, we don't usually think of our role in telling or listening to
everyday experiences as requiring any extraordinary skills. In contrast,

stories of traumatic experiences are both difficult to hear and difficult to tell. Listening to stories of victimization requires, then, a special technique—witnessing trauma—a specific way of listening in which the witness is able to "hear" what cannot be adequately articulated by language. Witnessing the testimony of others is an intersubjective process involving shared responsibility for the reliving and reexperiencing of the traumatic event. This listener assists the victim in reclaiming her subject position by helping her get outside the event rather than being lost in it. Telling one's story to empathetic others facilitates the recovery process by granting the narrator the distance necessary to empathize with her own self. Feminist philosopher Kelly Oliver (2000, 40) argues that this process of witnessing inherently requires address-ability and response-ability: "Subjectivity develops through address and addressability from and to others. Without an 'external' witness, we cannot develop or sustain the 'internal' witness necessary for the ability to interpret and represent our experience, which is necessary for subjectivity and more essentially for both individual and social transformation. And, if subordination is taken to the extreme of objectification, then the possibility of address, of witnessing, becomes destroyed and with it the possibility of subjectivity. Only when someone else listens to me can I listen to myself." This reclamation of being able to be a witness to oneself is essential for recovery: survivors not only struggle to survive so that they may tell their stories, but tell their stories so that they may survive (Laub 1992).

Learning to Listen

Witnessing trauma requires particular attention not just to the content of the story, but also to the emotions conveyed by the speaker, that is, her psychological responses to the events. In other words, empathy plays a central role in listening to stories of trauma. While it may be that I have never had the same experience as the person with whom I empathize, it is very likely that I have experienced feelings like the ones that are described. Because I know what it is like to feel frightened, sad, ashamed, hurt, betrayed, and so on, I can imaginatively access an individual's experience by recalling the same emotions expressed. In witnessing trauma, I call upon the memories of these feelings, eliciting them from the past to bring them to present awareness. Psychotherapists

John Wilson and Rhiannon Thomas (2004) describe this process of "empathetic attunement" as a way of connecting with a client's *being*, not just relating to what the narrator says. Importantly, I do not imagine how "I would feel" in that situation. To do so would prevent me from empathizing since the client may respond differently than I would. In this way, "identification" is a misleading term. It is not the case that I can empathize only with people who are like me, or that I can empathize with people only insofar as I am able to locate some way that we are the same. To do so privileges the listener, maintaining the otherness of the survivor and preventing her from regaining subjectivity insofar as she would be the object of another's knowledge. We might think of this use of empathy as a version of what feminist philosopher Maria Lugones (1987) calls "world"-traveling and loving perception. Rather than perceiving others arrogantly, as objects "for me" or "against me," "world"-traveling and loving perception involves understanding others fully as subjects. Although I do not identify with her experience in the strict sense of identity as sameness, I do identify with her in the sense that I identify the emotions she experiences, access my own memories of experiencing those emotions, and bring them to the surface of consciousness.

The first time I was called to the ER, I felt a mixture of excitement and nervousness. I had clocked over four hundred phone hours, not to mention over one hundred hours of training in crisis intervention, suicide prevention, and rape survivor advocacy. But this was my first time doing what I wanted to do most: advocate for a victim during the rape reporting process. As a feminist activist, I wanted to make a difference, and I knew how important my role could be for helping facilitate a survivor's recovery. I threw on a pair of jeans and a sweatshirt, told my partner that I wasn't sure when I would be back that night, and drove to the hospital. On my way there, I drilled myself on my crisis intervention skills: reflect her feelings, avoid judgment, tell her what to expect, and, most importantly, help her feel safe and in control.

Empathy is regularly conflated with two related and sometimes overlapping emotional experiences: sympathy and emotional contagion. Sympathy is a feeling of compassion for another and is colloquially distinguished by referring to sympathy as feeling *for* someone and empathy as feeling *with* him or her. It most significantly differs from empathy in two ways. First, sympathy entails an acceptance of the other's perspective on the situation while empathy brackets such judgment; and, second, sympathy need not entail the same emotion as the other person while empathy does. Emotional contagion, the involuntary sharing of emotions between two or more people, occurs when one experiences the same emotions as others simply by being near them, as if one "caught" the feeling like one may "catch a cold." The two most significant differences between emotional contagion and empathy are that the former is an involuntary emotional response while the latter is a deliberately cultivated skill, and emotional contagion collapses the distinction between individuals and empathy preserves it. Empathy navigates between sympathy and emotional contagion by avoiding collapse into either sameness or difference. It involves a kind of sharing of experience, both in the sense that the other person shares her experience with you and in the sense that by empathizing you share in the experience.

I was nervous, but confident that I was ready to be the empathetic advocate that was needed. But when I got to the hospital, I lost my bearings. I wasn't sure exactly where to go or what to do. I made my way past the registration desk, introduced myself to the victim, Carla, and to the attending nurse, and explained my role. Okay, now. Time to be the empathetic listener and advocate needed. The problem was, though, that Carla wasn't talking. She sat staring blankly into space, numbly watching the nurse take her vitals. I panicked. How was I supposed to reflect her feelings when I had almost nothing to go on? Surely, I wasn't going to ask her how she was doing. That would be absurd. I made a few attempts, something like, "You're scared," or "You're in shock," but it sounded so awkward. I wanted to gather information so that I could be useful, but I felt like anything I could think to ask would be at best prying or at worst asking her to relive what she probably didn't want to think about. I knew that Carla would have to tell and retell the details of what had happened to medical personnel and to the police, and I didn't want to add to the list of those who barraged her with questions. Instead, I just stood there silently for what seemed like hours. I felt that my empathy skills were failing me.

Holocaust survivor and psychoanalyst Dori Laub emphasizes the importance of recognizing, respecting, and meeting silence when listening to testimonies of trauma. Such silence bears witness to the impossibility of testimony, the impossibility of representing the experience in language, not only to others but even to oneself. A sign of her inability to claim her status as a subject of this experience, Carla's muteness echoed Kim's. The dehumanizing effect of human-inflicted violence threatens to become totalizing, trapping the survivor inside her experience. Laub (1992, 69) writes, "Trauma survivors live not with memories of the past, but with an event that could not and did not proceed through to its completion, has no ending, attained no closure, and therefore, as far as its survivors are concerned, continues into the present and is current is every respect." Without an independent frame of reference to understand the event, the survivor believes herself to be blameworthy, feeling shame and humiliation. She accepts the perpetrator's narrative and can feel no compassion toward herself. Her "inner witness," necessary for a sense of herself as a subjective agent, is annihilated. With Carla at the ER, I kept looking for what was visible, and what I heard was silence. The gap between us felt insurmountable. Was I too eager, too anxious, to be fully present with her and listen to her silence?

The triage nurse brought us to a waiting room, where Carla's sister was waiting. Again, I introduced myself and explained my role. A rape survivor advocate accompanies victims to the hospital emergency room, police station, or courthouse, and assists them throughout the rape reporting process, I recited. Carla's sister was interested in learning about what happened. I felt that I was of little help in that department. I could, however, give her some information about what to expect. I explained that the nurse would complete a rape kit and police would get the Carla's statement and take photographs. And, I explained that, if necessary, I could intervene on Carla's behalf in an attempt to ensure that the rape reporting process did not add to her experience of victimization. For example, I would make sure that she was examined by a SANE nurse specially trained to complete rape kits;[4] I could help acquire emergency contraception medication in case the Catholic hospital refused to administer it; or I could request a female officer to photograph injuries if the presence of a male would make Carla uncomfortable. After a few minutes, the nurse returned to take Carla to an examination room. I offered to come with her, but she declined. I was frustrated but eager to help somehow, so I tried to be supportive to Carla's sister. I said something like, "You're worried about your sister," and she opened up. We talked for a bit, and I was able to tell her what I knew about rape trauma syndrome. I desperately wanted to provide her with as much information as I could so that she would understand what her sister would likely experience. Carla would need a witness, and could perhaps find one in her sister, to help her rebuild her narrative self.

At the next advocate meeting, I talked about meeting Carla. I suspected that much of my discomfort was due to my inexperience. Yet I also worried that some of the gap between Carla and me was cultural. I was a twenty-five-year-old, white graduate student who had enough privilege to volunteer at a Crisis Center. Carla was older than me, Hispanic, with young children and no college education. I knew that cultural differences can interfere with two people understanding and trusting one another in everyday circumstances, and Carla and I were encountering each other in extraordinary ones. I announced that the Crisis Center needed to improve its services for Latinas in our community. We needed Spanish-speaking volunteers, and translator services available for our advocacy program. Over the course of the next several months, I commissioned a fellow graduate student, Viviana, to translate our outreach and educational materials into Spanish, and I met Aida, an organizer for the Latino Coalition, at a training on child abuse prevention for Hispanic families. Aida and I met regularly, sharing our stories, strategizing about integrating our efforts, and helping each other in many other ways: she with my Spanish, and I with her algebra.

Response-ability

Not only can the poverty of language and the collapse of one's inner witness inhibit the ability to tell one's story of trauma, but the refusal of others to listen or the fear that one's story will not be believed creates an additional obstacle to telling. Many survivors are aware that telling their stories involves great risk. For people who are members of racial, ethnic, and sexual minorities, one's claims are all too frequently met with incredulity, and any testimony will likely be itself on trial. Not only does the telling itself entail the reliving of the events, but to talk about one's trauma without being heard can exacerbate the damage. Laub recounts a conversation between psychoanalysts and historians regarding the testimony of a survivor of Auschwitz. The historians discounted the survivor's testimony because it conflicted with the known facts (only one chimney was destroyed, not four) and the events she observed were insignificant (the uprising failed). In their search for empirical truth, they insisted that this woman's story was not worth listening to. In contrast, the psychoanalysts insisted on the value of the Holocaust survivor's testimony regarding the uprising at Auschwitz. Rather than looking to verify the propositional content of her testimony, Laub and his colleagues heard a different kind of truth, the very possibility of the impossible, of survival and resistance: "She had come, indeed, to testify, not to the empirical number of the chimneys, but to resistance, to the affirmation of survival, to the breakage of the frame of death. . . . It is not merely her speech, but the very boundaries of silence which surround it, which attest, today as well as in the past, to this assertion of resistance" (Laub 1992, 62). The contrast between the historians and the psychoanalysts is remarkable. The former listen with their own agenda, carrying what they know into the listening enterprise, searching for consistency or inconsistency, and ultimately producing silence. The latter listen with an openness to receive the story the narrator transmits, willing to hear not only what is said but what is unsaid, discerning the meaning of its silences.

The importance of being nonjudgmental, in not judging testimony for its veracity and also in not judging a victim's choices, always made a lot of sense to me. My role was to be neither a therapist nor a police investigator. Instead, the witness takes the person in crisis as she presents herself, and provides a sounding board for her to decide, based on her own values, what to do. When I first started my training, I assumed that I would have trouble handling my own feelings regarding victims who decided not to report the violence that they experienced. But, instead, I found myself easily accepting when the caller refused to tell authorities for fear of retaliation or fear of not being believed. I empathized with the longing to try to contain the trauma in the past rather than revisit it. And when another volunteer expressed disbelief about one of the caller's stories—she was sure that the young woman was just "trying to get attention"—it didn't matter whether the story she was telling was an accurate, full description of what had happened to her. I had talked with her several times on the phone and once in person, and I was sure that *something* had happened to victimize her. Maybe it wasn't her stepfather as she had claimed, but she was clearly undergoing unbearable events and needed help. In our next phone conversation, I invited the young woman to attend the survivor's support group. I was determined to never be one of those people who thought a victim was lying.

In order to empathize successfully, the witness to trauma must work to set aside her own judgments about what is heard, focusing completely on the story told by the narrator. In order to maintain a nonjudgmental attitude, the witness brackets her own viewpoint regarding the events described in order to help the speaker explore her own. Narratives of trauma are true in the sense that they are descriptions of traumatic experience, of lived events that defy easy integration into propositional, empirically verifiable knowledge. This is not the truth sought after by the historian or courtroom. To listen as a witness to trauma requires, then, suspending judgments about accuracy to make way for empathizing with the narrator. This way of responding emotionally when witnessing trauma is, then, a deliberate, conscious emotional response that develops out of the listener's commitment to a set of judgments or principles aimed at validating the victim's experience and making a space for the victim's voice to be heard.

I tried not to stare as the nurse laid out a piece of paper for Jane to stand on as she undressed. Each piece of clothing was placed into a bag, along with the carefully folded paper she stood on. Jane put on a hospital gown, and sat on the table. I stood next to her and explained the evidence collection procedure. In contrast to Carla, Jane talked easily, almost chatty about what she had experienced. I held Jane's hand as the nurse asked intimate questions about what the attacker had done, seeking information about where he may have left evidence on her body, the site of violence. As she talked about a man entering her home, about what he looked like, about being afraid, the nurse completed a vaginal exam, carefully placing swabs into little manila envelopes.

Putting aside one's own feelings regarding the content of a victim's story is crucial. Otherwise, those reactions could get in the way of fully hearing the story, or worse, they could get in the way of allowing victims to tell their stories. The importance of reestablishing agency and voice weighs heavily, and the witness must work hard to foster rather than interfere with the restoration of the victim's autonomy. Even when a victim makes choices that the witness believes would be harmful, she must not pressure the victim, particularly since the victim's integrity as a subject is vulnerable. Sexual abuse survivor and writer Dorothy Allison (2010) describes this as a situation in which you are "unable to have your own reactions to be useful." If a person feels negatively judged, she will likely censor her story to avoid further judgment. This is especially true for rape survivors who are often stigmatized. To engage in analysis when listening is to regard the narrator's story as fallible, that the events perhaps didn't happen the way that they are described or that important pieces of the story may be missing. Rape survivors already approach bearing witness with an enormous amount of pressure to censor themselves. The social presumption that survivors of rape are at fault or lying quickly puts them on the defensive, and this presumption is often internalized. In addition, as women who are socialized to the caretaking role, rape survivors may censor their stories in an effort to protect the listener from the painful information therein.

Two police officers entered the room to take Jane's statement, and she nodded that, yes, she wanted me to stay. As Jane told her story to the officer, I felt uneasy, but in a very different way than in my advocacy experience with Carla. I was uncomfortable that both she and the nurse were making a big deal about the race of her attacker: earlier when I arrived at the ER, the nurse had whispered to me, "She was raped by a *black* guy!" I was well aware of how the archetype of the black male rapist of white women had been used to justify violence against black men. It has fed stereotypes of black male criminality and white female helplessness, and left a legacy of tension between the antiracism and feminist movements. I also understood how this trope minimized the harm to the majority of rape victims of intraracial sexual violence by presuming that it is somehow worse for a white woman to be raped by a black male than any other man. I had to keep swallowing my own thoughts and feelings so that I could fulfill my role. In that moment, my duty was to affirm the survivor's feelings regardless of the rationality or irrationality behind those feelings in order to help rebuild her sense of self.

Being able to bracket feelings doesn't mean that the witness lacks strong emotional responses to the story. That would be impossible. But the witness must be able to distinguish her emotional responses into two kinds. The first of these, the emotional response I have been describing as a kind of reflection or mirroring of the narrator's, is an empathetic emotional response. Witnessing trauma requires a deep emotional involvement with the experience of victims, as well as an ambiguous doubling of one's consciousness.[5] Empathy allows one to identify with another's emotional experiences while simultaneously maintaining awareness that those emotional experiences are not one's own. The emotions are both "mine" and "not-mine." They are mine in the sense that I experience emotions through empathy. Yet, these emotions are not-mine in the sense that they are reflective of those experienced by the storyteller, mirroring those belonging to another. The second, the emotional response that is bracketed, is a reactive emotional response. The reactive emotional response, on the other hand, is more clearly "mine." It reflects the listener's visceral response to what she witnesses. Arising from the listener's individual past experiences, beliefs, and values, it is a product of habit and socialization. Most importantly, it reflects the listener's judgment and evaluation of what she hears. Reactive feelings and judgments arise out of one's worldview, including broader sociocultural attitudes that, once reflected upon, the listener may or may not approve of.

At the next advocate meeting, I talked about meeting Jane and my discomfort. One of the other advocates conveyed a story of how she had told a black male detective that he should not interview the survivor she was working with because the woman's attacker was a black male. She thought that having him interview the survivor, who was white, would further traumatize her. I was conflicted. By her comment, it seemed that she thought that the victim's race, not sex, was what motivated the rape. The belief is that if one black man commits rape, then all black men reinvoke the experience of being raped; but in this case, the assumption links rape with blackness and not with maleness. I worried that such attitudes were not being interrogated for their harmful and discriminatory social impact: they perpetuate the stereotype of the black male rapist of white women; they ignore the use of this stereotype to regulate black male behavior and white female behavior; they render invisible the widespread rape of women of color; they minimize the harm to women of color and most white women who are raped; they obscure how racialized myths of womanhood delegitimize the rape claims of women of color; and they contribute to a discriminatory punishment disparity based on the race of the victim. At the same time, I had to acknowledge that the encounter of witnessing is not the space to challenge such attitudes. Regardless of the beliefs underlying a survivor's emotional response, the witness's role is to work toward affirming her autonomy.

While the empathetic emotional response is one of the most important tools in acquiring accurate information about the victim's experience of trauma, the reactive emotional response is an important tool in acquiring accurate information about the witness's underlying beliefs and values insofar as it is a reflection of the listener's past experience rather than the victim's. This, then, allows the witness to engage in critical self-reflection. For example, in listening to a rape survivor's story, I may find myself adhering to rape-supportive beliefs when I pass judgment on a victim's actions (what was she thinking when she agreed to go up to his room alone?) or choices (if she cared about what could happen to other women, she'd report this to the police!). Though it can be very frustrating—and easy to feel guilty—to discover that my reactions replicate the kinds of attitudes I struggle against, part of being accountable for my work entails personal transformation. I can also discover opportunities for social transformation. For example, witnessing trauma allows me to observe how medical professionals and law enforcement agents respond to victims, and these can motivate campaigns for reeducation and policy change.

Answering the Call

Listening as a witness to trauma is not a passive effort. It is an active process requiring the witness to share the responsibility of constructing the narrator's story. This entails asking open-ended questions, reflecting back to the narrator both what is said and what is unsaid, and responding to her needs. As Oliver (2001, 18) writes, "If subjectivity is the process of witnessing sustained through response-ability, then we have a responsibility to response-ability, to the ability to respond. We have an obligation not only to respond but also to respond in a way that opens up rather than closes off the possibility of response by others." While witnessing trauma is a dialogic, intersubjective process, it is not symmetrical. Although they share a common goal, the survivor-narrator and listener-witness play different roles. The survivor's status as a subject in the world is precarious; the traumatic event has threatened it with annihilation. The listener's subjectivity is more stable, and with the power to listen or refuse to listen, she carries great responsibility. The aim is not mutual understanding in the usual sense of each interlocutor gaining understanding of each other's perspective, but rather a process in which both parties focus on the restoration of one perspective, that of the survivor. And, in restoring the survivor's authority as a subject of her own narrative, the listener helps restore the survivor's agency.

Maria came to my office visibly upset. She had lost her textbook, and the exam was next week. I consoled her, offering to loan her my copy of the text to prepare for the exam. But Maria's distress did not subside. She said that this was the last straw; she was ready to give up. I could hear something that she wasn't saying. Almost instinctively I asked her whether she was thinking about suicide. She was, and she had a plan. None of her loved ones knew about her feelings. And, although she had been seeing a mental health professional, she could not promise to wait for her next appointment before hurting herself. Maria faced many responsibilities and couldn't bear them anymore. I told her that I could hear that she was overwhelmed and hopeless. I told her that I could also hear how much she cared about her loved ones and her future. Since I couldn't get her to promise that she wouldn't hurt herself before her doctor's appointment, I asked if she would promise to call me before she did anything to hurt herself. Not looking me in the eye, she agreed.

My crisis intervention training manual emphasizes the semantic root of the word "crisis," signaling both danger and opportunity: "A crisis is a critical turning point at which both danger and opportunity exist together. In fact, the semantic root of the word 'crisis' is the Greek word 'krinein,' meaning to decide. This indicates that a crisis is a turning point during which, by definition, there will be some change for the better or worse" (Stepich 2010, 9). Witnessing in the face of an emergency requires a delicate balancing between affirming autonomy and preserving bodily integrity. The witness takes more responsibility for the pacing of the interaction by asking probing questions to assess the danger, and may need to engage in a higher level of intrusiveness to make decisions about getting help. Suicidal individuals may need someone to help determine whether the risk is immediate and to send help if needed; victims of domestic violence may need help determining the extent of injury or threat and identifying safe places to retreat; and, those who are in need of food or shelter may need help locating community resources to assist them. At the same time, maintaining empathetic connection and minimizing intrusive intervention are essential for respecting the person's autonomy. These can be achieved by acknowledging the person's ambivalence about seeking help, by making contracts with her to not injure herself while talking, or by asking her to contact rescue services herself. But, it is *her* call.

A day later my phone rang; it was Maria. "I'm on the edge of the Golden Gate Bridge." I thanked her for keeping her promise to me. She replied, "I'll probably regret it later." I knew that she could be right, depending on her determination to end her life. Maria wouldn't agree to call 911, but she did give me permission to call them on her behalf and promised not to jump before I called her back. I explained the situation to the dispatch and was connected to the station at the bridge. They had questions for me that I couldn't answer: *exactly where* on the bridge is she? I was so mad at myself for not knowing the answer. I called Maria back, got her location as best as I could, and again asked her to promise not to jump before I called again. I was so scared that this extra step would be too much for her, but she agreed. I called the bridge police and told them where she was, and then quickly called her back. Her voicemail answered. I called again. The phone rang and rang, but no answer. I was worried that she had jumped or that the wind had knocked her down, but finally, she answered. Relieved, I again thanked her for keeping her promise to me. I waited on the phone with her until they arrived, trying to keep her talking, and panicking each time she was silent. After what seemed like an eternity, I could hear an officer in the background. "Ma'am. I'm here to help you down."

Trauma survivors are especially at risk for suicide. Because trauma's impact disrupts the survivor's relationship to her body, robs her of control over herself and her environment, and compromises her ability to construct a self-narrative, suicide can represent a survivor's attempt to gain control over herself, even if it is a permanent foreclosing of her future. The skills entailed in witnessing trauma—hearing both what is said and what is unsaid, affirming agency, and responding to the address of the other—can forge a connection between the victim and witness that opens an alternative way to reclaim one's embodied, autonomous, and narrative self.

Bearing Witnessing

Witnessing trauma is anything but easy. It requires maintaining full presence with suffering and the fact that this suffering is often imposed by other human beings. To be open and connect with a victim's experience is terrifying. The witness enters a world filled with fear, shame, and guilt, hearing what it is like to have one's bodily integrity violated, to be treated with disrespect and disdain, and to be reduced by another to the status of a nonperson. Allison (2010) describes it as "being present in the place you most don't want to be." It is heart-wrenching to care about victims when one is powerless to prevent or repair the harms done against them, and easy to feel guilty for it. Witnesses to trauma may experience nightmares, bouts of depression, and feelings of despair, numbness, and suicidal thoughts. Psychologists refer to these effects as a form of trauma called compassion fatigue, secondary trauma, or vicarious trauma. Wilson and Thomas (2004, 7) label this collection of symptoms "*traumatoid states*, a form of occupational stress which results from work with trauma survivors." Bearing witnessing thus requires awareness of and resisting the possible damage to one's own sense of self.

One technique for bearing witnessing involves narrating the witnessing process itself. At the Crisis Center, we called this "processing," a kind of debriefing technique I learned in my training. At the completion of a conversation, volunteers document the contact in writing, recording what was said by both speaker and listener. For particularly difficult situations, we discuss the contact with other volunteers either when changing shifts or during monthly meetings. Doing so provides a record of our activities, informs other volunteers about the situation in case the contact needs help later, and allows volunteers to assist each other in improving their skills. It also enables the listener to work through his or her own feelings regarding the situation. Processing is a way of witnessing to oneself, or in more difficult situations, enlisting the help of others to do so. This allows the listener to focus attention on his or her reactive emotional responses, to explore them, and to conduct some self-care to make sure that these feelings are given expression. Since the empathetic emotional response displaces the witness's voice in order to elicit the voice of the survivor, processing ensures that the listener does not lose his or her own narrative self when witnessing trauma.

Processing can also function as a tool for reeducation. Since the reactive emotional response is a product of acculturation and thus a reflection of larger sociocultural attitudes, processing allows the witness to examine his or her beliefs and attitudes. Describing one's own reactive emotional responses places them up against the values and principles that are deliberately cultivated through the empathetic emotional response. As I discussed earlier, it helps the witness challenge the larger sociocultural attitudes that have been internalized much like the empathetic emotional response attempts to intervene in the survivor's internalization of those attitudes. This promotes the witness's autonomous self insofar as one can work in a community of activists to effect social change. One of the most rewarding projects for me was self-defense training geared specifically for women survivors of violence. Together, as witnesses and survivors, we explored our embodied selves, building new habits of physical and emotional confidence.

Arguably, bearing witnessing is more than just a coping mechanism; it is also the means by which witnessing trauma is possible. An effective witness to trauma connects with survivors without collapsing the boundaries between self and other. In the process, two narratives are written. Not only does the witness assist survivors in constructing their self-narrative, but the survivor also constructs her own self-narrative as an agent of change. Through witnessing trauma, the status of victims is changed from object to subject of a narrative, and through critical self-reflection, the listener develops into a more empathetic and responsible witness. While the strands of theory and practice are often in tension, competing with each other at the site of trauma, they need each other. But this need is fulfilled not just by practicing theory or by theorizing practice, but by deliberately transforming ourselves and our world.

NOTES

1 I want to thank everyone at the Lafayette Crisis Center for teaching me so much: the skills I gained have served me well beyond the Center. Thanks to the organizers of the 2010 "New Directions in Trauma Studies: Bridging Theory and Practice" for allowing me to present parts of this essay and introducing me to the inspiring scholars included in the program, and especially to Monica Casper and Eric Wertheimer for pushing this essay to be more than it was. Thanks also to Martha Fineman and the Emory University School of Law for supporting my visit to the Feminism and Legal Theory Project, during which I started this essay. And very special thanks to my dear-

est friend and colleague Liora Gubkin Malicdem for her at times desperately needed encouragement, suggestions, and insight.

2 For several of these experiences, the survivors have graciously granted me permission to use their names and stories. For others, I have no way of contacting the survivors, and so have created new names and left out any identifying information in order to maintain confidentiality.

3 This discussion of the limits of representing trauma is especially influenced by Liora Gubkin (2007). On the insufficiency of language to describe traumatic experiences, see, for example, Delbo (1995) and Jacobs ([1861] 2013). On trauma's destruction of one's ability to narrate even to oneself, see, for example, Felman and Laub (1992).

4 SANE is the acronym for sexual assault nurse examiner.

5 W. E. B. Du Bois's (1903) term "double consciousness" has been used by both critical race and feminist theorists to describe a feature of psychological oppression. For example, see Bartky (1990). But here I am invoking the term in a different light, using Iris Marion Young's (2005) description of pregnant embodiment for inspiration.

13

Documenting Disaster

Hurricane Katrina and One Family's Saga

REBECCA HANKINS AND AKUA DUKU ANOKYE

In the United States, "trauma," "disaster," and "catastrophe" have often been defined as moments that reveal our best imagined communities, that bring us together in spirit and action, events that make us proud of our national belonging. After the bombing of Pearl Harbor and, more recently, after the terrorist attacks of September 11, 2001, historians, librarians, educators, social scientists, and archivists have been called upon to chronicle the lives of survivors—to capture and record their stories so as to ensure that we have not only the "official" accounts, but the reactions of those impacted beneath the view of political history and its narratives of power. We owe a debt of gratitude to librarians and historians at the Library of Congress for the project "After the Day of Infamy: 'Man-on-the-Street' Interviews Following the Attack on Pearl Harbor." The archivists understood that only through documentary accounts would we preserve the memory of that day for future generations, especially once the survivors had perished. We witnessed similar projects developed to record popular accounts of the attacks of 9/11. The Library of Congress, once again, enlisted librarians, archivists, and historians in capturing stories for the project "Witness and Response: September 11 Acquisitions at the Library of Congress." The uses of oral history to capture the responses of those who have witnessed trauma— first responders, families who suffer the loss of loved ones—allow future generations the opportunity to hear and see these events not merely through the filter of broadcast media, or of historiography, but more immediately through the voices of those affected.

An event must be understood in all its problematic, inspiring, and even reprehensible perspectives. Documenting the experience of Hurricane Katrina survivors and those who supported them offered opportunities for scholarly and survivor collaboration, and as a result a multistate project was created in 2005 called "In the Wake of the Hurricanes: A Coalition Effort to Collect Our Stories and Rebuild Our Culture."[1] With support from the Louisiana Folklife Program at Louisiana Tech University, spearheaded by Professor Susan Roach, the coalition gathered academics, scholars, and community activists to assist those affected by Hurricanes Katrina and Rita in reconnecting with their communities and cultures. In our case, a multigenerational African American family presents voices that are often missing from the "official" historical record. A willingness to reconsider oral histories as a strategic tool in documenting historical events and disasters has brought awareness that we have begun to realize in highlighting the experiences of people of color who suffer contemporary trauma.

This oral history project, focused on the impact of the storm on the Hankins family, provides an opportunity to fill in some of the gaps in the larger cultural narrative about shared experiences of ordinary people caught up in an extraordinary event. This multigenerational African American family is typical of many throughout metropolitan New Orleans. They consist of the working class, the working poor, students, homeowners, apartment dwellers, business owners, and first responders. Their stories are told here via oral histories taken a few months after Hurricane Katrina and then again five years later, on the anniversary of the disaster. Our subjects speak about what community means to them, the government's response to the disaster, their feelings of alienation from the political and civil spheres, and pervasive and deeply entrenched racism. Finally, the stories project what the future might hold for their beloved city and its people.

African Americans in New Orleans

New Orleans has been said to be the most European of America's cities. But for the majority of its residents, it has also been the most traditional of American cities, with the vestiges of slavery firmly in place. One need consider only that the defining case of the nineteenth century for blacks concerned a New Orleans man of color, Homer Plessy, the litigant in *Plessy v. Ferguson*, which institutionalized the "separate but equal" doctrine and

Figure 13.1. Left to right, front row: Hawah (black scarf), Muhammad Shajad, Sajidah Bagel; second row: Salih (dreads), Ahmad (cap), Fatimah (pink top); back row: Nafisah (floral scarf), Muhammad Abdush Shakur, Salimah (black top), and Rebecca Hankins (blue scarf)

legitimized Jim Crow laws. The dissenting judge, Justice Harlan, expressed prophetic wisdom about the effect of the decision: "For the Plessy majority and for the dissent, for white supporters and white opponents of segregation, white over black was to continue, as a certainty, 'for all time.'"[2]

Disenfranchisement and disparity in the allocation of resources and power—that is, de facto "separate but equal" status—has continued into the present. The neglect that the African American population experienced in New Orleans, both prior to and after Hurricane Katrina, is reflected in impoverished communities, one of the poorest educational systems in the nation, and an overabundance of low-wage service jobs. Systemic failures in New Orleans, conditions that have created a permanent underclass, are widely known and discussed. As New Orleans City Council member Cynthia Willard-Lewis has said about the Ninth Ward, a predominantly black area decimated by Katrina, "this is a community with many economic challenges—chronic and systemic poverty in a core group."[3] She states further, "Poor education worsens the effects of concentrated poverty and extends its reach into every area of black life." These preexisting conditions within New Orleans's black community *exponentially magnified* the trauma of the Katrina survivors. Michael Eric Dyson, in his discussion of the Middle Passage, suggests a connection between Katrina and slavery: "This most recent tragedy harkened back even further: the deadly waters of slavery's middle passage flooded the black collective memory. One of the unifying themes of slavery and storms in the black imagination is the traumatic dispersal of black folk across rugged, even resistant, geographies."[4] The analogy is enhanced when we consider that what caused the displacement of people was the flooding of New Orleans when the levees broke, forcing families to flee and thus reproducing the diasporic separation of family members.

Sadly, the oral histories lend a great deal of credence to this narrative of life pre–and post–Hurricane Katrina. Many in the black community in New Orleans believe that during Hurricane Betsy in the 1960s, the levies were dynamited to save the French Quarter, flooding black neighborhoods and killing scores of residents. The oral narratives from Katrina reinforce the historical perception among the black community that black life is cheap, and often to be sacrificed in the service of landed white commercial power, in New Orleans.

***

The Hankins children had traveled with friends twice to College Station, Texas, to avoid potential storms during the 2005 hurricane season,[5] only to have them pass the city without harm. Staying abreast of Katrina's movements, there was a general feeling among many in the family that this was unlike anything they had experienced in more than twenty years of living in New Orleans. In 1998, they escaped severe damage from Hurricane Georges by driving to Baton Rouge, a two-hour trip that took over ten hours. On the weekend of August 26–28, 2005, the upgrade of the storm to a Category 5 hurricane, coupled with Mayor Nagin's late mandatory evacuation order, forced everyone to rethink the strategy of *waiting out the storm*. Various broadcast media conveyed news of the possibly devastating impact of this storm to the New Orleans community, and the Hankins family, once again, began to flee to College Station. By Monday morning, August 29, there were fifteen family and friends from Louisiana in a small, three-bedroom duplex there.

When Katrina made landfall and reports of the levee breaches circulated, everyone remained glued to televisions sets. Stunned by the drama as it unfolded, they wondered about stranded friends and colleagues back home. They watched in horror as water engulfed the cities of Chalmette and New Orleans. Chalmette, where many of the Hankins family lived, with all the toxic chemicals and oil refineries housed there, was totally underwater. Following weeks of the emotional aftermath of Katrina, the Hankins family began to realize that life in College Station would be the fate of the now nineteen evacuees.

Survival stories can appear imaginary, fragmented, or disjointed, and this is typical of those who have undergone traumatic experiences. Yet the stories also speak of recovery and resiliency as the subjects struggle to literally remake and move forward with their lives. Understanding and acknowledging symptoms related to posttraumatic stress disorder (PTSD), as defined in the *Diagnostic and Statistical Manual of Mental Disorders* (*DSM-IV-TR*; American Psychiatric Association 2000), provides a framework for recovery. Symptoms of Katrina victims are recognizable in the three *DSM* symptom clusters listed below:

1. Reexperiencing symptoms: intense psychological distress, physiological reactivity, and exposure to internal or external cues that symbolize or resemble aspects of traumatic event (fear of heavy rain, lack of permanence, loss of feelings of security);
2. Avoidant symptoms: marked diminished interest or participation in significant activities; feelings of detachment or estrangement from others; restricted range of affect (unable to experience loving feelings); sense of foreshortened future (not expecting to have a career, a marriage, a childhood, or normal lifespan);
3. Hyperarousal symptoms: difficulty falling or staying asleep; irritability or outbursts of anger; exaggerated startle response; difficulty concentrating; or hypervigilance.[6]

The narratives embody many of the symptoms subjects displayed throughout their ordeal of escaping the hurricane and in the aftermath, as they attempted to recover their lives. The most prevalent set of symptoms displayed initially was *avoidant symptoms*, the deliberate need to disconnect from what was happening in New Orleans; there was an increasing lack of interest and a sense of detachment from what was going on. As the realization of the extent of devastation became known, *hyperarousal symptoms* set in for many of the victims, with many becoming hypervigilant about storms, often seeing them as precursors to flooding and loss of life. The emergency planning that many residents had in place failed them, prompting rethinking of any permanent or long-term decisions because of the uncertainty of life in New Orleans.

Reexperiencing symptoms have been the more permanent and frequent reactions displayed by Hankins family oral reports. Careers have been put on hold, relationships have broken, and drug addiction and estrangement have affected some of the participants. Coming to grips with the loss of everything and continually rediscovering these losses reinforce the lack of permanence. The Katrina disaster and the lack of appropriate and timely responses subjected victims to serious threats of harm to life, physical integrity, and their children, spouses, close relatives, and homes. The sudden destruction of homes and communities, the pain of seeing or hearing of loved ones, neighbors, and friends who had been killed or injured, and fear, terror, and helplessness heighten the anxiety. Ultimately, the Katrina disaster led families such as the Hankins clan to experience long-term exile from their homes, the integrity of the extended family, and the communities to which they were devoted. For these Katrina survivors, it has been an ongoing struggle, with many of them successfully facing the challenges, but some ultimately succumbing to trauma's effects.

The Hankins Family Narratives

The Hankins's immediate family is not native to New Orleans, having migrated from Michigan to Louisiana to find a better life. In the tradition of many of their black ancestors who had at one point traveled from the Deep South to northern states to escape racism and oppression, the Hankins family's migration back to the South in 1984 was consistent with a shift in populations that was occurring all over the South: "Following a net loss of almost 300,000 Blacks in the second half of the 1960s, the South had a small net gain in 1970–75, which increased to over 100,000 in 1975–80 and almost 200,000 in 1985–89. . . . Then during 1990–95, the South had an unprecedented net in movement of over 300,000 Blacks into the region."[7]

New Orleans, with its creole culture, Marie Laveau, Congo Square, the birthplace of jazz, a celebrated cultural and artistic community, and a "New South" that promised a fresh start, was hard to resist. Unfortunately for the Hankins family and many other residents of New Orleans, the 1985 failures of the oil and gas industry in concert with the failed policies of city government forced the region's economy into a state of depression. Many African Americans switched to survival mode as the city rapidly transformed from lucrative oil field work to a minimum-

Figure 13.2. Rachel Washington

wage service industry dependent on tourism. The patriarch of the family, Dwight Handara Hankins, notes the shift in the population:

> Generally speaking, New Orleans for black people, at least, was not a good place to earn a living. . . . There was not a go-getter type of mentality in New Orleans's community and culture, it is more like just trying to get by. . . . Everybody recognizes the strength of the culture of New Orleans, but truthfully it was only appreciated from a distance. You know, the people who maintain the culture who are the culture are the ones who are suffering the most economically and being deprived the most politically.[8]

The people of New Orleans would discover that the city had neither the infrastructure nor the will to take care of many of its citizens, a fact that would play out on the world stage with Hurricane Katrina.

Twenty-two-year-old Rachel Washington Hankins, married to Salih Hankins, was born and raised in Louisiana. Rachel, Salih, and brother Muhammad Shajad Hankins lived in Chalmette, Louisiana, approximately twenty minutes by car from New Orleans. "I like the cultural aspect of the region. . . . If you walk down the streets people say 'hi' whether they know you or not; people were very familiar. It was very peaceful and quiet. . . . All of my family mostly stayed in New Orleans

and the surrounding areas and we would get together quite often, especially on weekends, go bowling, go out to eat, spend time together."[9] Rachel was an undergraduate social work student at Southern University
at New Orleans, a historically black university. Her working-class family had lived in the Chalmette/New Orleans area for over three generations; she was one of the first to attend college. For Rachel, the stories of
Hurricane Betsy influenced her thinking about Hurricane Katrina: "My
mom and my dad told me that when Betsy came they actually blew the
levies in the Ninth Ward and St. Bernard Parish to protect the uptown
and downtown areas. . . . I was thinking they may do the same thing to
us again."[10] She stayed behind to help her mother and ten other family
members leave New Orleans. They drove to Texas and were helped by
a church in Jasper, Texas, before she was reunited with her husband in
College Station. They lost everything to Katrina, including their home,
two cars, and most of their household goods. Her family was dispersed
to Tennessee, Texas, Florida, and Colorado.

Rachel talks about her initial response after evacuating from New
Orleans, noting that she did not pay much attention to the coverage of
the storm and felt very distant from events. She talks about not listening
to the news until days after the evacuation, a manifestation of avoidant
symptoms: "The first week I was kind of detached, it was impersonal to
me, it's not that bad." After the first week, she started to hear news about
the destruction and people who were in desperate circumstances, and
she became more concerned and attentive to the news. She also thought
about not returning to New Orleans because of the devastation, but she
and her husband did return, moving back to a hotel in downtown New
Orleans so that she could finish her education. Her husband, Salih, talks
about the difficulty of finding a community when they returned: "The
neighborhoods are different, they are not people you know, no longer
family-oriented the way it used to be, not that community type feel."[11]
They eventually found a home in their old neighborhood in Chalmette,
where Rachel's mom and sister had moved, also. Rachel finished a master's degree in social work, and she and Salih now live in Webster, Texas.

For those who have never experienced an evacuation, it is difficult to
explain. Many left New Orleans with only the clothing on their backs
and were happy to have a modest mode of transportation away from certain death. It can take hours to get out of a city like New Orleans that is

surrounded by water and has very few exit points. There are two options: I-10 east or I-10 west, depending on whether you are heading toward Texas or Mississippi. Creating an orderly flow is strategic for a smooth evacuation, so the government's implementation of a timely contra flow (or lane reversal) on the highways can be crucial. Dwight Handara Hankins talks about the problems he faced leaving New Orleans:

> They really should have started the contra flow across the bridge on the west bank or at least downtown so that [the] majority of the people could get on the contra flow downtown and head on out the city. So consequently it took us two hours just to get from the cemetery on I-10, the Pontchartrain Express Way to where the contra flow started which was around the Causeway somewhere around there. . . . Normally a five-minute drive, it took us almost two hours because we were in that traffic jam, people's cars were breaking down, . . . because it was an emergency situation people were just trying to get out. People were walking, people were on bikes, you know, people were driving vehicles that they would not normally drive because it was a life-and-death situation as far as people know, so we finally got to the contra flow and we headed on out.[12]

Before Katrina, Dwight Hankins was a self-employed electrician and worked on many of the large events that came to New Orleans. While in the city, he recognized the trauma that many of the residents were experiencing and sought the help of a group of educators and psychologists from the University of Missouri–Columbia's International Center for Psychosocial Trauma, eventually assisting them in hosting two workshops on mental health and trauma for area schoolteachers and activists.

The medical and mental health systems in New Orleans have long been underfunded, but after Katrina the systems were chronically in crisis mode. As psychiatrist and mental health scholar Bruce D. Perry notes, "Even before Katrina we were drowning our front-line child care providers, our educators, our child welfare workers and our mental health providers. . . . To these overwhelmed services we will be adding hundreds of thousands of children."[13] Nevertheless, the governor of Louisiana continued to *cut* resources for mental health facilities and services. Mental health is not the only problem faced by returning residents; crime, education, and housing have been critical obstacles.

Especially housing. Housing costs have increased exponentially since Katrina, pricing many former residents out of their old neighborhoods. The Oxfam America report "Mirror on America" notes that "82,000 apartments were damaged or destroyed by Katrina and Rita, but the highest official estimate proposes to replace only about 25,000 afford- able units. . . . Full recovery is possible only when affordable homes are coupled with secure, decent jobs."[14] Post-Katrina, Dwight Handara Hankins lived in uptown New Orleans until the lack of a stable income forced him to return to College Station, Texas. He now resides in Hous- ton, where he works as an electrician while also remaining active in the Islamic community.

Sajidah Bagel Hankins, twenty-two, speaks about her ordeal of leav- ing with her two children and fiancé, Lee Williams:

> The night before (Saturday) filled up on gas . . . we left New Orleans at
> about 10:30 (a.m. Sunday) and made it to Shreveport at four o'clock in the
> morning. Shreveport is only a five-hour drive; five hours because we had
> to go out of Louisiana into Mississippi, drove a little up into Mississippi,
> and then went back into Louisiana. That's how we had to do it because the
> traffic was so bad and I was so tired. We were in Hattiesburg [Mississippi]
> and I was so tired from driving and I said we should just stop and Lee
> said, no we can't stop because this is where the hurricane is going to hit.
> And I wanted to stop because I was just so tired, but he said no come on
> we have to keep going. Good thing we did, because we would have been
> right there in Hattiesburg right where the eye of the storm hit. I'm glad I
> just got the strength to just drive.[15]

Pre-Katrina, Sajidah and Lee were part of the working poor but upwardly mobile, looking to purchase a home. Lee was a manager at one of the restaurants in New Orleans. They left just before Katrina, traveled to Shreveport to be near Lee's family, and then went to College Station to be near the other Hankins family members. Less than six months after their evacuation, Lee was called back to manage a restaurant on the Westbank of New Orleans, so they left College Station. Their lives since have been up and down, characterized by estrangement and recon- ciliation, and they have struggled to maintain a healthy and supportive relationship. They are both working to get their lives back on track.

Figure 13.3sajidah Bagel Hankins

Sajidah is a student at Delgado Community College, working toward a degree in criminal law.

Fatimah Hankins, her husband Lawrence Sylvan, their three children, and their two foster sons were forced to leave their close-knit community in Marrero, Louisiana. The Sylvan family, natives of New Orleans, also included Lawrence's mother, sisters, and brother, all living in the same neighborhood. A working-class family, they were childhood friends of the Hankins children. Two days before Katrina hit New Orleans, they packed up and drove to College Station to be with family. Lawrence's mother and one sister moved to Dallas and another sister and her family moved to Georgia. Again, the separation and dispersal of families increased stress and trauma on this once tight-knit family. Fatimah speaks about her children and the struggle to adapt to new surroundings:

> My oldest son Khalil he wanted to go see his cousins and I tried to explain to him that we were staying in another state now and that he couldn't just pick up and go right around the corner and see them. He didn't understand why, but as time went on he got better. And my two youngest they really didn't care, and my two foster children Ernest and Alvin it affected them a lot more. Because not only were they with me, but they were away from their families in another state in another school.[16]

After almost a year in Texas, Lawrence and Fatimah returned to Louisiana. They decided against moving back to New Orleans due to the uncertainty of life there, and moved to Opelousas, about two hours from New Orleans. But they found the isolation too difficult, and so moved to the Westbank of New Orleans, in Marrero. They bought a house, but they struggle to maintain the mortgage. Fatimah has enrolled in school and is a sophomore at Delgado Community College majoring in engineering.

Though some of those who had arrived to College Station had high hopes of making a new life, their dreams were daunted by unforgiving and biased treatment from some of the citizens of that town. Vincent Holmes, childhood friend of the Hankins, also came to College Station and talks about his experience in this new city: "Locally, in the beginning everybody was pretty nice, but towards the . . . like now [2006] they are not so nice anymore. . . . I live in a complex and I have a landlord and every time he sees me he constantly remarks on Hurricane Katrina, how lazy the people are from New Orleans, they don't want to find jobs."[17] Vincent was a small business owner in New Orleans, an Air Force veteran, so these remarks were particularly problematic. But as time wore on, we heard such negative comments from many throughout the country, including politicians. Texas notable Kinky Friedman spoke for many when he called Katrina survivors "crackheads and thugs."[18] Katrina survivor became a pejorative designation that marked one as an ingrate, lazy, and a tax burden. In spite of the negatives, Vincent stayed in College Station and opened two businesses. Five years later, he had moved to Clear Lake, Texas, where he owns a karate school and, with his girlfriend, recently welcomed a son to their household.

Menelik Mitchell, thirty-one years of age, son of the matriarch in the Hankins family, was in the Air Force National Guard Reserves living at the base in Belle Chase, Louisiana, until they were evacuated due to flooding. He returned to New Orleans from the army base in Lafayette on Tuesday, the day after Katrina hit, to assist with supplying food and water to the stranded people in the Superdome and Convention Center. He talks about the work they did to alleviate suffering:

> It was kind of crazy to see all the food, like you would go out there for four hours and you might fill maybe twenty helicopters up with food and

water . . . go back to the hanger where you staying and you watch TV
and you seeing all these people that are starving and the people on the
west bank that they are starving and need water . . . and we just see
pallets and pallets and pallets of water and tractor trailers filled with water, . . . and we were just begging to drive out there to give water to them,
but they wouldn't let us . . . because "we" weren't given weapons.[19]

He later accompanied the Kenyon Corporation in the process of body
retrieval and recovery: "You might not see nothing except everything is
destroyed then you look over the couch, everything is mud and black
but you keep looking and there might be a body there. We found bodies
up in the backyard under trees, or just lying in the yard."[20] Menelik talks
about the spike in suicides of friends in the military since Katrina. He
initially had trouble sleeping and adjusting to civilian life, as he experienced feelings of alienation and hopelessness. He decided to finish his
education, completing a degree in sociology at Southern University of
New Orleans, and is now seeking a teaching job in Houston. He is typical of many Katrina survivors trying to move on with their lives who
attained an education and then again left the city.

Shajad was a straight-A student at Nunez Community College in
Chalmette and wanted to be a doctor. The disruption to his life has been
monumental. In Chalmette, he and his brother were anchors for each
other, sharing expenses and engaging in healthy academic competition.
His school was within walking distance, and he had a plan for how he
would achieve his dream of attending medical school. Due to his Katrina
displacement, he lost everything and his life was derailed. He also displayed PTSD symptoms from his ordeal: "I think it has numbed me because you don't want to imagine that people you know is getting messed
up like that. You don't want to imagine that 'your boy' is on a roof or
something like that because it was crazy."[21] After six months of floun-
dering in an attempt to find a job and unsuccessfully trying to reenter
school in College Station, Shajad returned to Louisiana, where he lived
with his brother and sister-in-law and enrolled in Nunez to finish up his
associate's degree. In 2010, he moved back to College Station and now
lives with his mother, works, and struggles to get his life back on track.

Of the more than nineteen family and friends of the Hankins family who evacuated, only Fatimah and Bagel with their families continue

to live in the New Orleans area. Their tight-knit group of family and friends now are living either in Texas or Georgia. Erica Hackett, another childhood friend, and her son Tyree lived in Algiers, Louisiana, across the street from Sajidah. Erica initially fled to Mississippi with her mother and stepfather, but she eventually moved to College Station to be near her close friends in the Hankins family. Her attempts to find normalcy continued to elude her, and she returned to Algiers in December 2005. Erica was working in a low-skilled job in New Orleans, but became involved with the drug culture. She and Sajidah had moved into a house in New Orleans, but their relationship frayed and they barely spoke, finally moving apart. Erica has undergone three stints in New Orleans prisons for drug use and was on parole at the time of this writing.

Race, Responsibility, and Recovery

When we couple personal loss with the physical destruction of New Orleans, we see that Katrina was not only an avoidable tragedy, but also a crime with many villains and victims. From historical neglect of the levee systems to the abandonment of rescue efforts, local, state, and federal governments all share responsibility for this disaster and its aftermath. As the saga of Katrina continues to unfold and those affected by it fade from the headlines, we who continue to see the victims and the pathologies that evolved from this ordeal ask ourselves many questions: What can we do to help recover lives lost? How can we take action now to prevent such losses from occurring in the future? How do we minimize the mental and physical trauma of these events? And finally, how do we hold our governments accountable?

As parents and friends, we lament the slowness of recovery and the bureaucracy that chronically dehumanizes our families and those of many others. We also see the long-term impacts of the storm and some of the triumphs of the people affected. Of the nineteen Hankins family and friends that came to College Station, we interviewed twelve. In 2011, additional interviews were conducted with four friends who stayed during the storm and two additional "first responders." We will continue interviewing individuals affected by Katrina, expanding our interviews to cover others outside of the Hankins family to provide comparative

Figure 13.4. Flooded homes and streets in the Lower Ninth Ward in New Orleans

data, simultaneously documenting the long-term recovery of the family and of New Orleans.

This family is in many ways a microcosm of the state of Louisiana and especially the city of New Orleans. Our study offers an important sociological and psychological analysis of what occurs after a devastating trauma impacts a related group of people, including how they attempt to reconnect and revitalize their lives after a tragedy. These stories account how one family, the Hankins, like many other families dispersed by the Katrina disaster, have experienced symptoms characterized as PTSD. Muhammad Shajad exhibits marked diminished interest and participation in significant activities like education; Fatimah cannot explain the increase in irritability or outbursts of anger that led to her arrest on charges of spousal abuse; and Salih's hypervigilance when it rains are but three examples of PTSD observed in the Hankins family. Ultimately, the stories speak of lost communities and ongoing challenges to rebuild lives. The stories are told with humor, sadness, dignity, indignation, and love. As family members and members of the academic community, we continue to document the ongoing saga of the Hankins family because we know that Katrina will never be over for them. It remains a defining moment in many of their lives, and its aftermath will continue to have an impact on their (and our) lives.

As we document disasters and trauma through oral history, we must ask ourselves many questions: When is close (relations) too close? When is it "too soon" to look back? What are the next steps? How do we (can we) objectively document these stories? Are we asking the right questions? How do we avoid retraumatizing? What are the lessons learned? And how do we help these families heal? There are now thousands of oral history sites at which one can download or listen to reactions to America's tragedies and triumphs, from large national projects to smaller community ones. Such stories capture the tangled history of floods, fires, families, revolutions, and social change.

For African Americans trying to tell their stories in the aftermath of Katrina, it will take a significant amount of time to recover. The pain of acknowledging this reality for African Americans comes through succinctly in the words of Lawrence Sylvan, husband of Fatimah Hankins, as he sums up how many in the New Orleans community view the "American dream" in the aftermath of Hurricane Katrina:

> I feel like the people that we have in power to make change have done a mediocre job at best. I think that people are happy knowing that there are people doing bad because of Katrina. I think our federal government has proven what everybody already suspected, that we can't trust them. . . . And as great of a country as they say America is, the land of the free, this great country has only been the land of the free to one race, and to every other race and every other ethnic background it's been the land of trial and pain and I think that Katrina was a reflection of that trial and pain.[22]

NOTES

1 See http://www.louisianafolklife.org/katrina.html.

2 *Plessy v. Ferguson*, 163 U.S. 537, 559 (1896) (Harlan, J., dissenting).

3 Ibid., 78.

4 Dyson (2006, 75).

5 Hurricane season is a fact of life in Louisiana and throughout the South, beginning in June and lasting until November. William Gray, head of the Tropical Meteorology Project at Colorado State University, projected that during the 2005 hurricane

season "there would be twenty named storms, twice the average. That estimate, which seemed so extravagant before the season began, was ultimately short: there were thirty named storms in 2005. Furthermore, Gray predicted that six major hurricanes would develop in the Atlantic, three times the average (there were indeed six) and said that there was a 77 percent chance that one would strike the United States" (Brinkley 2006, 75).

6 University of Missouri–Columbia, International Center for Psychosocial Trauma (2006, 15–16).

7 Fuguitt, Fulton, and Beale (2001, 1).

8 Dwight Handara Hankins (DHH), transcribed interview, October 7, 2006, 2–3.

9 Rachel Washington Hankins (RWH), interview, December 14, 2005.

10 RWH interview.

11 Salih Hankins, interview, October 7, 2006.

12 DHH, 3–4.

13 Bruce D. Perry, MD, PhD, "The Real Crisis of Katrina," *Zero*, http://www.vachss.com/guest_dispatches/katrina-tragedy.html.

14 Oxfam America (2008, 4).

15 Sajidah Bagel Hankins, interview, October 7, 2006.

16 Fatimah Hankins Sylvan, interview, December 20, 2005.

17 Vincent Holmes, interview, October 12, 2006.

18 Dailykos.com, September 12, 2006, http://www.dailykos.com/story/2006/09/12/245710/-Kinky-calls-Katrina-Evacuees-crackheads-and-thugs.

19 Menelik Mitchell, interview, October 7, 2006.

20 Ibid., 4.

21 Muhammad Shajad Hankins, interview, October 12, 2006.

22 Lawrence Sylvan, interview, October 6, 2006.

14

A Cure for Bitterness

DOROTHY ALLISON

Almost twenty years ago, I started writing an essay called "A Cure for Bitterness." I was invited to go talk to a bunch of psychologists. I was going to take the gig because it was in Santa Cruz, and I figured I could run off to the beach and they'd put me up in a nice hotel because psychologists have a lot of money. And then I started thinking what I want to say to these . . . I'm going to use bad language. Be warned. What did I want to say to these sons of bitches? As different from me as I could imagine, people with whom I have had a long history of difficulty. With those people who interpret and explain and examine trauma survivors, I have great difficulty.

So I started outlining why, in fact, I was bitter at them. And it quickly expanded to why, in fact, I was bitter and what were the virtues of being bitter. And isn't it a goddamned wonderful thing that sometimes we can just glory in bitterness? It may not surprise you to know that I did not finish the essay. I had an excuse. I got really sick and couldn't go, and today all day I've been feverish.

I think because in fact I find talking about this really, really difficult. One of the things I loved about Monica's presentation to me was that she wanted to put together these really separate strands of academia, theory, philosophy, and of practice and of experience. These are not things that go together easily or dovetail in any way that we can explain. And we are sometimes adversaries, competitors, claiming this territory and that is mean and does not help. It leads us nowhere useful.

Today, I heard this word, which I've heard before: *selah*. Pause, stop for a minute, take a breath, pace your breath, think, think. Take a breath. This work speaks to people who have been very near to death. This work speaks of people who have experienced what no one wants to experience: grief, pain, loss, damage.

We talk about healing. We talk about all the ways in which we can categorize our responses, shape not just narrative and theory but practice to be useful, and I engage in that conversation constantly. I need to be useful. Now do I need that because I was raped at the age of five or because I was fortunate enough to get a college education and read a hell of a lot of Heidegger and theory?

I am a teacher and a writer, and these are very different worlds. As a writer and as a teacher of writers, what I know about narrative, what I know about language is painfully, stringently insistent on the spare. I don't give you an account of the rape of Bone in *Bastard Out of Carolina*. I give you as little information as possible. It took me thirty drafts to write that chapter; thirty drafts in which in almost every case what I was doing was taking words out. What I was doing was avoiding any, any reference, any image, any language choice that would have evoked for you anything else you had ever read on the subject of rape of twelve-year-old girls.

I wanted new. I wanted you to *selah*. I wanted you to stop. Oh hell with that; I wanted to rip your insides out and force you up against the wall and make you be in that place where that child was. And as a writer, what I know is to step away from all that intense language and go for least language, the most spare image to somehow trick you into being in the room with something you do not want to be in the room with. That's what we do as writers; that's how it works.

Now I didn't start thirty years ago. I started forty years ago. I'm sixty-one. I started trying to figure out how to write in my early twenties. Oh hell, I was writin' poems when I was eight, nine, twelve, but I was bad. In fact, I think I fit standards for terrible. I think that you can only be as good as you're willing to be bad in the beginning. You can only get strength from being pitiful and broken. You get where that's coming from?

The lesson that I was taught as a young writer was that there were subjects that were not to be spoken. The lessons that I was given, particularly as a young woman writer, were that to be a great writer I had to avoid any narrative of which I spoke of my own lived experience. There was this concept of literature, and this concept had a category of purity that did not extend to memoir but certainly did not extend to fictionalizing your own experience. That was and remains to this day deeply suspicious. We're uncomfortable with it.

You may have lived through some trauma, but that does not entitle you to create narrative about it; at least not by many of the literary critics and not to a certain extent by the minds of many readers. Now hold that idea. Put it next to this other idea. We love to know gossip. And we want all the dirty details. We want to know the color of the panties. We want to know exactly how much blood was shed. We want to hear the screaming on the page and goddamn that the book that says "based on a true story"—we will buy that book before we will buy a novel.

It's been this huge shift in the literary marketplace. Memoir is canonized and popularized in part, I believe, by our worst impulses, our lust for gossip. But in part also by what I think of as one of our best impulses. We want a correction to lies. We want to know what is true. We want our lives and our true lived experience to be taken seriously. Even if I grow up in a Westchester suburb with a well-employed daddy and a voting mama who could cook, I want to know that what I see on the page is a true version and I want to be able to tell the difference.

And the secret to being able to tell the difference is to trust the narrative. Now I'm old enough to have grown up in a world in which I did not trust the narratives I was given. I knew they were false. I read stories about rape. They were bullshit. I read stories about poverty. I read stories about southerners. I read stories about queers. And they were so unrelentingly, terribly false that it ate out of me my sense of being part of the world.

If I live in a world in which my experience is not reflected back to me, then maybe I'm not real enough; maybe I'm not real at all. Maybe I'm fiction. When our children read only fictions that reflect nothing of themselves back to them, we cripple them. That is a trauma: to see yourself never in the world. To feel yourself so unspeakable, forbidden, dangerous.

We need memoir. We need nonfiction narrative. We need it defined and presented to us. We need those people to walk through the streets with brotherly hands saying yes, goddamn it, that's what it was like. And to speak to us in the language fair enough and powerful enough to make us inside their lives, to take us in and make us feel.

And what is the use of that? That suffering, what is the use of suffering? It changes you. Not always in good ways. For it to be a good change, you got to do some work with it. It is not sufficient merely to have been in pain. No, much as I'd like to reward all of you who have survived being in pain. You know, you know the work that you have to do.

All day I have been going around and listening to people talk, talking of terrible things: of death, of loss, of being hated, of stigma. Oh, and speaking mostly between two languages: this personal "I'm grateful to be alive" language and this other language that I admire but don't use too well, this academic language that uses references to people I do vaguely remember reading some of but am no longer up to date on what they said. Half the time, I don't know what you people are talking about except that I do know what you're talking about because you listened to Maurice this morning.

You slowed down. You've been speaking very, very plainly and carefully. The questions you've been asking. The suffering is noble. Agency, you talk about agency. You talk about being in the narrative. You tell me stories. You need a few more stories. Just by way of critique, you need a few more stories and fewer references to Heidegger. What is the use of story?

Story done well, we believe. Even fiction we believe. It is reflecting back to us the world in which we live. And it does it in the best possible way, because it shows us not only terrible things, but the possibility of being great souls. It shows us, in fact, the use of suffering. My job, I have two, well three. I got this child. I'm a mom, therefore I'm required to put him in the world somewhat sane and educated and gentle and feminist and oh the list I got for what I have to do as a mom is almost more than any human being should have to bear.

And then I am a writer and I am a slow writer, which is humiliating. "I thought she was going to publish that book." I was. I'm almost done. I have almost become that computer joke, real soon now. You know that one? The new software release is coming real soon now. Three years later, I come back. It's coming real soon now. I'm almost done.

And then, I am a teacher and it is the nature of the kind of teaching I do—and I mostly teach writing, some literature but mostly writing—and it is the nature of the young people who will come to work with me because of much of what I have published.

I get the children of terror. I get the survivors of nightmares. I get the broken, the damaged, the terrified. I get kids who come in with a notebook and can't talk. I get kids who when they talk, stutter. I get kids who tell jokes continually or tell horrific sexual adventures terribly. Anything to avoid going where they hope I'm going to take them.

My job as a teacher is to take them. To take them safely—love that word don't you?—past all their fears into the narrative that dogs their every moment. Now some of you know what I'm talking about. You work with these hurt young people. Young people, sixty, seventy, we're different as writers. We define young in a different way. If you've not had an article published, you're still young. I don't care how old you are.

But when I go and work in high schools or on reservations or in housing projects, and I sit across from a fifteen-year-old who can't talk but who can put a list of words on a page, my job is to be both impassive, to sit there with my face calm while they tell me terrible, terrible, horrific things. And then to be fully present, sometimes to weep, sometimes to just slide around the table and put my hands on them. You've got to watch that. I've got to be careful.

My job is to be in the room with the unspeakable, the impossible, the completely-to-be-avoided experience. Let me tell you, narrative is far easier to be with than the narrator. You know this because you teach. And they are bitter. You know this. You run into it, I have no doubt.

They are full of rage and grief, inappropriate emotions. Resentment. The resentment of a child who has been raped and has been afraid to acknowledge it, well that's bigger than earthquakes. It burns. Most of all it burns the narrator. They live in a cauldron of bitterness; the story of their lives when they can even begin to tell you. When they can begin to shape it into story.

And when that story happens, you close your eyes; you step back. You step away. You make lists of words. Some words you'll use; some you will avoid. You work your way around to it. Most narration begins with avoidance. Can't say that, can't say that. It'd kill my mama to know I survived that.

Can't say that, can't say that. Look who the world would think I am if they knew I lived through that. There are some things you are sure should have killed you and if you're alive, if it didn't kill you, well then you must not have been good enough to have died.

Look in the face of a fifteen-year-old boy who is sure he should have died. And if he speaks it out loud, he will die. And your job is to sit with him into the narrative, into the story. Practice, philosophy, theory. Sometimes I read the book of Job for relief. *For relief.*

And over here where I live, where many of you live, it's a razor. We are squatting above it. We are frog walking forward trying not to slice ourselves to bits. But the reality is, there is no safe, right action.

The secret of this work is that you must accustom yourself to discomfort. And you have to redefine what that means. You have to be in the room with horror. You have to take deep breaths; sometimes you're not even allowed to have the emotions you're having to do the work. You'll have to get to them later. But in the work, sometimes you have to put them aside.

That's razor squatting. That's trying to be of use. That's trying to bend theory and academic understanding and all of those explanations and studies and information that you have acquired over long, long years of work and turning it into something that is a tool. And along the way, you have to figure out that no tool that destroys you is genuinely useful.

It means you have to forgive yourself for not having been raped at five. For not having been shot or near murdered. Easier, easier to be in the support group with the other people who have had your experience; you know this. Easier, easier to look at it all as story.

And we can talk about how to craft the story, but we're squatting on a razor. We're walking between narrative and experience and we're in the room with people who need us, need us to be fully adult, grown up, helpful, useful, useful in big, complicated, layered, textured ways.

When *Bastard Out of Carolina* was published, I had to go around and talk to reporters. I recommend getting a job cleaning septic tanks versus that. Because reporters have an agenda and what they want most from you is that moment where you break down and give them an emotion that they can write about. They have a short list of the emotions that they want from you. One is rage. They love that one. The other is grief. Best of all if you just have a breakdown right in front of them. If you collapse sobbing and couldn't go on, Lord God, they'd win a Pulitzer. They try really hard to provoke that.

They also believe absolutely, which to a certain extent our culture believes, that all writers, that we are a particular kind of creature, savants in some ways. Gifted, give you that; but damaged. All writers are damaged. Narrative is ascribed to a therapeutic process; not necessarily a cure for the disease but the whole idea is you wrote that to purge yourself. You wrote that to heal yourself. You fix things by making it a story. Wouldn't it be nice to think so?

You heal yourself by writing that book. I must have heard that two or three times a day for the whole of the six weeks I was running around trying to sell novels. You fixed yourself. God. The book fixed you didn't it? Writing the book fixed you. That book. God.

Those of you who work with trauma survivors know that yes, creating the story, creating the narrative, is useful and it has the possibility for a lot of healing work to be done. But it fixes nothing; changes nothing. That work we do in engagement with our story is separate from the narrative we construct for it.

And truthfully, no one comes to write about experiencing horrific events. No one writes about death or loss or grief without having already done so much of the work. You have to find a place to stand that is safe and strong and solid, and it's going to move under you as you do the work, but you have to have done that work first. You have to have found a way to live with your own story before you make a story you can give other people.

You know what is grace? You know what is wonderful? The best damn thing about it, you get to lie. Let me speak of the glories of fiction. Let me speak of the glory of taking your lived experience and making it different. Yes, yes, God yes, to figure out what really happened is vital, is wonderful. And if you have been through any of these experiences that I have heard recounted today, you do have to shape a story and wonderful, wonderful if the story you shape is a heroic narrative. God damn if you become a warrior for feminism or Christ or democracy or whatever the fuck serves your purpose to get through it alive and semi-sane.

Glory, glory if you can make that story all good, I give you the license. But I also give you the license to make it small and mean and needle sharp. To scrape the bones of everyone who wasn't raped at five. The thing I know that you have to make peace with is that bitter need to hurt the world back. Out of it can come extraordinary story, powerful narrative, life-changing poetry.

And none of it will happen if you're always trying to be good, saintly, forgiving. I forgive you, Jesus take my sin. Jesus takes my sin a little bit better when I'm frank about my sin. When I'm honest with myself, bitter, bitter, the crying desire to hurt the world back.

You know that.

Think about your worst moment. If you can admit it to yourself, you know that hot heat chain that you felt; the humiliation, the horror of discovering yourself capable not only of rage but the need to hurt people, to shake them up, to tell your mama a story that will break her heart. To forgive yourself that, then you can begin the narrative; then you can begin to shape story.

What I've heard over and over today, the people who go where I think I try desperately to go. I'm not sure about healing. I am not sure how it is accomplished. I know and I have read so many books about all of the exercises you can do, about all of the practices.

I know that for me going to consciousness-raising groups in the early women's movement gave me a way not to be ashamed in the world. To begin to talk about the scary big subjects: being an incest survivor, being beaten, being a lesbian. All the ways I could figure out how to talk about that grew, became deeper, became purposeful in conversations with other women who had shared those experiences.

And I know that as a writer, when I began to write those stories and share them with other writers, and other writers would come back to me and say "you might want to take that sentence out." That one—that sentence—I couldn't get past that sentence. And then I had to think: do I want to never get past that sentence? There's a kind of glory in that. I could fuck them up forever. Or do I want to change it just enough that they'll take it in and feel it, be with me where I want them to be and go somewhere different?

I believe absolutely in activism, in engagement, in being part of a community. I believe in widening your notion of your life. Oh, there were years when I couldn't come talk to you. I was a very doctrinaire lesbian feminist and you got men in this room; there's testicles under the tables. I did not go where that was the case.

And then I began to feel small and scared. One of the corrections I trust in my life is, anything I do that leads me back to feeling small and scared and bitter has something wrong with it, and I got to look again. My correction was to start engaging with that other gender on a meaningful basis. It required that I talk to gay male poets. I thought they were almost women.

I could kind of feel my way and then I made my world bigger and started talking to heterosexuals, scary people, people whose traumas I did not understand. Then I made my world bigger and I had to start talking to people who scared the shit out of me, people of color, rich people.

This may be the only talk you'll ever hear in which rich people and people of color are equated for scariness. Bitterness, damage, this is what I know. If you were raped at five or seven, nine, thirteen, twenty-four, seventy-eight, you have in you a hurt place. You have in you damage. You know what happens when you have a hurt place and you learn to live with it; you learn to move around it, limping on that cracked knee, stumbling on those sore feet.

You adjust your life to the damage and then you have to come to a point where you've got to reclaim, let go of the damage. Somehow become that normative figure, the one that could walk easily, the one that doesn't limp. So let me be really clear. I don't genuinely believe in the normative. I don't think any of us started out little God's babies, little pristine angelic creatures of light and love. I actually think we all started out fucked up.

I know that I think this because of my family background, but give it to me. You got family background. You got damaged mamas and angry daddies, drunken cousins. You've got first lovers who said the worst possible thing to you at the worst possible moment, cut you right to the bone. We start out fucked up and we learn to deal with it. We develop muscles around the damage.

Some kinds of fucked up last a lifetime, some kinds of fucked up never, never to be fixed. I will limp forever. I know this. I know this. I have sat with my sisters and talked about why it is that three of us—so different, almost unbelievably different—have the same disability, that if there is a son of a bitch in the room and it's a boy, my sisters are right over there buying him a drink. And if it's a girl, I'm over at her side. Talk to me, honey. Be mean to me. I got a piece of damage needs that.

What we learn in crafting the story of our lives is some way to love ourselves even in the midst of our horror. To forgive ourselves, our broken damaged hurt places, an appreciation for the muscle we have created in order to survive.

And what we learn as theorists and practitioners, academics, writers, is to look at scary impossible situations with complex, reasonable, nuanced attention. We create a way to understand what is unexplainable, and two or three things I tried to figure out what I genuinely know.

But eventually it just became more and more about what I do not know; do not understand. Two or three things I know for sure, but none of them is why a man would beat a child. None of them is why anyone would rape a child.

Two or three, four or five, dozens; the things we do not know become the subjects of our lectures, our stories. And let me just say frankly, especially after having listened to all the panels today, when you make your narratives, let's be clear your narratives are fictions. They're beautiful, they're wonderful, they reference reality; but then again all good fiction references reality.

What I see you doing is creating narratives that assign meaning and purpose to a struggle that sometimes seems hopeless, endless, debilitating, and shameful. I know that what you're doing is creating purposeful narrative. You're going for redemption. You're going for meaning. You're looking for a cure.

But you in this world have read enough to know there is no cure. There are techniques for making it possible for survival. There are strategies that we can explore that remake how our culture deals with the very events that are embodied under the label trauma.

We are the leavening to the salt-crusted fear of this society that only wants to read terrible stories on paperback covers at a distance. And if they're going to see that narrator, they want them carefully positioned on Oprah's couch, kind of respectful, kind of honorable, kind of animalistic, kind of gossipy sexually exciting.

Ooh, she was raped. You think she liked it? The worst impulses, the meanest impulses, the place where as a culture our damage is almost universal that we are fascinated with the horrible, that we use it as a way to reassure ourselves of our own safety, our protected place.

You know none of that is true. You know that the narrative that says these things only happen to people like that; people not me. You know, terrible things happen to us all the time. When terrible things happen to me, I read poetry. I may be the only one in the room whose iPod is half full of poets. Muriel Rukeyser, that gold in the mouth. Adrienne Rich, taking me diving into the wreck. Gary Snyder, somehow convincing me that I can walk in mountainous places and be safe. Layers and textures and Seamus Heaney showing me history and layers and scary, scary, scary stories.

This summer we lost Ai (Ogawa). Maybe some of you got a chance to meet her. I met her twenty-five years ago in New York. I listened to her read poetry downtown. And she read a complete fiction. She read a narrative she invented, herself as Billy the Kid. Herself as a young boy who shoots first his little sister and then his mama and his daddy. Who walks through the dust with a gun slapping the side of his knee and says in her glorious voice, "I'm a wind out of hell and I'll break your heart."

When I am at my worst, when I am in the middle of the night unable to sleep, walking back and forth despairing that anything will ever be different, that there are still raped five-year-olds, that there are still terrified adolescents, that there is still a world of lies being preached to me and mine, I walk back and forth in my living room with my little dog and the cats up on the couch staring at me.

I walk back and forth and I recite out loud poems. I'm a wind out of hell and I'll break your heart. And sometimes that's exactly what I want; bitter and mean and to hurt you, make you feel how hurt I have been. And then sometimes it's Ai's voice, her face and where she took it. I'm a wind out of hell; I'm a wind out of hell. Just to know I am, I'll break your heart.

Healing, I don't know. The nobility of suffering; I've got questions about that. But the creation of language that sustains. The letting go of violence and bitterness and hatred, well I believe in that. I believe in that to save myself, to not be who they tried to make me, to resist being what I couldn't be too easily.

Last thing I want to tell you, this book I've been writing, this book that's near killed me; it's called *She Who*. It started out to be a book about a young woman who survived being assaulted in a parking garage in San Francisco and thrown off the roof, who goes into a coma, whose mother goes crazy trying to rescue her daughter. And when the girl wakes up, she's lost great portions of her memory; doesn't know what happened. Her mama becomes an antiviolence organizer and a colossal pain in the ass.

I wanted to explore what that would be like. This golden girl, the one I threw off the roof, Casey, she's a Stanford student about to graduate. A golden child going off to be a lawyer and rich and oh yeah, she's a lesbian but she's got a good-looking girlfriend and her mama adores her. And her mama's a member of the parents' union, and all that stuff.

I based her on young people I actually met while guest teaching at various universities around the world including Stanford alum. I have to apologize to some of them for what I did to that child. I broke that child on the page. Trauma, well baby wait until you read it.

But it stopped, because that wasn't really what my heart was needing to write about. Because what fascinated me, what still fascinates me, is what you do, it's what happens *after*. Not that you were raped, but that you're not dead. That you have to lift your head, figure out how to move through the world. I had to figure out if you never remember the most terrible event of your life—and Casey never remembers the assault—who do you become and how do you recover?

I had to write a narrative of damage that is explicit about the damage but with carefully chosen crafted words about the thing I'm not even sure I believe in: recovery, healing, who you make yourself. Let us just say, she fights a lot with her mother, something I believe all people should attempt to write on the page. I think boys should fight with their daddies and girls with their mamas and figure it all out. Say impossible, horrible things. Then you don't have to say them to your actual mothers. That's a useful exercise.

But the great challenge that I faced, it really is the question of how you survive what no one believes is survivable. How do you claim dignity when everyone in the world saw you carted away, ripped, shredded, you were on the nightly news? Reporters got to have their moment with you, make you a thing. How you become a human creature again.

That's what narrative does. That's the deep thing narrative can do. You do that thing when you take your time, when you place yourself in the room with people who have survived the unsurvivable, the unspeakable, the horrible. You take a breath. You take care. You be truthful. You cure your own bitterness by doing the work. It is the only solution I know.

Jesus might forgive you. Actually, based on your Baptist upbringing you go even halfway, he'll forgive you. But that won't fix it. You have to forgive yourself. You have to do useful work. You have to be in the room with me.

BIBLIOGRAPHY

Abraham, Nicholas, and Maria Torok. 1994. *The Shell and the Kernel: Renewals of Psychoanalysis*. Vol. 1. Edited and translated by Nicholas T. Rand. Chicago: University of Chicago Press.

Ackerman, Elliot L. 2006. "Relearning Storm Troop Tactics: The Battle for Fallujah." *Marine Corps Gazette*, September, 47–52.

Agamben, Giorgio. 2005. *State of Exception*. Translated by Kevin Attell. Chicago: University of Chicago Press.

Ai, Amy L., and Christopher Peterson. 2004. "Symptoms, Religious Coping, and Positive Attitudes of Refugees from Kosovar War." In *Focus on Posttraumatic Stress Disorder Research*, edited by Thomas A. Corales, 122–56. Hauppauge, NY: Nova.

Allison, Dorothy. 2010. "A Cure for Bitterness." Keynote address presented at the New Approaches to Trauma: Bridging Theory and Practice conference at Arizona State University, Phoenix, October 7.

American Psychiatric Association (APA). 2000. *Diagnostic and Statistical Manual of Mental Disorders*. 4th ed., text revision. Washington, DC: APA.

Amnesty International. 2000. "Real Scale of Atrocities in Chechnya: New Evidence of Cover-Up." http://reliefweb.int/report/russian-federation/real-scale-atrocities-chechnya-new-evidence-cover.

Anderson, Charles, and Marian MacCurdy. 2000. *Writing and Healing: Toward an Informed Practice*. Urbana, IL: National Council of Teachers of English.

Anderson, Col. Gary W. 2004. "Fallujah and the Future of Urban Operations." *Marine Corps Gazette*, November 2004, 52.

Angelou, Maya. 1969. *I Know Why the Caged Bird Sings*. New York: Random House.

Anthias, F., and Yuval-Davis, N. 1989. "Introduction." In *Woman, Nation, State*, edited by N. Yuval-Davis and F. Anthias, 1–16. Basingstoke: Macmillan.

Arendt, Hannah. 1959. *The Human Condition: A Study of the Central Dilemmas Facing Modern Man*. Garden City, NY: Doubleday.

Argenti-Pillen, Alexandra. 2000. "The Discourse on Trauma in Non-Western Cultural Contexts." In *International Handbook of Human Response to Trauma*, edited by Arieh Y. Shalev, Rachel Yehuda, and Alexander McFarlane, 87–102. New York: Kluwer.

———. 2003. *Masking Terror: How Women Contain Violence in Southern Sri Lanka*. Philadelphia: University of Pennsylvania Press.

Argo, Nicole. 2006. "The Role of Social Context in Terrorist Attacks." *Chronicle of Higher Education*, January 13. Accessed June 29, 2011. http://newschool.academia. edu/NicholeArgo/Papers/8203/The_Role_of_Social_Context_in_Terrorist_Attacks.

Arutunyan, Anna. 2011. "Many Motives in Budanov Murder." *Moscow Times*, June 14. Accessed June 29, 2011. http://www.themoscownews.com/ crime/20110614/188750662.html.

Ashford, M.-W., and Y. Huet-Vaughn. 1997. "The Impact of War on Women." In *War and Public Health*, edited by Barry S. Levy and Victor W. Sidel, 186–96. Oxford: Oxford University Press.

Atran, Scott. 2003. "Genesis of Suicide Terrorism." *Science* 299(5612): 1534–39.

———. 2004. "Mishandling Suicide Terrorism." *Washington Quarterly* 27(3): 67–90.

Atwood, Margaret. 2003. *Orxy and Crake*. New York: Anchor.

Badiou, Alain. 2005. *Being and Event*. Translated by Oliver Feltham. New York: Continuum.

Baiev, Khassan, and Nicholas Daniloff. 2006. "Russia's Public Health Catastrophe in Chechnya." Speech delivered at the Woodrow Wilson International Center for Scholars, Washington, DC, June 12.

Balasingham, Adele. 2003. *The Will to Freedom: An Inside View of Tamil Resistance*. London: Fairmax.

Ball, Karyn. 2000. "Introduction: Trauma and Its Institutional Destinies." *Cultural Critique* 46: 1–44.

Banash, David. 2013. *Collage Culture: Readymades, Meaning, and the Age of Consumption*. Amsterdam: Editions Rodopi.

Barber, Charles. 2013. "We Live in the Age of Trauma." *Salon*, May 1. http://www.salon. com/2013/05/01/we_live_in_the_age_of_trauma/.

Bar-On, Dan. 1989. *Legacy of Silence: Encounters with Children of the Third Reich*. Cambridge, MA: Harvard University Press.

Bartholomae, David. 1995. "Writing with Teachers: A Conversation with Peter Elbow." In *Cross-Talk in Composition Theory: A Reader*, edited by Victor Villanueva, 479–88. Urbana, IL: National Council of Teachers of English.

Bartky, Sandra Lee. 1990. *Femininity and Domination: Studies in the Phenomenology of Oppression*. New York: Routledge.

Basayev, Usam. 2009. "Holiday for Plaits." *Prague Watchdog*, September 16. Accessed June 15, 2011. http://www.watchdog. cz/?show=000000-000024-000002-000022&lang=1.

BBC News. 2001. "Colonel Accused of Murder in Chechnya Stands Trial." November 4. Accessed March 9, 2011. http://news.bbc.co.uk/1/hi/events/newsnight/1274747.stm.

———. 2002. "Support for Hostage-Takers Strong in Chechen Refugee Camps." *NTV Mir*, October 28.

———. 2003. "Colonel Jailed for Chechen Murder." http://news.bbc.co.uk/2/hi/europe/3095003.stm.

Beckett, Samuel. 1955. "The Unnamable." In *Three Novels*, 281–407. New York: Grove Press.

Benhabib, Seyla. 1992. *Situating the Self: Gender, Community and Postmodernism in Contemporary Ethics*. New York: Routledge.

Benjamin, Walter. 1968. *Illuminations: Essays and Reflections*. New York: Schocken Books.

Berger, Alan L., and Naomi Berger, eds. 2001. *Second Generation Voices: Reflections by Children of Holocaust Survivors & Perpetrators*. Syracuse, NY: Syracuse University Press.

Berger, James. 1999. *After the End: Representations of Post-apocalypse*. Minneapolis: University of Minnesota Press.

Bergson, Henri. 1946. *The Creative Mind*. New York: Philosophical Library.

———. 2001. *Time and Freewill*. Translated by F. L. Pogson. Mineola, NY: Dover.

Berko, Anat, and Edna Erez. 2007. "Gender, Palestinian Women, and Terrorism: Women's Liberation or Oppression?" *Studies in Conflict and Terrorism* 30(6): 493–519.

Berman, Jeffrey. 2001. *Risky Writing*. Amherst: University of Massachusetts Press.

Berns, Nancy. 2011. *Closure: The Rush to End Grief and What It Costs Us*. Philadelphia: Temple University Press.

Bersanova, Zalpa. 2004. "Values Stronger Than War." Speech presented at Radio Free Europe, July 30.

Betancourt, Theresa S., Robert T. Brennan, Julia Rubin-Smith, Garrett M. Fitzmaurice, and Stephen E. Gilman. 2010. "Sierra Leone's Former Child Soldiers: A Longitudinal Study of Risk, Protective Factors, and Mental Health." *Journal of the American Academy of Child and Adolescent Psychiatry* 49(6): 606–15.

Betancourt, Theresa S., and Timothy Williams. 2008. "Building an Evidence Base on Mental Health Interventions for Children Affected by Armed Conflict." *Intervention* 6: 39–56.

Beyler, Clara. 2003. "Messengers of Death, Female Suicide Bombers." Herzliya: Institute for Counterterrorism. Accessed January 15, 2011. www.ict.org.il/articles/article-det.cfm?articleid=471.

———. 2006. "Using Palestinian Women as Bombs." *New York Sun*, November 15. Accessed June 30, 2011. http://www.nysun.com/article/43574.

Biro, Matthew. 2009. *The Dada Cyborg: Visions of the New Human in Weimar Berlin*. Minneapolis: University of Minnesota Press.

Bishop, Wendy. 1997. *Teaching Lives: Essays and Stories*. Logan: Utah State University Press.

Blanchot, Maurice. 1995. *The Writing of Disaster*. Translated by Ann Smock. Lincoln: University of Nebraska Press.

Bloom, Mia. 2005. *Dying to Kill: The Allure of Suicide Terror*. New York: Columbia University Press.

Bohner, Gerd. 2001. "Writing about Rape: Use of the Passive Voice and Other Distancing Text Features as an Expression of Perceived Responsibility of the Victim." *British Journal of Social Psychology* 40(4): 515–29.

Bollas, Christopher. 1989. *The Shadow of the Object: Psychoanalysis of the Unthought Known*. New York: Columbia University Press.

Bondurant, Barrie. 2001. "University Women's Acknowledgement of Rape." *Violence Against Women* 7(3): 294–314.

Bordo, Susan. 1993. *Unbearable Weight: Feminism, Western Culture, and the Body.* Berkeley: University of California Press.

Borrowman, Shane, ed. 2005. *Trauma and the Teaching of Writing.* Albany: State University of New York Press.

Botting, Fred, and Scott Wilson, eds. 1998. *Bataille: A Critical Reader.* Oxford: Blackwell.

Brand, Alice. 1989. *The Psychology of Writing: The Affective Experience.* New York: Greenwood Press.

Brinkley, Douglas. 2006. *The Great Deluge: Hurricane Katrina, New Orleans, and the Mississippi Gulf Coast.* New York: HarperCollins.

Brison, Susan J. 1997. "Outliving Oneself: Trauma, Memory, and Personal Identity." In *Feminists Rethink the Self*, edited by Diana Tietjens Meyers, 12–39. Boulder, CO: Westview.

———. 1998. "Surviving Sexual Violence: A Philosophical Perspective." In *Violence Against Women: Philosophical Perspectives*, edited by Stanley G. French, Wanda Teays, and Laura Martha Purdy, 11–26. Ithaca: Cornell.

———. 1999. "Trauma Narratives and the Remaking of the Self." In *Acts of Memory*, edited by Mieke Bal, Jonathan Crewe, and Leo Spitzer, 39–54. Hanover: University Press of New England.

———. 2003. *Aftermath: Violence and the Remaking of a Self.* Princeton: Princeton University Press.

Butler, Judith. 2004. "Bracha's Eurydice." *Theory, Culture, & Society* 21(1): 95–100.

Camp, Dick. 2009. *Operation Phantom Fury: The Assault and Capture of Fallujah, Iraq.* Minneapolis: Zenith Press.

Campbell, Rebecca, Tracy Sefl, and Courtney E. Ahrens. 2004. "The Impact of Rape on Women's Sexual Health Risk Behaviors." *Health Psychology* 23(1): 67–74.

Campbell, Rebecca, and Sharon M. Wasco. 2005. "Understanding Rape and Sexual Assault: 20 Years of Progress and Future Directions." *Journal of Interpersonal Violence* 20(1): 127–31.

Canguilhem, Georges. (1966) 1991. *The Normal and the Pathological.* Translated by Carolyn R. Fawcett and Robert S. Cohen. New York: Zone Books.

Caputi, Jane. 2003. "Everyday Pornography." In *Gender, Race, and Class in Media: A Text Reader*, edited by Gail Dine and Jean M. Humez, 434–50. Thousand Oaks, CA: Sage.

Card, Claudia. 1996. "Rape as a Weapon of War." *Hypatia* 4(1): 5–18.

Carpenter, Laura M., and Monica J. Casper. 2009. "Global Intimacies: Innovating the HPV Vaccine for Women's Health." *WSQ: Women's Studies Quarterly* 37(1–2): 80–100.

Caruth, Cathy, ed. 1995. *Trauma: Explorations in Memory.* Baltimore: Johns Hopkins University Press.

———. 1996. *Unclaimed Experience: Trauma, Narrative, and History.* Baltimore: Johns Hopkins University Press.

———. 1997. "Traumatic Awakenings." In *Violence, Identity, and Self-Determination*, edited by Hent de Vries, 208–22. Palo Alto: Stanford University Press.

Casarjian, Robin. 1992. *Forgiveness: A Bold Choice for a Peaceful Heart*. New York: Bantam Books.

Casper, Monica J. 2014. "A Ruin of Elephants: Trans-Species Love, Labor, and Loss." *Oppositional Conversations* (Winter). http://cargocollective.com/OppositionalConversations_Iii/A-Ruin-of-Elephants-Trans-Species-Love-Labor-and-Loss.

Casper, Monica J., and Laura M. Carpenter. 2008. "Sex, Drugs, and Politics: The HPV Vaccine for Cervical Cancer." *Sociology of Health & Illness* 30(6): 886–99.

Casper, Monica J., and Lisa Jean Moore. 2009. "Seen but Not Heard: Consequences of Innocence Lost." In *Missing Bodies: The Politics of Visibility*, edited by Monica J. Casper and Lisa Jean Moore, 25–56. New York: New York University Press.

Caucasian Knot. 2011. "In Chechnya Father Is Arrested on Suspicion of Murdering Two Young Women." *Кавказский Узел*, June 29. Accessed June 29, 2011. http://chechnya.kavkaz-uzel.ru/articles/188110/.

Caywood, Cynthia L., and Gillian R. Overing, eds. 1987. *Teaching Writing: Pedagogy, Gender, and Equity*. Albany: State University of New York Press.

Chaudhry, Lubna Nazir, and Corrine Bertram. 2009. "Liberation Psychology and the Contours of Agency in the Margins: Narrating Trauma and Reconstruction in Post-conflict Karachi." *Feminism & Psychology* 19: 298–312.

Chechen. 2007. "Traditions and Customs." Islamicboard.com, October 27. Accessed June 15, 2011. http://www.islamicboard.com/general/52766-traditions-customs.html.

Cho, Grace M. 2008. *Haunting the Korean Diaspora: Shame, Secrecy, and the Forgotten War*. Minneapolis: University of Minnesota Press.

Cixous, Hélène. 1976. "The Laugh of the Medusa." Translated by Keith Cohen and Paula Cohen. *Signs* 4(1): 875–93.

Clarke, Stephanie B., Shireen L. Rizvi, and Patricia A. Resick. 2008. "Borderline Personality Characteristics and Treatment Outcome in Cognitive-Behavioral Treatments for PTSD in Female Rape Victims." *Behavior Therapy* 39(1): 72–78.

Clough, Patricia Ticineto. 2009. "Troubling the Sociological Imagination: Methodological Considerations." Keynote address presented at the Sociological Reimagination: Crisis and Critique Today symposium, Graduate Center at the City University of New York, November 20.

Collins, John J., ed. 2000. *The Encyclopedia of Apocalypticism: Volume 1*. London: Continuum.

Conley, Brigit. 2004. "For the Women of Chechnya, Hope Dies Last." *Journal of Human Rights* 3(3): 331–42.

Connors, Robert J. 1987. "Personal Writing Assignments." *College Composition and Communication* 38(2):166–83.

Conoscenti, Lauren M., and Richard J. McNally. 2006. "Health Complaints in Acknowledged and Unacknowledged Rape Victims." *Journal of Anxiety Disorders* 20(3): 372–79.

Cooke, Miriam. 1997. *Women and the War Story*. Berkeley: University of California Press.

———. 2000. "Women, Religion, and the Postcolonial Arab World." *Cultural Critique* 45: 150–84.

Cooper, H. H. A. 1978. "Psychopath as Terrorist." *Legal Medical Quarterly* 2: 253–62.

Crenshaw, M. 1998. "The Logic of Terrorism." In Reich, *Origins of Terrorism*, 7–24.

Creswell, John W. 1998. *Qualitative Inquiry and Research Design: Choosing among Five Traditions*. Thousand Oaks, CA: Sage.

Csordias, Thomas. 1994. *Embodiment and Experience*. London: Cambridge University Press.

Daniloff, Ruth. 2007. "A Determined Spirit Guides Grozny." *International Herald Tribune*, November 14. Accessed August 15, 2010. http://www.iht.com/bin/print-friendly.php?id=8334151.

Dargis, Manohla. 2010. "Hacker with Ink on Back and Big Chip on Shoulder." *New York Times*, March 18, 2010. Accessed October 29, 2011. http://movies.nytimes.com/2010/03/19/movies/19girl.html.

Das, Veena. 1997. "Language and Body: Transactions in the Construction of Pain." In Kleinman, Das, and Lock, *Social Suffering*, 67–91.

Das, Veena, and Arthur Kleinman. 2001. "Introduction." In *Remaking a World: Violence, Social Suffering, and Recovery*, edited by Veena Das, Arthur Kleinman, Margaret Lock, Mamphela Ramphele, and Pamela Reynolds, 1–3. Berkeley: University of California Press.

Davenport, Donna S. 1991. "The Functions of Anger and Forgiveness: Guidelines for Psychotherapy with Victims." *Psychotherapy: Theory, Research, Practice, Training* 28(1): 140–44.

Delbo, Charlotte. 1995. *Auschwitz and After*. Translated by Rosette C. Lamont. New Haven: Yale University Press.

Deleuze, Gilles. 1990. *Bergsonism*. Translated by Hugh Tomlinson and Barbara Habberjam. Brooklyn: Zone.

Derrida, Jacques. 1984. "No Apocalypse, Not Now (Full Speed Ahead, Seven Missiles, Seven Missives)." *Diacritics* 14: 20.

———. 1988. *The Ear of the Other: Otobiography, Transference, Translation*. Lincoln: University of Nebraska Press.

———. 1994. *Specters of Marx*. New York: Routledge.

———. (1997) 2001. *On Cosmopolitanism and Forgiveness*. Translated by Routledge. New York: Routledge.

Desalvo, Louise. 1999. *Writing as a Way of Healing: How Telling Our Stories Transforms Our Lives*. Boston: Beacon.

Doherty, Brigid. 1997. "'See: *We Are All Neurasthenics!*' or, The Trauma of Dada Montage." *Critical Inquiry* 24(1) : 82–132.

Dowler, Lorraine. 1998. "And They Think I'm Just a Nice Old Lady: Women and War in Belfast, Northern Ireland." *Gender, Place and Culture* 5(2): 159–76.

Du Bois, W. E. B. 1902. *The Souls of Black Folk*. Chicago: A.C. McClurg.

Dunlop, John. 2003. "The October 2002 Moscow Hostage-Taking Incident." *Radio Free Europe*, December 13. Accessed June 30, 2011. http://www.nord-ost.org/today/the-october-2002-moscow-hostage-taking-incident-part-2_en.html.

Dyer-Witheford, Nick, and Greig de Peuter. 2009. *Games of Empire: Global Capitalism and Video Games*. Minneapolis: University of Minnesota Press.

Dyson, Michael Eric. 2006. "Great Migrations." In Trout, *After the Storm*, 75–84.

Ebert, Roger. 2010. "Review: *The Girl with the Dragon Tattoo*." Accessed May 2, 2011. http://rogerebert.suntimes.com/apps/pbcs.dll/article?AID=/20100317/REVIEWS/100319981/-1/RSS.

Eisenstein, Zillah. 2000. "Writing Bodies on the Nation for the Globe." In Ranehod-Nillson and Tetreault, *Women, States, and Nationalism*, 35–54.

Elshtain, Jean Bethke. 1987. *Women and War*. New York: Basic Books.

Enloe, Cynthia. 2000. *Maneuvers: The International Politics of Militarizing Women's Lives*. Berkeley: University of California Press.

———. 2005. "Foreword." In *(En)gendering the War on Terror: War Stories*, edited by Krista Hunt and Kim Rygiel, vii–x. Denver: Ashgate.

Enright, Robert D., David L. Eastin, Sandra Golden, and Issidoros Sarinopoulos. 1992. "Interpersonal Forgiveness within the Helping Professions: An Attempt to Resolve Differences of Opinion." *Counseling and Values* 36(2): 84–103.

Enright, Robert D., and Richard P. Fitzgibbons. 2000. *Helping Clients Forgive: An Empirical Guide for Resolving Anger and Restoring Hope*. Washington, DC: American Psychological Association.

Erichsen, John Eric. 1867. *On Railway and Other Injuries of the Nervous System*. Philadelphia: Henry C. Lea.

Fahs, Breanne. 2011. *Performing Sex: The Making and Unmaking of Women's Erotic Lives*. Albany: State University of New York Press.

Faigley, Lester. 1992. *Fragments of Rationality: Postmodernity and the Subject of Composition*. Pittsburgh: University of Pittsburgh Press.

Faravelli, Carlo, Alice Giugni, Stefano Salvatori, and Valdo Ricca. 2004. "Psychopathology after Rape." *American Journal of Psychiatry* 161(8): 1483–85.

Farley, Anthony Paul. 2006. "The Station." In Trout, *After the Storm*, 147–59.

Fassin, Didier, and Richard Rechtman. 2009. *The Empire of Trauma: An Inquiry into the Condition of Victimhood*. Princeton: Princeton University Press.

Felman, Shoshana, and Dori Laub. 1992. *Testimony: Crises of Witnessing in Literature, Psychoanalysis, and History*. New York: Routledge.

Fighel, Y. 2003. "Palestinian Islamic Jihad and Female Suicide Bombers." Institute for Counterterrorism, October 6. Accessed March 19, 2011. http://www.ict.org/articele/articledet.cfm?articleid=499.

Flowe, Heather D., Ebbe B. Ebbesen, and Anila Putcha-Bhagavatula. 2007. "Rape Shield Laws and Sexual Behavior Evidence: Effects of Consent Level and Women's Sexual History on Rape Allegations." *Law and Human Behavior* 31(2): 159–75.

Foucault, Michel. 1980. *The History of Sexuality: Volume 1: An Introduction*. Translated by Robert Hurley. New York: Vintage.

Freedman, Suzanne. 1998. "Forgiveness and Reconciliation: The Importance of Under-standing how they Differ." *Counseling and Values* 42(3): 200–216.

Frye, Marilyn. 1983. *The Politics of Reality: Essays in Feminist Theory*. Trumansburg, NY: Crossing Press.

———. 1997. "Some Reflections on Separatism and Power." In *Feminist Social Thought: A Reader*, edited by Diana Tietjens Meyers, 406–14. New York: Routledge.

Fuguitt, Glenn V., John A. Fulton, and Calvin L. Beale, eds. 2001. "The Shifting Patterns of Black Migration into and from the Nonmetropolitan South, 1965–95." Washing-ton, DC: US Department of Agriculture, Economic Research Service.

Gannett, Cynthia. 1995. "The Stories of Our Lives Become Our Lives: Journals, Diaries, and Academic Discourse." In *Feminine Principles and Women's Experience in Ameri-can Composition and Rhetoric*, edited by Louise Wetherbee Phelps and Janet Emig, 109–36. Pittsburgh: University of Pittsburgh Press.

Garrison, Carole. 2006. "Sirens of Death: Role of Women in Terrorism Past, Present, and Future." *Journal of Criminal Justice & Security* 8(3–4): 332–39.

Gidycz, Christine A., Lindsay M. Orchowski, Carrie R. King, and Cindy L. Rich. 2008. "Sexual Victimization and Health-Risk Behaviors: A Prospective Analysis of Col-lege Women." *Journal of Interpersonal Violence* 23(6): 744–63.

Giles, Wenona Mary, and Jennifer Hyndman. 2004. *Sites of Violence: Gender and Con-flict Zones*. Berkeley: University of California Press.

The Girl with the Dragon Tattoo. 2010. Directed by Niels Arden Oplev. Chicago: Music Box Films Home Entertainment.

Giroday, Gabrielle. 2010. "Russia's Black Widows." *Maissoneuve*, March 29. Ac-cessed June 15, 2011. http://maisonneuve.org/pressroom/article/2010/mar/29/maisonneuve-vault-russias-black-widows/.

Goggin, Peter, and Maureen Daly Goggin. 2005. "Presence in Absence: Discourses and Teaching (In, On, and About) Trauma." In Borrowman, *Trauma and the Teaching of Writing*, 29–51.

Gordon, Avery. 1997. *Ghostly Matters: Haunting and the Sociological Imagination*. Min-neapolis: University of Minnesota Press.

Gordon, Kristina C., Donald H. Baucom, and Douglas K. Snyder. 2005. "Treating Couples Recovering from Infidelity: An Integrative Approach." *Journal of Clinical Psychology* 61(11): 1393–1405.

Grant, R. 2005. "The Fallujah Model." *Air Force Magazine*, February.

Griffin, Susan. 1993. *A Chorus of Stones: The Private Life of War*. New York: Anchor.

Groskop, Viv. 2004. "The Beslan Atrocity: The Black Widows: Women at Heart of the Terror Cells: Moscow Theatre Siege Survivors Say Female Terrorists Out for Revenge Were Most Chilling of Their Captors." *Observer*, September 5, 4.

Grosz, Elizabeth. 1994. *Volatile Bodies: Toward a Corporeal Feminism*. Bloomington: Indiana University Press.

Gubkin, Liora. 2007. *You Shall Tell Your Children: Holocaust Memory in American Passover Ritual*. New Brunswick, NJ: Rutgers University Press.

Guerette, Sarah M., and Sandra L. Caron. 2007. "Assessing the Impact of Acquaintance Rape: Interviews with Women Who Are Victims/Survivors of Sexual Assault while in College." *Journal of College Student Psychotherapy* 22(2): 31–50.

Guerlac, Susan. 2009. *Thinking in Time: An Introduction to Henri Bergson.* Ithaca, NY: Cornell University Press.

Guletkin, Kubra. 2007. "Women's Engagement in Terrorism: What Motivates Females to Join Terrorist Organizations?" In *Understanding Terrorism: Analysis of Social and Psychological Aspects*, edited by Suleyman Ozeen, Ismail Dincer Gunes, and Diab M. Al-Babayneh, 167–75. New York: IOS Press.

Gunawardena, A. 2006. "Female Black Tigers: A Different Breed of Cat." In Schweitzer, *Female Suicide Bombers*, 81–90.

Haddad, Simon. 2004. "A Comparative Study of Lebanese and Palestinian Perceptions of Suicide Bombings: The Role of Militant Islam and Socio-Economic Status." *International Journal of Comparative Sociology* 45(5): 337–63.

Hage, Ghassan. 2003. "'Comes a Time We Are All Enthusiasm': Understanding Palestinian Suicide Bombing in Times of Exighophobia." *Public Culture* 15(1): 65–89.

Hale, Sondra. 1999. "Mothers and Militias: Islamic State Construction of Women Citizens of Sudan." *Citizenship Studies* 3(3): 373–86.

Haraway, Donna. 1988. "Situated Knowledges: The Science Question in Feminism and the Privilege of Partial Perspective." *Feminist Studies* 14(3): 575–99.

Hargrave, Terry D., Janet Froeschle, and Yvette Castillo. 2009. "Forgiveness and Spirituality: Elements of Healing in Relationships." In *Spiritual Resources in Family Therapy*, 2nd ed., edited by Froma Walsh, 301–22. New York: Guilford.

Harries, Martin. 2007. *Forgetting Lot's Wife.* New York: Fordham University Press.

Harrington, Ellen Burton. 2007. "Nation, Identity, and the Fascination with Forensic Science in Sherlock Holmes and CSI." *International Journal of Cultural Studies* 10(3): 365–82.

Harrison, Robert Pogue. 1992. *Forests: The Shadow of Civilization.* Chicago: University of Chicago Press.

Herman, Judith. 1997. *Trauma and Recovery: The Aftermath of Violence.* New York: HarperCollins.

Hirschauer, Stefan. 2006. "Animated Corpses: Communicating with Post Mortals in an Anatomical Exhibition." *Body & Society* 12(4): 25–52.

Hocquenghem, Guy, Jean Danet, and Michel Foucault. 1980. "The Danger of Child Sexuality." *Semiotext(e).* Retrieved April 2, 2011. http://www.ipce.info/ipceweb/Library/danger.htm

Hoffman, Bruce. 1998. *Inside Terrorism.* New York: Columbia University Press.

Holmgren, Mike. 1993. "Forgiveness and the Intrinsic Value of Persons." *American Philosophical Quarterly* 30: 341–52.

Hugo, Victor. 1862. *Les Miserables.* New York: Dodd, Mead.

Human Rights Watch (HRW). 2000a. "More Evidence of Rape by Russian Forces in Chechnya." Accessed March 17, 2011. www.hrw.org/press/2000/03/checho330.htm

———. 2000b. "Rape Allegations Surface in Chechnya." Accessed March 17, 2011. www. hrw.org/press/2000/01/chech0120.htm.

———. 2000c. *Welcome to Hell: Arbitrary Detention, Torture and Extortion in Chechnya*. New York: Human Rights Press.

———. 2011. *You Dress According to Their Rules: Enforcement of an Islamic Dress Code for Women in Chechnya*. New York: Human Rights Watch.

International Rescue Committee (IRC). 2006. "Gender-Based Violence Technical Assessment." September.

Israilov, Artur. 2008. "Dress Code for Chechen Women." Institute for War and Peace. Reporting: Caucasus Reporting Service, January 9. https://iwpr.net/global-voices/dress-code-chechen-women

Jacobs, Harriet A. (1861) 2013. *Incidents in the Life of a Slave Girl*. New York: Dover.

Jaimoukha, A. 2005. *The Chechens: A Handbook*. London: Routledge.

Jentz, Terri. 2006. *Strange Piece of Paradise*. New York: Picador.

Jewkes, Yvonne. 2004. *Media and Crime*. London: Sage.

Johnson, Denis. 1985. *Fiskadoro*. New York: Harper.

Jordan, Jan. 2004. "Beyond Belief? Police, Rape and Women's Credibility." *International Journal of Policy and Practice* 4(1): 29–59.

Jordan, Kim, and Myriam Denov. 2007. "Birds of Freedom? Perspectives on Female Emancipation and Sri Lanka's Liberation Tigers of Tamil Eelam." *Journal of International Women's Studies* 9(1): 42–62.

Kahn, Arnold S. 2004. "2003 Carolyn Sherif Award Address: What College Women Do and Do Not Experience as Rape." *Psychology of Women Quarterly* 28(1): 9–15.

Kahn, Arnold S., Jennifer Jackson, Christine Kully, Kelly Badger, and Jessica Halvorsen. 2003. "Calling It Rape: Differences in Experiences of Women Who Do or Do Not Label Their Sexual Assault as Rape." *Psychology of Women Quarterly* 27(3): 233–42.

Kaplan, E. Ann. 2005. *Trauma Culture: The Politics of Terror and Loss in the Media and Literature*. New Brunswick, NJ: Rutgers University Press.

Kavkazcenter. 2011. "Chechen Connection: Chechen Female Fighters "Discovered" in Afghanistan." February 1. Accessed June 27, 2011. http://www.kavkazcenter.com/eng/content/2011/02/01/13447.shtml.

Kelley, Douglas L. 1998. "The Communication of Forgiveness." *Communication Studies* 49(3): 255–71.

———. 2001. "Common Perspectives of Forgiveness." Presentation at the National Communication Association conference, Atlanta, November.

———. 2012. "Forgiveness as Restoration: The Search for Well-Being, Reconciliation, and Relational Justice." In *Positive Interpersonal Communication*, edited by T. Socha and M. Pitts, 193–210. Frankfurt: Peter Lang.

Kienzler, Hanna. 2008. "Debating War-Trauma and Post-Traumatic Stress Disorder (PTSD) in an Interdisciplinary Arena." *Social Science & Medicine* 67: 218–27.

Kingston, Maxine Hong. 1989. *The Woman Warrior: Memoirs of a Girlhood among Ghosts*. New York: Vintage.

"Kinky Calls Katrina Evacuees 'Crackheads and Thugs.'" 2006. Dailykos.com, September 12. http://www.dailykos.com/ story/2006/09/12/245710/-Kinky-calls-Katrina-Evacuees-crackheads-and-thugs.

Kishovsky, Sophia. 2010. "Chechnya Coerces Women on Dress, Activists Say." *New York Times*, September 27. Accessed June 15, 2011. http://www.nytimes.com/2010/09/28/world/europe/28iht-chechnya.html.

Kleinman, Arthur. 1997. "'Everything That Really Matters': Social Suffering, Subjectivity, and the Remaking of Human Experience in a Disordering World." *Harvard Theological Review* 90(3): 315–35.

Kleinman, Arthur, Veena Das, and Margaret Lock, eds. 1997. *Social Suffering*. Berkeley: University of California Press.

Kleinman, Arthur, and Joan Kleinman. 1994. "How Bodies Remember: Social Memory and Bodily Experience of Criticism, Resistance, and Delegitimation Following China's Cultural Revolution." *New Literary History* 25(3): 707–23.

Knight, W. Andy, and Tanya Narozhna. 2005. "Rape and Other War Crimes in Chechnya: Is There a Role for the International Criminal Court?" York University. Accessed March 15, 2011. http://www.yorku.ca/soi/_Vol_5_1/_HTML/Knight_Narozhna.html.

Koss, Mary P. 1985. "The Hidden Rape Victim: Personality, Attitudinal, and Situational Characteristics." *Psychology of Women Quarterly* 9(2): 193–212.

Koss, Mary P., Christine A. Gidycz, and Nadine Wisniewski. 1987. "The Scope of Rape: Incidence and Prevalence of Sexual Aggression and Victimization in a National Sample of Higher Education Students." *Journal of Clinical and Consulting Psychology* 55(2): 162–70.

Koss, Mary P., Lori Heise, and Nancy C. Russo. 1994. "The Global Health Burden of Rape." *Psychology of Women Quarterly* 18(4): 509–37.

Krasnov, V. N. 2008. "Russia: Psychological Prerequisites and Consequences of Suicide Terrorism." In Sharpe, *Suicide Bombers*, 82–97.

Kreuger, Alan B., and Jitka Malecková. 2002. "Education, Poverty, Political Violence and Terrorism: Is There a Causal Connection?" National Bureau of Economic Research Working Paper W9074. Accessed March 17, 2011. http://papers.nber.org/papers/W9074.

Kristeva, Julia. 1984. *Revolution in Poetic Language*. New York: Columbia University Press.

Kunsa, Ashley. 2009. "'Maps of the World in Its Becoming': Post-Apocalyptic Naming in Cormac McCarthy's *The Road*." *Journal of Modern Literature* 33: 57–74.

Kunstler, James Howard. 2008. *World Made by Hand*. New York: Grove Press.

Kuppers, Petra. 2004. "Visions of Anatomy: Exhibitions and Dense Bodies." *Differences: A Journal of Feminist Cultural Studies* 15(3): 123–56.

Kurczab-Redlich, Krystyna. 2002. "Torture and Rape Stalk the Streets of Chechnya." *Guardian*, October 27. Accessed June 27, 2011. http://www.guardian.co.uk/world/2002/oct/27/chechnya.russia2.

LaCapra, Dominick. 1998. *History and Memory after Auschwitz*. Ithaca, NY: Cornell University Press.

———. 2001. *Writing History, Writing Trauma*. Baltimore: Johns Hopkins University Press.

Lachkar, Joan. 2006. "The Psychopathology of Terrorism: A Cultural V Spot." Accessed June 29, 2011. http://www.primal-page.com/lachkar.htm.

Lahnait, F. 2008. "Female Suicide Bombers: Victims or Murderers?" In Sharpe, *Suicide Bombers*, 71–86.

Lapidus, Gail W. 1984. "Ethnonationalism and Political Stability: The Soviet Case." *World Politics* 36(4): 555–80.

Larsson, Stieg. 2008. *The Girl with the Dragon Tattoo*. New York: Knopf.

Latour, Bruno. 2004. "Why Has Critique Run Out of Steam? From Matters of Fact to Matters of Concern." *Critical Inquiry* 30: 225–48.

Laub, Dori. 1992. "Bearing Witness or the Vicissitudes of Listening." In *Testimony: Crises of Witnessing in Literature, Psychoanalysis, and History*, 57–74. New York: Routledge.

Leder, Drew. 1990. *The Absent Body*. Chicago: University of Chicago Press.

LeDoux, Joseph. 1996. *The Emotional Brain*. New York: Touchstone.

Leininger, Madeleine. "Evaluation Criteria and Critique of Qualitative Research Studies." In *Critical Issues in Qualitative Research Methods*, edited by Janice M. Morse, 95–115. Thousand Oaks, CA: Sage.

Levenson, Jill S., and David A. D'Amora. 2007. "Social Policies Designed to Prevent Sexual Violence: The Emperor's New Clothes?" *Criminal Justice Policy Review* 18(2): 168–99.

Leys, Ruth. 2000. *Trauma: A Genealogy*. Chicago: University of Chicago Press.

Liberakina, Marina. 1996. "Women and the War in Chechnya." OWL: Women Plus. Accessed March 9, 2011. http://www.owl.ru/eng/womplus/1996/gender.htm.

Library of Congress, American Memory Collections. 2003. "After the Day of Infamy: 'Man-on-the-Street' Interviews Following the Attack on Pearl Harbor." Accessed June 6, 2007. http://memory.loc.gov/ammem/afcphhtml/afcphhome.html.

———. n.d. "Witness and Response: September 11 Acquisitions at the Library of Congress." Accessed May 14, 2007. http://www.loc.gov/exhibits/911/.

Lieven, Anatoly. 1998. *Chechnya: Tombstone of Russian Power*. New Haven: Yale University Press.

Linke, Uli. 2005. "Touching the Corpse: The Unmaking of Memory in the Body Museum." *Anthropology Today* 21(5): 13.

Littleton, Heather, and Carmen R. Breitkopf. 2006. "Coping with the Experience of Rape." *Psychology of Women Quarterly* 30(1): 106–16.

Littleton, Heather L., Deborah L. Rhatigan, and Danny Axsom. 2007. "Unacknowledged Rape: How Much Do We Know about the Hidden Rape Victim?" *Journal of Aggression, Maltreatment & Trauma* 14(4): 57–74.

Lock, Margaret. 1993. "Cultivating the Body: Anthropology and Epistemologies of Bodily. Practice and Techniques." *Annual Review of Anthropology* 22: 133–55.

Lugones, Maria. 1987. "Playfulness, 'World'-Traveling and Loving Perception." *Hypatia* 2(2): 3–21.

MacKinnon, Catharine A. 1994. "Rape, Genocide, and Women's Human Rights." *Harvard Women's Law Journal* 17: 5–16.

Malabou, Catherine. 2012. *The New Wounded: From Neurosis to Brain Damage*. Translated by Steven Miller. New York: Fordham University Press.

Mallot, Edward. 2006. "Body Politics and the Body Politic." *Interventions: International Journal of Postcolonial Studies* 8(2): 165–77.

Manchanda, Rita. 2001. "Ambivalent Gains in South Asian Conflicts." In Meintjes, Pillay, and Turshen, *Aftermath*, 99–121.

Martin, Elaine K., Casey T. Taft, and Patricia A. Resick. 2007. "A Review of Marital Rape." *Aggression and Violent Behavior* 12(3): 329–47.

Martin, Emily. 1987. *The Woman in the Body: A Cultural Analysis of Reproduction*. Boston: Beacon.

Marx, Brian P., Victoria Van Wie, and Alan M. Gross. 1996. "Date Rape Risk Factors: A Review and Methodological Critique of the Literature." *Aggression and Violent Behavior* 1(1): 27–45.

Mbembe, Achille. 2003. "Necropolitics." *Public Culture* 15(1): 11–40.

McCarthy, Cormac. 2006. *The Road*. New York: Vintage.

McCloskey, Laura Ann, and Jennifer A. Bailey. 2000. "The Intergenerational Transmission Risk for Child Sexual Abuse." *Journal of Interpersonal Violence* 15(10): 1019–35.

McCullough, Michael E., Kenneth I. Pargament, and Carl E. Thoresen, eds. 2000. *Forgiveness: Theory, Research, and Practice*. New York: Guilford.

McGlothlin, Erin. 2006. *Second-Generation Holocaust Literature: Legacies of Survival and Perpetration*. Rochester, NY: Camden House.

McMullin, Darcy, and Jacquelyn W. White. 2006. "Long-Term Effects of Labeling a Rape Experience." *Psychology of Women Quarterly* 30(1): 96–105.

Meares, Russell. 2000. *Intimacy and Alienation*. London: Routledge.

Médecins Sans Frontières. 2004. "The Trauma of Ongoing Conflict and Displacement in Chechnya: Quantitative Assessment of Living Conditions, and Psychosocial and General Health Status among War Displaced in Chechnya and Ingushetia." *Conflict and Health* 1(4): 4.

Medical Foundation for the Care of Victims of Torture. 2004. *Rape and Other Torture in the Chechnya Conflict: Documented Evidence from Asylum Seekers Arriving in the United Kingdom*. Accessed March 10, 2009. http://www.torturecare.org.uk/node/2102.

Meier, Andrew. 2005. *Chechnya: To the Heart of a Conflict*. New York: Norton.

Meintjes, Sheila, Anu Pillay, and Meredeth Turshen, eds. 2001. *The Aftermath: Women in Post-Conflict Transformation*. London: Zed Books.

Meister, Robert. 2011. *After Evil: A Politics of Human Rights*. New York: Columbia University Press.

Memorial. 2000. "Appeal to the PACE to the UN-Commission of Human Rights to the OSCE to the European Union." June 26. Accessed March 10, 2009. http://www.radicalparty.org/humanrights/cecenia/appeal_cecenia.htm.

Merleau-Ponty, Maurice. 1964. "Indirect Language and the Voices of Silence." In *Signs*, translated by Richard C. McCleary. Evanston: Northwestern University Press.

———. 1969. *Phenomenology of Perception*. Translated by Colin Smith. London: Routledge.

Michaels, Anne. 1996. *Fugitive Pieces*. Toronto: McClelland & Stewart.

Middle Eastern Media Research Institute (MEMRI). 2002. "Wafa Idris: The Celebration of the First Female Palestinian Suicide Bomber—Part III." MEMRI Inquiry and Analysis Series 85, February 14. Accessed March 28, 2011. http://memri.org/bin/articles.cgi?Page=archives&Area=ia&ID=IA8502.

Miller, K. E., and A. Rasmussen. 2010. "War Exposure, Daily Stressors, and Mental Health in Conflict and Post-conflict Settings: Bridging the Divide between Trauma-Focused and Psychosocial Frameworks." *Social Science & Medicine* 70(1): 7–16.

Miller, Nancy K., and Jason Tougaw. 2002. "Introduction: Extremities." In *Extremities: Trauma, Testimony, and Community*, edited by Nancy K. Miller and Jason Tougaw, 1–24. Champaign: University of Illinois Press.

Mitscherlich, Alexander, and Margarete Mitscherlich. 1984. *The Inability to Mourn: Principles of Collective Behavior*. New York: Grove/Atlantic.

Mohler-Kuo, Meichun, George W. Dowdall, Mary P. Koss, and Henry Wechsler. 2004. "Correlates of Rape while Intoxicated in a National Sample of College Women." *Journal of Studies on Alcohol* 65(1): 37–45.

Moore, Lisa Jean, and Monica J. Casper. 2014. *The Body: Social and Cultural Dissections*. London: Routledge.

Morrison, Daniel R., and Monica J. Casper. 2012. "Intersections of Disability Studies and Critical Trauma Studies: A Provocation." *Disability Studies Quarterly* 32(2). http://dsq-sds.org/article/view/3189/3073.

Morrison, Toni. 1987. *Beloved*. New York: Knopf.

Mullet, Etienne, Michelle Girard, and Parul Bakhshi. 2004. "Conceptualizations of Forgiveness." *European Psychologist* 9(2): 78–86.

Myers, Kevin. 2004. "The Terrible Sight of a Female Terrorist." *Sunday Telegraph* (London), October 27, 26.

Nalbantian, Suzanne. 2011. *The Memory Process: Neuroscientific and Humanistic Perspectives*. Cambridge, MA: MIT Press.

Nandy, Ashis. 2009. *The Intimate Enemy: Loss and Recovery of Self under Colonialism*. Oxford: Oxford University Press.

Neal, Arthur G. 2005. *National Trauma and Collective Memory: Extraordinary Events in the American Experience*. New York: M.E. Sharpe.

Nekrich, A. M. 1978. *The Punished Peoples*. Translated by George Saunders. New York: Norton.

Nivat, Anne. 2001. *Chienne de Guerre*. New York: PublicAffairs.

———. 2003. "Brutality and Indifference: The Russian Army in Chechnya." *Crimes of War Project Magazine, Chechnya: The World Looks Away*, April 18, 18–19.

———. 2005. "The Black Widows: Chechen Women Join the Fight for Independence— and Allah." *Studies in Conflict and Terrorism* 28(5): 413–19.

O'Brien, Tim. 1995. *In the Lake of the Woods*. New York: Penguin.

Olesen, Virginia. 1992. "Extraordinary Events and Mundane Ailments: The Contextual Dialectics of the Embodied Self." In *Investigating Subjectivity: Research on Lived Experience*, edited by Carolyn Ellis and Michael G. Flaherty, 205–20. Newbury Park, CA: Sage.

Oliver, Kelly. 2000. "Beyond Recognition: Witnessing Ethics." *Philosophy Today* 44(1): 31–43.

———. 2001. *Witnessing: Beyond Recognition*. Minneapolis: University of Minnesota Press.

Olujic, Maria. 1998. "Embodiment of Terror: Gender Violence in Peacetime and War-time in Croatia and Bosnia and Herzegovina." *Medical Anthropology Quarterly* 12: 31–50.

Open Society Institute. 2008. "Women's Rights and Social Change in Chechnya." Talk, May 5. Accessed March 17, 2009. http://www.soros.org/initiatives/women/events/chechnya_20080505.

Orr, Jackie. 2006. *Panic Diaries: A Genealogy of Panic Disorder*. Durham, NC: Duke University Press.

Oushakine, Serguei Alex. 2006. "The Politics of Pity: Domesticating Loss in a Russian Province." *American Anthropologist* 108(2): 297–311.

Owen, William F. 1984. "Interpretive Themes in Relational Communication." *Quarterly Journal of Speech* 70(3): 274–87.

Oxfam America. 2008. "Mirror on America: How the State of Gulf Coast Recovery Reflects on Us All." Accessed September 2008. http://www.oxfamamerica.org/files/mirror-on-america.pdf.

Pandolfo, Stefania. 1997. *The Impasse of the Angels: Scenes from a Moroccan Space of Memory*. Chicago: University of Chicago Press.

Pape, Robert A. 2005. *Dying to Win: The Strategic Logic of Suicide Terrorism*. New York: Random House.

Parillo, Kathleen M., Robert C. Freeman, and Paul Young. 2003. "Association between Child Sexual Abuse and Sexual Revictimization in Adulthood among Women Sex Partners of Injection Drug Users." *Violence and Victims* 18(4): 473–84.

Payne, Jessica D., Lynn Nadel, Willoughby B. Britton, and W. Jake Jacobs. 2008. "The Biopsychology of Trauma and Memory." In *Memory and Emotions*, edited by Daniel Reisberg and Paula Hertel, 76–125. Oxford: Oxford University Press.

Payne, Michelle. 2000. *Bodily Discourses: When Students Write about Abuse and Eating Disorders*. Portsmouth, NH: Boynton/Cook.

Pearson, Patricia. 1997. *When She Was Bad: Violent Women and the Myth of Innocence*. New York: Random House.

Pennebaker, James. 1990. *Opening Up: The Healing Power of Expressing Emotions*. New York: Guilford.

Pérez, Emma. 1999. *The Decolonial Imaginary: Writing Chicanas into History*. Bloomington: University of Indiana Press.

Peteet, Julie. 1994. "Male Gender and Rituals of Resistance in the Palestinian 'Intifada': A Cultural Politics of Violence." *American Ethnologist* 21(1): 31–49.

Peterson, Scott. 2005. "Can Fallujah Be Rebuilt?" *Christian Science Monitor*, November 28.

Peterson, Zoë D., and Charlene L. Muehlenhard. 2004. "Was It Rape? The Function of Women's Rape Myth Acceptance and Definitions of Sex in Labeling Their Own Experiences." *Sex Roles* 51(3–4): 129–44.

Pfeiffer, Kathleen. 1993. "A Comment on 'Crossing Lines.'" *College English* 55(6): 669–71.

Pfohl, Stephen. 1992. *Death at the Parasite Café: Social Science (Fictions) and the Postmodern*. New York: St. Martin's.

Pitcher, Linda. 1998. "'The Divine Impatience': Ritual, Narrative, and Symbolization in the Practice of Martyrdom in Palestine." *Medical Anthropology Quarterly* 12(1): 8–30.

Pohl, J. Otto. 2000. "Stalin's Genocide Against the 'Repressed Peoples.'" *Journal of Genocide Research* 2(2): 267–93.

Pohl, Michaela. 2002. "'It Cannot Be That Our Graves Will Be Here': Chechen and Ingush Deportees in Kazakhstan, 1944–1957." *Journal of Genocide Research* 4(3): 401–30.

———. 2004. "From the Chechen People: Anti-Soviet Protest 1944–46." Chechnya Advocacy Network, February 20. Accessed March 9, 2011. http://www.chechnyaadvocacy.org/history/From%20the%20Chechen%20people%20-%20MPohl.pdf.

Politkovskaya, Anna. 2001. *A Dirty War: A Russian Reporter in Chechnya*. Edited and translated by John Crowfoot. London: Harvill.

———. 2002. "Children of Chechen 'Spezoperations.'" *Novaya Gazeta*, May 29. Accessed March 9, 2009. www.tketjenien.dk/baggrund/politkovskaya.html.

———. 2003. *A Small Corner of Hell: Dispatches from Chechnya by Anna Politkovskaya*. Translated by Alexander Burry and Tatiana Tulchinsky. Chicago: University of Chicago Press.

"Professor: Shooter's Writing Dripped with Anger." 2007. *CNN*. http://www.cnn.com/2007/US/04/17/vtech.shooting/index.html.

Raccioppi, Linda, and Katherine O'Sullivan. 2000. "Engendering Nation and National Identity." In Ranehod-Nillson and Tetreault, *Women, States, and Nationalism*, 18–34.

Rambo, Shelly. 2008. "Beyond Redemption? Reading Cormac McCarthy's *The Road* after the End of the World." *Studies in the Literary Imagination* 41: 99–120.

Ramphele, Mamphela. 1997. "Political Widowhood in South Africa: The Embodiment of Ambiguity." In Kleinman, Das, and Lock, *Social Suffering*, 99–118.

Ranehod-Nillson, Sita, and Mary Ann Tetreault, eds. 2000. *Women, States, and Nationalism: At Home in the Nation?* London: Routledge.

Reich, Walter, ed. 1998. *Origins of Terrorism: Psychologies, Ideologies, Theologies, States of Mind*. Washington, DC: Woodrow Wilson Center Press.

Renner, Walter, and Ingrid Salem. 2009. "Post-Traumatic Stress in Asylum Seekers and Refugees from Chechnya, Afghanistan, and West Africa: Gender Differences in Symptomatology and Coping." *International Journal of Social Psychiatry* 55(2): 99–108.

Reuter, Cristoph. 2004. *My Life Is a Weapon: A Modern History of Suicide Bombing.* Princeton: Princeton University Press.

Reynolds, Maura. 2000. "War Has No Rules for Russian Forces Fighting in Chechnya." *Los Angeles Times*, September 17. Accessed June 15, 2011. http://articles.latimes. com/2000/sep/17/news/mn-22524.

Rickels, Laurence A. 2002. *Nazi Psychoanalysis, Volume II: Crypto-Fetishism.* Minneapolis: University of Minnesota Press.

Ricoeur, Paul. 2004. *Memory, History, Forgetting.* Translated by Kathleen Bamey and David Pellaeur. Chicago: University of Chicago Press.

Ricolfi, Luca. 2005. "Palestinians, 1981–2003." In *Making Sense of Suicide Missions*, edited by Diego Gambetta, 77–129. London: Oxford University Press.

Ridd, Rosemary, and Helen Calloway, eds. 1986. *Caught Up in Conflict: Women's Responses to Political Strife.* London: Macmillan.

The Road. 2009. Directed by John Hillcoat. New York: Dimension Films.

Rogers, Kim Lacy, Selma Leydesdorff, and Graham Dawson. 2002. *Trauma and Life Stories: International Perspectives.* New York: Routledge.

Romanyshyn, Robert. 1989. *Technology as Symptom and Dream.* New York: Routledge.

Rose, Nikolas. 2006. *The Politics of Life Itself: Biomedicine, Power, and Subjectivity in the Twenty-First Century.* Princeton: Princeton University Press.

Rose, Nikolas, and Joelle M. Abi-Rached. 2013. *Neuro: The New Brain Sciences and the Management of the Mind.* Princeton: Princeton University Press.

Rosen, Elizabeth. 2008. *Apocalyptic Transformation: The Apocalyptic and the Postmodern Imagination.* Lanham, MD: Lexington Books.

Rotar, Igor. 2002. "Under the Green Banner: Islamic Radicals in Russia and the Former Soviet Union." *Religion, State & Society* 30(2): 89–153.

Rousseva, Valentina. 2004. "Rape and Sexual Assault in Chechnya." *Culture, Society & Praxis* 3(1): 64–67.

Rozee, Patricia D. 2005. "Rape Resistance: Successes and Challenges." In *The Handbook of Women, Psychology, and the Law*, edited by Andrea Barnes, 265–79. Hoboken, NJ: John Wiley.

Rubin, Gayle. 1993. "Thinking Sex: Notes for a Radical Theory of the Politics of Sexuality." In *The Lesbian and Gay Studies Reader*, edited by Henry Abelove, Michele Aina Barale, and David M. Halperin, 3–42. New York: Routledge.

Ruggiero, Kenneth J., Daniel W. Smith, Rochelle F. Hanson, Heidi S. Resnick, Benjamin E. Saunders, Dean G. Kilpatrick, and Connie L. Best. 2004. "Is Disclosure of Childhood Rape Associated with Mental Health Outcome? Results from the National Women's Study." *Child Maltreatment* 9(1): 62–77.

Russell, John. 2008. "Terrorists, Bandits, Spooks and Thieves: Russian Demonisation of the Chechens Before and Since 9/11." *Third World Quarterly* 26(1): 101–16.

"Russia: Chechen Mass Grave Found." 2008. Agence France Presse, June 21, sec. A, col. 0.

Sable, Marjorie R., Fran Danis, Denise L. Mauzy, and Sarah K. Gallagher. 2006. "Barriers to Reporting Sexual Assault for Women and Men: Perspectives of College Students." *Journal of American College Health* 55(3): 157–62.

Sarkar, N. N., and Rina Sarkar. 2005. "Sexual Assault on Woman: Its Impact on Her Life and Living in Society." *Sexual and Relationship Therapy* 20(4): 407–19.

Sattler, J. 2005. "Operation Al Fajr. . . ." *Marine Corps Gazette* 89(7): 12–17.

Saul, Jack. 2013. *Collective Trauma, Collective Healing: Promoting Community Resilience in the Aftermath of Disaster*. New York: Routledge.

Savage, Charlie. 2011. "As Acts of War or Despair, Suicides Rattle a Prison." *New York Times*, April 24. Accessed June 27, 2011. http://www.nytimes.com/2011/04/25/world/guantanamo-files-suicide-as-act-of-war-or-despair.html?src=recg.

Scahill, Jeremy. 2007. *Blackwater: The Rise of the World's Most Powerful Mercenary Army*. New York: Nation Books.

Scarry, Elaine. 1985. *The Body in Pain: The Making and Unmaking of the World*. New York: Oxford University Press.

Scheper-Hughes, Nancy. 2001. "Maternal Thinking and the Politics of War." *Peace Review* 8(3): 353–59.

Scheper-Hughes, Nancy, and Margaret M. Lock. 1987. "The Mindful Body: A Prolegomenon to Future Work in Medical Anthropology." *Medical Anthropology Quarterly* 1(1): 6–41.

Schwab, Gabriele M. 1997. "Words and Moods: The Transference of Literary Knowledge." *SubStance* 26(3): 107–27.

———. 2010. *Haunting Legacies: Violent Histories and Transgenerational Trauma*. New York: Columbia University Press.

Schweitzer, Yoram, ed. 2006. *Female Suicide Bombers: Dying for Equality?* Memo 84. Tel Aviv: Jaffee Center for Strategic Studies.

Seierstad, Anne. 2008. *Angel of Grozny*. New York: Basic Books.

Shabad, Peter. 2000. "The Most Intimate of Creations: Symptoms as Memorials to One's Lonely Suffering." In *Symbolic Loss: The Ambiguity of Mourning and Memory at Century's End*, edited by Peter Homans, 197–212. Charlottesville: University of Virginia Press.

Sharpe, M., ed. 2008. *Suicide Bombers: The Psychological, Religious and Other Imperatives*. New York: IOS Press.

Shcheblanova, Veronika, and Elena Yarskaya-Smirnova. 2009. "Explanations of Female Terrorism: Discourses about Chechen Terrorists in the Russian Mass Media: 'Easy Girls,' 'Coarse Women' or Fighters?" In *Gender Dynamics and Post-conflict Reconstruction*, edited by Christine Eifler and Ruth Seifert, 245–68. Frankfurt: Peter Lang.

Shermatova, Sanovar, and Alexander Tait. 2003a. "Шестеро из бараевских. Айшат. Амнат. Марьям. Секилат. Аймани. Раяна." *Moscow News*, April 29.

———. 2003b. "Six of Barayev's." *Moscow News*, April 29.

Sideris, Tina. 2003. "War, Gender and Culture: Mozambican Women Refugees." *Social Science & Medicine* 56: 713–24.

Siebers, Tobin. 2008. *Disability Theory*. Ann Arbor: University of Michigan Press.

Silove, Derrick. 1999. "The Psychosocial Effects of Torture, Mass Human Rights Violations, and Refugee Trauma: Toward an Integrated Conceptual Framework." *Journal of Nervous & Mental Disease* 187(4): 200–207.

Simmons, William Paul, and Monica J. Casper. 2012. "Culpability, Social Triage, and Structural Violence in the Aftermath of Katrina." *Perspectives on Politics* 10(3): 675–86.

Sjoberg, Laura, and Caron E. Gentry. 2007. *Mothers, Monsters, Whores: Women's Violence in Global Politics*. London: Zed Books.

Skaine, Rosemary. 2006. *Female Suicide Bombers*. Jefferson, NC: McFarland.

Sloan, Stephen. 2006. "Voices of Katrina." Mississippi History Now, Mississippi Historical Society, August. Accessed June 20, 2007. http://mshistorynow.mdah.state.ms.us/articles/253/voices-of-katrina.

Smedes, Lewis B. 1996. *The Art of Forgiving: When You Need to Forgive and Don't Know How*. Nashville, TN: Moorings.

Smith, Jonathan A. 1995. "Semi-structured Interviewing and Qualitative Analysis." In *Rethinking Methods in Psychology*, edited by Jonathan A. Smith, Rom Harre, and Luk Van Langenhove, 9–26. London: Sage.

Speckhard, Anne. 2005. "Understanding Suicide Terrorism: Countering Human Bombs and Their Senders." In *Topics in Terrorism: Toward a Transatlantic Consensus on the Nature of the Threat*, vol. 1, edited by Jason S. Purcell and Joshua D. Weintraub, 1–22. Washington, DC: Atlantic Council.

Speckhard, Anne, and Khapta Akhmedova. 2006. "The Making of a Martyr: Chechen Suicide Terrorism." *Studies in Conflict and Terrorism* 29(5): 1–65.

Spielberg, Steven, dir. 2005. *War of the Worlds*. Paramount/DreamWorks. Film.

Spivak, Gayatri. 1988. "Can the Subaltern Speak?" In *Marxism and the Interpretation of Culture*, edited by Cary Nelson and Lawrence Grossberg, 271–313. Champaign: University of Illinois Press.

Stearns, Peter. 1994. *American Cool: Constructing a Twentieth-Century Emotional Style*. New York: New York University Press.

Stepich, Don. 2010. *Lafayette Crisis Center Volunteer Training Manual*. 5th ed. Lafayette, IN: Lafayette Crisis Center.

Stevens, Maurice. 2010. "Trauma Is as 'Trauma' Does: The Politics of Affect in Catastrophic Times." Keynote address presented at the New Approaches to Trauma: Bridging Theory and Practice conference at Arizona State University, Phoenix, October 7.

———. 2011. "Trauma's Essential Bodies." In *Corpus: An Interdisciplinary Reader on Bodies and Knowledge*, edited by Monica J. Casper and Paisley Currah, 171–86. New York: Palgrave Macmillan.

———. 2014. "Before Aftercatastrophe." *Oppositional Conversations* 2. http://www.oppositionalconversations.org/.

———. In Progress. *Catastrophe's Glow: A Critical Trauma Theory for Chaotic Times*.

Stoop, David A., and James Masteller. 1991. *Forgiving Our Parents, Forgiving Ourselves: Healing Adult Children of Dysfunctional Families*. Ann Arbor, MI: Vine Books.

Strauss, Anselm, and Juliet Corbin. 1998. *Basics of Qualitative Research: Techniques and Procedures for Developing Grounded Theory*. Thousand Oaks, CA: Sage.

Sturken, Marita. 1997. *Tangled Memories: The Vietnam War, the AIDS Epidemic, and the Politics of Remembering*. Berkeley: University of California Press.

———. 2007. *Tourists of History: Memory, Kitsch, and Consumerism from Oklahoma City to Ground Zero*. Durham, NC: Duke University Press.

Summerfield, Derek. 2004. "Cross-Cultural Perspectives on the Medicalization of Human Suffering." In *Posttraumatic Stress Disorder: Issues and Controversies*, edited by Gerald M. Rosen, 233–45. New York: John Wiley.

Szczepaniková, Alice. 2004. "Gender on the Move: Gender and Family Relations among Chechens in the Czech Refugee Camp." Master's thesis, Central European University.

Tal, Kali. 1996. *Worlds of Hurt: Reading the Literatures of Trauma*. Cambridge: Cambridge University Press.

Tambiah, Stanley J. 1996. *Leveling Crowds: Ethnonationalist Conflict and Collective Violence in South Asia*. Berkeley: University of California Press.

Tambiah, Yasmin. 2005. "Turncoat Bodies—Sexuality and Sex Work under Militarization in Sri Lanka." *Gender & Society* 19(2): 243–61.

Tellis, Katharine M., and Casia C. Spohn. 2008. "The Sexual Stratification Hypothesis Revisited: Testing Assumptions about Simple Versus Aggravated Rape." *Journal of Criminal Justice* 36(3): 252–61.

Thompson, Neil, and Mary Walsh. 2010. "The Existential Basis of Trauma." *Journal of Social Work Practice* 24(4): 377–89.

Thompson, Richard, and Stephen A. Madigan. 2005. *Memory: The Key to Consciousness*. Washington, DC: Joseph Henry Press.

Tilly, Charles. 2002. "Violence, Terror and Politics as Usual." *Boston Review*. Accessed February 17, 2011. http://bostonreview.net/archives/BR27.3/tilly.html.

Tjaden, Patricia, and Nancy Thoennes. 2000a. "Extent, Nature, and Consequences of Intimate Partner Violence: Findings from the National Violence against Women Survey." Washington, DC: US Department of Justice.

———. 2000b. "Prevalence and Consequences of Male-to-Female and Female-to-Male Intimate Partner Violence as Measured by the National Violence against Women Survey." *Violence Against Women* 6(2): 142–61.

Tobin, Lad. 2004. *Reading Student Writing: Confessions, Meditations, and Rants*. Portsmouth, NH: Boynton/Cook.

Todeschini, Maya. 2001. "The Bombs Womb? Women and the Atom Bomb." In *Remaking a World: Violence, Social Suffering, and Recovery*, edited by Veena Das, Margaret Lock, Arthur Kleinman, Mamphela Ramphele, and Pamela Reynolds, 102–55. Berkeley: University of California Press.

Tracy, Steven R. 1999. "Sexual Abuse and Forgiveness." *Journal of Psychology and Theology* 27(3): 219–29.

Trout, David Dante, ed. 2006. *After the Storm: Black Intellectuals Explore the Meaning of Hurricane Katrina*. New York: New Press.

Tutu, Desmond. 1999. *No Future without Forgiveness*. New York: Doubleday.

Ullman, Sarah E., Stephanie M. Townsend, Henrietta H. Filipas, and Laura L. Starzynski. 2007. "Structural Models of the Relations of Assault Severity, Social Support, Avoidance Coping, Self-blame, and PTSD among Sexual Assault Survivors." *Psychology of Women Quarterly* 31(1): 23–37.

United Nations. 2006. "Integration of the Human Rights of Women and a Gender Perspective: Violence Against Women." Report of the Special Rapporteur on Violence Against Women, Its Causes and Consequences, Commission on Human Rights, Sixty-Second Session, Item 12(a) of the Provisional Agenda.

United Nations Entity for Gender Equality and the Empowerment of Women. 2011. "Gender-Based Violence." Accessed December 2, 2011. http://www.unifem.org/gender_issues/women_war_peace/gender_based_violence.php.

University of California, Santa Cruz. 2008. "Rape Prevention Education: Rape Statistics." Accessed January 1, 2008. www2.ucsc.edu.

University of Missouri–Columbia, International Center for Psychosocial Trauma. 2006. "Promoting Hope for the Survivors of Katrina: Training Course in Trauma Psychology & Psychiatry to Help Traumatized Children and Their Families." Workshop presented at Tulane University, New Orleans, November 11–12.

Unrepresented Nations and Peoples Organization. 2009. "Chechen Republic of Ichkeria." Accessed June 15, 2011. http://www.unpo.org/content/view/7865/100/.

Usta, Jinan, Jo Ann M. Farver, and Lama Zein. 2008. "Women, War, and Violence: Surviving the Experience." *Journal of Women's Health* 17(5): 793–804.

Valentine, Gill. 1989. "The Geographies of Women's Fear." *Area* 21, no. 4: 385–90.

van der Kolk, Bessel A., Alexander C. McFarlane, and Lars Weisaeth. 1996. *Traumatic Stress: The Effects of Overwhelming Experience on Mind, Body, and Society*. New York: Guilford.

van der Kolk, Bessel, and Onno van der Hart. 1995. "The Intrusive Past." In Caruth, *Trauma*, 158–82.

Vickroy, Laurie. 2002. *Trauma and Survival in Contemporary Fiction*. Charlottesville: University of Virginia Press.

Victor, Barbara. 2003. *Army of Roses: Inside the World of Palestinian Women Suicide Bombers*. New York: Rodale.

Victoroff, Jeff. 2005. "The Mind of the Terrorist: A Review and Critique of Psychological Approaches." *Journal of Conflict Resolution* 49(1): 3–42.

Vojdik, Valorie. 2003. "The Invisibility of Gender in War." *Duke Journal of Gender Law & Policy* 9: 261–70.

von Hagens, Gunter. 2006. *Body Worlds: The Exhibition of Real Human Bodies*. Heidelberg: Arts & Sciences.

Von Knop, Katharina. 2007. "The Female Jihad: Al Qaeda's Women." *Studies in Conflict and Terrorism* 30(5): 397–414.

Waas, Joost, Anke van der Kwaak, and Maurice Bloem. 2003. "Psychotrauma in Moluccan Refugees in Indonesia." *Disaster Prevention and Management* 12(4): 328–35.

Walby, Sylvia. 1992. "Woman and Nation." *International Journal of Comparative Sociology* 33(1–2): 81–100.

Waldron, Vincent R., and Douglas L. Kelley. 2008. *Communicating Forgiveness*. Thousand Oaks, CA: Sage.

Weir, Fred. 2011. "Report: Chechen Women Attacked with Paintball Guns for 'Immodest' Dress." *Christian Science Monitor*, March 11. Accessed

June 30, 2011. http://www.csmonitor.com/World/Europe/2011/0311/
Report-Chechen-women-attacked-with-paintball-guns-for-immodest-dress.

Weiss, Meira. 1997. "War Bodies, Hedonist Bodies: Dialectics of the Collective and the Individual in Israeli Society." *American Ethnologist* 24(4): 813–32.

———. 2001. "The Body of the Nation: Terrorism and the Embodiment of Nationalism in Contemporary Israel." *Anthropological Quarterly* 75(1): 37–62.

West, Jessica. 2004–5. "Feminist IR and the Case of the 'Black Widows': Reproducing Gendered Divisions." *Innovations: A Journal of Politics* 5: 1–16.

White, John Valery. 2006. "The Persistence of Race Politics and the Restraint of Recovery in Katrina's Wake." In Trout, *After the Storm*, 41–62.

Whitehead, Anne. 2004. *Trauma Fiction*. Edinburgh: Edinburgh University Press.

Wiesenthal, Simon. 1998. *The Sunflower: On the Possibilities and Limits of Forgiveness*. New York: Schocken Books.

Williams, Brian G. 2000. "Commemorating 'The Deportation' in Post-Soviet Chechnya: The Role of Memorialization and Collective Memory in the 1994–1996 and 1999–2000 Russo-Chechen Wars." *History & Memory* 12(1): 101–34.

Willse, Craig, and Greg Goldberg. 2008. "Losses and Returns: The Soldier in Trauma." In *The Affective Turn: Theorizing the Social*, edited by Patricia Clough with Jean Halley, 264–85. Durham, NC: Duke University Press.

Wilson, Elizabeth A. 2004. *Psychosomatic: Feminism and the Neurological Body*. Durham, NC: Duke University Press.

Wilson, John, and Rhiannon B. Thomas. 2004. *Empathy in the Treatment of Trauma and PTSD*. New York: Brunner-Routledge.

Wines, Michael. 2001. "Colonel's Trial Puts Russian Justice to Test." *New York Times*, March 18.

Wirth-Nesher, Hana. 1994. *What Is Jewish Literature?* Philadelphia: Jewish Publication Society.

Witherell, Carol, and Nel Noddings. 1991. *Stories Lives Tell: Narrative and Dialogue in Education*. New York: Teachers College Press.

Wolitzky-Taylor, Kate B., Kenneth J. Ruggiero, Carla K. Danielson, Heidi S. Resnick, Rochelle F. Hanson, Daniel W. Smith, Benjamin E. Saunders, and Dean G. Kilpatrick. 2008. "Prevalence and Correlates of Dating Violence in a National Sample of Adolescents." *Journal of the American Academy of Child and Adolescent Psychiatry* 47(7): 755–62.

Woliver, Laura R. 2002. *The Political Geographies of Pregnancy*. Champaign: University of Illinois Press.

Woolf, Virginia. 1929. *A Room of One's Own*. Orlando: Harcourt Press.

Worthington, Everett L., Jr., ed. 2005. *Handbook of Forgiveness*. New York: Brunner-Routledge.

Worthington, Everett L., and Michael Scherer. 2004. "Forgiveness Is an Emotion-Focused Coping Strategy That Can Reduce Health Risks and Promote Health Resilience: Theory, Review, and Hypotheses." *Psychology & Health* 19(3): 385–405.

Yamadayev, Ruslan. 2002. "Oni priatshutsia za zhenskiye spiny, pozor!" [They hide behind women's backs, what a shame!]. *Komsomolskaya Pravda*, October 25, 4.

Young, Allan. 1997. *The Harmony of Illusions: Inventing Post-traumatic Stress Disorder.* Princeton: Princeton University Press.

Young, Iris Marion. 2005. *On Female Body Experience: "Throwing Like a Girl" and Other Essays*. Oxford: Oxford University Press.

Yuval-Davis, Nira. 1996. "Human Security and the 'Gendered Politics' of Belonging." Paper delivered at the Symposium on Justice, Equality and Dependency in the "Postsocialist" Condition, Warwick University, March 22.

———. 1997. *Gender & Nation*. London: Sage.

Zarakhovich, Yu. 2001. "Who's on Trial? What the Trial of a Russian Colonel for the Murder of a Chechen Girl Says about the State of Russia." *Time Magazine, Europe*, April 3.

ABOUT THE CONTRIBUTORS

Dorothy Allison is a self-described feminist, working-class storyteller, Southern expatriate, sometime poet, and happily born-again Californian. Recipient of numerous awards and fellowships, she is the author of the short story collection *Trash*; a chapbook of poetry, *The Women Who Hate Me*; the widely taught books *Skin: Talking about Race, Class, and Literature* and *Two or Three Things I Know for Sure*; and the novels *Bastard Out of Carolina* and *Cavedweller*, both of which were made into movies. She teaches and lectures frequently and is currently finishing a novel titled *She Who*.

Akua Duku Anokye is Associate Professor of Africana Language, Literature, and Culture at Arizona State University. She is a sociolinguist, and her research focuses on African Diaspora orality and literacy practices, folklore, discourse analysis, and oral history with a specialization in Ghanaian culture, religion, storytelling, and dance. She is currently working on a book manuscript, *Nana Esi and Other People's Children*, about a Ghanaian ancestress/deity who serves as the archetype for African Diaspora women's literature and community motherhood activism.

Francine Banner is Associate Professor of Sociology at the University of Michigan, Dearborn. She holds a PhD in justice studies from Arizona State University and a JD from NYU School of Law. She has published extensively in the areas of gender, political violence, and state violence, and her work recently was voted as "Best New Voice in Gender Studies" by the AALS Section on Women in Legal Education.

Monica J. Casper is Professor of Gender and Women's Studies and Associate Dean for Academic Affairs in the College of Social and Behavioral Sciences at the University of Arizona. She is coauthor of *The Body: Social and Cultural Dissections* and coeditor of *Missing Bodies: The Politics of*

Visibility; author of *The Making of the Unborn Patient: A Social Anatomy of Fetal Surgery*; editor of *Synthetic Planet: Chemical Politics and the Hazards of Modern Life*; and coeditor of *Corpus: An Interdisciplinary Reader on Bodies and Knowledge*. She is also coeditor of the NYU Press book series *Biopolitics: Medicine, Technoscience, and Health in the Twenty-First Century* and a Managing Editor of *The Feminist Wire*. She writes fiction and creative nonfiction, and her hybrid essay "Oculus" was nominated for a Pushcart Prize.

Breanne Fahs is Associate Professor of Women and Gender Studies at Arizona State University and a practicing Clinical Psychologist specializing in couples work, sexuality issues, gender identity, and trauma recovery. Her scholarship focuses on three major areas: women's subjective accounts of their bodies and sexuality, radical feminism, and social movements and political socialization. She is the author of *Performing Sex: The Making and Unmaking of Women's Erotic Lives* and *Valerie Solanas: The Defiant Life of the Woman Who Wrote SCUM (and Shot Andy Warhol)*, and coeditor of *The Moral Panics of Sexuality*.

Carmen Goman completed her BA and MA in communication studies at Arizona State University. She is pursuing a PhD in communication studies at Georgia State University. Her research focuses on forgiveness from health and philosophical perspectives.

Amy Hodges Hamilton is Associate Professor of English at Belmont University in Nashville, Tennessee. Her research and teaching interests center on personal writing, feminist theory, and healing and the arts. She has served on panels as a specialist in writing and healing, including presentations at Vanderbilt University Medical Center and a Healing and the Arts panel at Florida State University's *Seven Days of Opening Nights*. She coauthored her first essay on the subject of loss and trauma with her mentor, Wendy Bishop, in *Trauma and the Teaching of Writing* (NYU Press, 2005). She also served as the founding director of Vanderbilt University's Writing Studio from 2005 to 2006 and continues to support writing programs both inside and outside the academy.

Rebecca Hankins is a Certified Archivist/Librarian and Associate Professor at Texas A&M University. Her research interests include the African diaspora, women and gender studies, diversity in academia, and Muslims and Islam in speculative fiction. She is the author of articles on Black feminist writers, Islamic science fiction and fantasy, oral history, library/archival practices, and more.

Debra Jackson is Associate Professor of Philosophy at California State University, Bakersfield. Her research interests include legal, political, and epistemological issues regarding gender and race, especially with regard to sexual violence against women. She has served as a Crisis Intervention Volunteer and Rape Survivor Advocate at the Lafayette Crisis Center, a Project Coordinator for the Greater Lafayette Sexual Assault Prevention Coalition, and a Crisis Training Certification Presenter at the Alliance Against Family Violence and Sexual Assault.

Douglas Kelley is Professor of Communication Studies at Arizona State University. His scholarship focuses on communication in interpersonal relationships, especially as it relates to marriage and forgiveness. His 1998 study on the communication of forgiveness launched a decade's worth of work focusing on various forgiveness processes. His most recent book, *Marital Communication*, was published in 2012. He has been nominated for various teaching awards and takes great pride in the creation of a service-learning course in which students work with children and youth in inner-city contexts.

Martin Beck Matuštík is Lincoln Professor of Ethics and Religion at Arizona State University. His research and writing interests include critical theory, social and political philosophy, nineteenth- and twentieth-century continental philosophy, and philosophy of religion. He is the author of *Postnational Identity: Critical Theory and Existential Philosophy in Habermas, Kierkegaard, and Havel*; *Specters of Liberation: Great Refusals in the New World Order*; *Jürgen Habermas: A Philosophical-Political Profile*; *Radical Evil and the Scarcity of Hope: Postsecular Meditations*; and most recently, *Out of Silence: Repair Across Generations*.

Jackie Orr is Associate Professor of Sociology at Syracuse University; she teaches and writes in the fields of cultural politics and performance, critical technoscience studies, and contemporary theory. Her book, *Panic Diaries: A Genealogy of Panic Disorder* (2006), conjures a performative sociology of the entangled histories of militarization, cybernetics, and scientific desire animating the language of psychic dis-ease and collective terror. She coedited a special issue on "Enchantment" for *Women's Studies Quarterly* (2012), and published essays on "Punk Justice" in the *Scholar & Feminist Online* (2013) and "a possible history of oblivion" in *Social Text: Periscope* (2013). For the past two decades she has experimented with live performance and visual/sound montage as methods for remaking public memory and insurgent knowledges. Her most recent performance piece on the deep time of catastrophe and the BP oil spill, *Slow Disaster at the Digital Edge*, debuted at the University of Chicago's Center for Contemporary Theory in April 2012.

Gabriele M. Schwab is Chancellor's Professor of English and Comparative Literature at the University of California, Irvine. Her research interests include critical theory, psychoanalysis, feminism, cultural theories, literature and anthropology, and twentieth- and twenty-first-century comparative literatures with an emphasis on the Americas. She is the author or editor of numerous publications, including the books *Subjects Without Selves: Transitional Texts in Modern Fiction*; *The Mirror and the Killer-Queen: Otherness in Literary Language*; *Haunting Legacies: Violent Histories and Transgenerational Trauma*; and *Imaginary Ethnographies: Literature, Subjectivity, Culture* (winner of the 2014 Choice Award). Her edited collections include *Accelerating Possession: Global Futures of Property and Personhood* (with Bill Mauer); *Derrida, Deleuze, Psychoanalysis*; and *Clones, Fakes and Posthumans: Cultures of Replication* (with Philomena Essed). Currently she is working on a new book titled *Haunted Ecologies* and a collaborative project with Simon J. Ortiz, titled *Children of Fire, Children of Water*.

Maurice E. Stevens is Associate Professor of Comparative Studies at The Ohio State University. He teaches theories and methods of interdisciplinary cultural and technological studies. His current research focuses on the emergence and application of critical trauma theory in clinical, social, and institutional contexts. In addition to publishing nearly a dozen articles and guest editing an issue of the journal *Oppositional Conversations*, he has published his first book, titled *Troubling Beginnings: Trans(per)forming African-American History and Identity*, and is currently working on a second book called *Catastrophe's Glow: A Critical Trauma Theory for Chaotic Times*. He has also worked as a Mental/Behavioral Health Counselor.

Shahla Talebi is Associate Professor of Religious Studies at Arizona State University. A native of Iran, she lived through the 1979 Revolution and the Iran-Iraq War, and left Iran in 1994 for the United States. Her research interests include self-sacrifice and martyrdom, violence, memory, trauma, death, and commemoration. Her book, *Ghosts of Revolution: Rekindled Memories of Imprisonment in Iran*, received the 2011 Choice Award for Outstanding Academic Title, an Honorable Mention for the 2011 Prose Award in autobiography/biography, and the 2012 Independent Publisher Gold Medal Book Award for autobiography/memoir.

Eric Wertheimer is Professor of English and Associate Vice Provost of the Graduate College at Arizona State University. He is Founding Director of ASU's Center for Critical Inquiry and Cultural Studies, and he is faculty director of ASU's Digital Humanities Initiative. He is the author of *Underwriting: The Poetics of Insurance in Early America* and *Imagined Empires: Incas, Aztecs, and the New World of American Literature, 1771–1876*, as well as many works of poetry and prose. *Mylar*, his first book of poetry, was published in 2012.

Amanda Wicks holds a PhD in English from Louisiana State University. Her research concentrates on collective and cultural memory in contemporary literature and film.

INDEX

addiction, 68, 188, 198–99; and alcohol, 66–67, 199; and drugs, 40, 51, 66, 191, 197, 232, 240. *See also* mental health

adolescence, 24, 63–64, 185; and sexting, 64, 76. *See also* childhood; family; mothering; parenting

affect, 22–23, 180, 244, 249; and emotional contagion, 214; expression, 185; and feelings, 31–36; and forgiveness, 90; politics of, 19–36

Afghanistan, 54, 124, 173, 188. *See also* Iraq; war

Agamben, Giorgio, 58

agency, 25, 28, 70–71, 222, 247; embodied, 210–11; political, 9, 41; and recovery, 33, 197, 218, 222–23. *See also* social justice

alienation, 239. *See also* Durkheim, Emile

Allison, Dorothy, 205, 219, 244–55; and *Bastard Out of Carolina*, 249

American studies, 4

Amnesty International, 59

Angelou, Maya, 196

Anokye, Akua Duku, 15, 227–43. *See also* emergency services; Hurricane Katrina; natural disaster; oral history

Arendt, Hannah, 78, 210

Banner, Francine, 9, 37–60. *See also* Chechnya

Beckett, Samuel, 111–12, 116. *See also* silence

Benjamin, Walter, 106–9, 157, 160, 162, 167, 171

Berger, Alan, 88–90, 92–93, 95. *See also* Berger, Alan and Naomi; Holocaust

Berger, Alan and Naomi, 125. *See also* Berger, Alan; Holocaust

Berger, James, 138–39

Bergson, Henri, 144–45

biopolitics, 8, 11, 23, 35–36; and death, 159; of war, 157–176

Bishop, Wendy, 184, 188, 204. *See also* pedagogy; writing

Blanchot, Maurice, 135, 155

body, 22; in critical trauma studies, 4; and effects of trauma, 37–38, 54–55, 185; and embodiment, 9, 14, 26, 29–31, 33, 225; and plastination, 158–62; and war, 53. *See also* Body Worlds; brain

Body Worlds, 13, 158–62, 175–76. *See also* von Hagens, Gunther

Bollas, Christopher, 119

Bordo, Susan, 75

brain, 5; and hippocampus, 153; and neuroscience, 4–5; and traumatic injury, 4, 31. *See also* body

Brand, Alice, 184–85

Brison, Susan, 61, 152, 208–9, 211. *See also* rape; sexual violence; trauma

Butler, Judith, 166

capitalism, 31, 167. *See also* neoliberalism

Caruth, Cathy, 3, 136, 140, 150, 152, 154–56, 179, 207–9. *See also* forgetting; memory; trauma

Casper, Monica J., 1–16

Catholic Church, 88, 94

tics of, 23; collective, 50, 53–57, 131,173, 227–28, 240–42; as culture bound syndrome, 74–76; definitions of, 3–4, 20, 26–27, 39–40; as diagnostic category, 9; discourse of, 5; documenting, 227–28; effects of, 14, 185, 206–9, 223; effects on families, 227–43; feminist perspectives on, 38; geopolitical, 9, 37; and health outcomes, 37–38, 185; historical, 10, 13, 78–97; ideologies of, 32; and language, 8, 168; as method, 170, 172; and pedagogy, 179–204; and performance, 157–76; politics of, 10, 57; psychiatry, 58; and race, 228; and recovery, 180, 254; sexual, 61–77; and space, 143–50; survivors, 206, 231; theory, 6–7, 205; and time, 143–50; transgenerational, 11–12, 120, 125–26, 132. *See also* critical trauma studies; posttraumatic stress disorder; suffering; trauma work
trauma work, 6–7, 224. *See also* recovery; trauma
traumatization, 8. *See also* trauma; trauma work

United Nations, 45–46, 59–60. *See also* human rights

violence, 3, 209; committed by women, 60; culture of, 65; domestic, 45, 56, 222; gender based, 45–48; honor killings, 47, 56; mass, 190; and militarization, 160; political, 39, 50–56; state sponsored, 173; structural, 21, 39, 56, 172; of war, 163–174. *See also* rape; sexual violence; torture; war
Virginia Tech, 190
visual culture, 19. *See also* imaging; media

von Hagens, Gunther, 13, 158–62. *See also* body; Body Worlds

Waldron, Vincent R., 78–82. *See also* forgiveness
war, 3–4, 163–74; and birth rate, 43–44; crimes, 59; and intelligence technologies, 164; in Iraq and Afghanistan, 162–74; Russo-Chechen war, 37–60; stories, 117–18; veterans, 24, 208; and World War I, 13, 82, 163, 170; and World War II, 43, 82, 122–34, 129, 134. *See also* colonialism; imperialism; militarization; nationalism; Marine Corps; terrorism; torture
Wertheimer, Eric, 1–16
Wicks, Amanda, 13, 135–56. *See also* McCarthy, Cormac
Wiesenthal, Simon, 10, 78–97. *See also* forgiveness; Holocaust; *The Sunflower*
witnessing, 14–15, 152, 205–6, 211–12, 218–21, 224–25; and listening, 212–16. *See also* memory; recovery; rehabilitation; silence; therapy
women, 41–45; and activism, 49; and birth rate, 43–44; and bodies, 42–45; and identity development, 74; incarcerated, 12; and mental health, 52; roles in war, 45–48; suicide bombers, 9, 37–60; and trauma, 220; and writing, 181. *See also* feminism; gender; intersectionality; masculinity; patriarchy; sexism
Woolf, Virginia, 181, 195
writing, academic, 181–82, 185; and historical trauma, 124–25; oral history, 198–99; personal, 192–93, 128; as therapeutic, 183–84. *See also* language; narrative; storytelling

Young, Iris Marion, 226